To ████████

Happy Reenacting

Paul Wilson

HIMMLER'S CAVALRY
The Equestrian SS, 1930-1945

HIMMLER'S CAVALRY
The Equestrian SS, 1930-1945

Paul J. Wilson

Schiffer Military History
Atglen, PA

Acknowledgments
I am indebted to several people for their invaluable assistance in the completion of this book. Johnpeter H. Grill, my major professor during my graduate study at Mississippi State University, introduced me to the topic and provided guidance and support throughout the preparation of a dissertation on the Equestrian SS. Dr. Grill has been an outstanding mentor and friend. I also want to express my appreciation to the Nicholls State University Faculty Research Council for providing funds to complete my research. Further appreciation is expressed to Alfred N. Delahaye, Robert Allen Alexander, and John H. Dennis for helpful suggestions on style and content. By formatting my manuscript, Jenny Schexnayder spared me unnecessary grief. Deborah A. Lillie's photography skills improved the quality of many of the photographs in this book. Mark C. Yerger forwarded my manuscript to Schiffer Publishing, Ltd., and has provided information and photographs used in this book. I am grateful for his assistance in seeing my manuscript improved and published. I received patient assistance from several archivists at the National Archives in Washington D.C., the National Archives II in College Park, Maryland, the Bundesarchiv Berlin, the Institut für Zeitgeschichte in Munich, and the Zentrale Stelle der Landesjustizverwaltungen in Ludwigsburg. Finally, I thank Schiffer Publishing, Ltd., and designer-editor Robert Biondi for accepting my manuscript and trusting my judgment.

Paul J. Wilson, Ph.D.
1999

Dedication:
To my parents, Anne and Burt

Book Design by Robert Biondi.

Printed in China.
ISBN: 0-7643-1112-3

We are always looking for people to write books on new and related subjects. If you have an idea for a book, please contact us at the address below.

Published by Schiffer Publishing Ltd.
4880 Lower Valley Road
Atglen, PA 19310 USA
Phone: (610) 593-1777
FAX: (610) 593-2002
E-mail: Schifferbk@aol.com.
Visit our web site at: www.schifferbooks.com
Please write for a free catalog.
This book may be purchased from the publisher.
Please include $3.95 postage.
Try your bookstore first.

In Europe, Schiffer books are distributed by:
Bushwood Books
6 Marksbury Ave.
Kew Gardens
Surrey TW9 4JF
England
Phone: 44 (0)208 392-8585
FAX: 44 (0)208 392-9876
E-mail: Bushwd@aol.com.
Free postage in the UK. Europe: air mail at cost.
Try your bookstore first.

Contents

Introduction

At the end of World War I, emerging from the chaos of defeat and revolution was Germany's first democracy, the Weimar Republic. Burdened by a dictated peace at Versailles and attendant economic crises, Weimar earned the enmity of countless Germans. The government's greatest critics charged its founders, the Social Democrats, with treason. Millions accepted Field Marshall Paul von Hindenburg's version of events: "The German army was stabbed in the back." Opposition groups multiplied. Weimar rapidly became the unwanted republic, a fragile democracy awaiting collapse.

Into this political cauldron stepped an obscure Austrian, Adolf Hitler, and his radical right-wing movement, National Socialism. Beer hall harangues gained publicity and support for the future dictator, but a pathetic attempt at revolution in 1923 earned him a five-year prison sentence. Banned across Germany were both the Nazi Party and its paramilitary organization of stormtroopers, the SA (*Sturmabteilung*). After serving less than a year of his sentence, Hitler returned to guide the reorganized Nazi Party. The reconstituted SA, however, raised his suspicions. What was needed for personal protection, he believed, was a Praetorian Guard of unquestioning loyalty. In 1925 it began as the SS (*Schutzstaffel*).

No other Nazi organization has achieved such notoriety. Under Heinrich Himmler's leadership, the SS developed into an all-powerful instrument of terror that wielded immense authority throughout Germany and its occupied territories. Called "the dynamic core of the National Socialist state" by one historian, it symbolized Nazi Germany's mono-lithic state-sanctioned terror.[1] Yet scholarship has exposed the SS as no monolith, but a multi-dimensional behemoth of components with distinct functions. What began as a small group of bodyguards, political spies, and strong-armed thugs later developed into a complex, multi-faceted organization.

The SS was involved in a wide variety of activities. It conducted ancestral, archeological, and medical research, and provided assistance to unwed mothers and their children. Its agricultural and industrial em-pire produced building materials, mineral water, textiles, bread, cutlery, porcelain, and other products. Few areas of political and social life in Nazi Germany avoided its presence. The SS influenced the diplomatic corps and judicial system, guarded the Reich Chancellery, and dispatched armed divisions throughout Europe during World War II. It controlled the police, the secret service, its own judicial system, as well as the concen-tration and extermination camps. Because the SS murdered millions, par-ticularly Jews, the Nuremberg Tribunal condemned it as a criminal orga-nization.

At the post-war trials in Nuremberg, the tribunal accused the SS and six other Nazi organizations of being criminal.[2] In effect, the tribunal de-clared that these organizations engaged in conspiracies to carry out the criminal purposes of the Nazi regime. The SS, it ruled, actively partici-pated in the events resulting in Germany's aggressive war, and during the war it committed war crimes and crimes against humanity. The SS exter-minated Jews and others regarded as undesirable, and it ran the concen-tration camp system, thereby committing criminal acts which logically resulted from the organization's ideology. The tribunal labeled as criminals all members of the SS after September 1, 1939. It excluded, however, the Equestrian SS – the SS riding units – from its decision. This exemption appears puzzling and in part reflects the tribunal's inability to comprehend the complex SS organization.[3]

The SS officially began in April 1925 as a headquarters guard for Adolf Hitler. This select group of from ten to twenty trustworthy and devoted Nazis scattered in several cities became subordinate to the SA (*Sturmabteilung*), the Storm Troopers of the original Nazi paramilitary organization. The initial duties of the SS generally mirrored those of its parent organization, the SA. SS members protected Nazi speakers at rallies and party meetings, and they performed such menial tasks as recruiting new party members, distributing Nazi literature, and seeking subscribers and advertisers for the *Völkischer Beobachter*, the Nazi Party newspaper.[4]

In its initial years, the SS hardly revealed its potential. But, on January 6, 1929, Hitler appointed Heinrich Himmler as Supreme SS Leader (*Reichsführer* SS). When Himmler assumed leadership of the approximately 280-man group, he intended to strengthen it and mold it into an indispensable Nazi organization. Himmler envisioned the SS as a new nobility, an elite group based on superior racial attributes, to replace the traditional aristocratic and industrial ruling classes. A gifted organizer, he realized results almost immediately. In less than a year SS membership quadrupled; by January 1933, the SS had an enlistment of over 50,000.[5]

By this time the SS had become distinguishable from the SA in both appearance and function. In 1930 the SS adopted its characteristic black uniform – black tie, black pants, black cap with a death's head insignia (skull and crossbones), and swastika armbands bordered in black. The SS became essentially a police and security force for Hitler and prominent Nazi Party officials. It could also be relied on to execute Hitler's orders, even those against officials within the party. In 1931 the Berlin SS helped suppress the Stennes Putsch, an attempt by SA leader Walter Stennes to defy Hitler, and in late June and early July 1934 the SS assisted in purging the SA of Ernst Röhm and other prominent leaders to appease the army and conservatives. A grateful Hitler returned the favor. Within days of the purge, the SS became independent of the SA.[6]

Institutionally, the SS branched out into several distinct components, almost all of which developed after January 1933 when Hitler became chancellor. The sole exception to this institutional evolution, the SS security service, emerged in 1931 under Reinhard Heydrich, a cashiered navy officer. In 1932 it became the SD (*Sicherheitsdienst*), an intelligence agency for the SS, the Nazi Party, and the Nazi hierarchy. Two significant, specialized, full-time groups were the Death's Head Formations (*Totenkopfverbände*), concentration camp guards, and the SS Militarized Troops (*Verfügungstruppen*), special duty forces who were the forerunners of the Waffen SS, the armed SS which fought in World War II. These two organizations provided Himmler with an ever-increasing number of armed forces during the pre-war years.

With the creation of new SS organizations, Himmler designated the original SS formation as the General (*Allgemeine*) SS. The General SS remained a single unit with no officially recognized components (although SD members also belonged to the General SS). It consisted primarily of part-time "volunteer political soldiers," as viewed by Himmler, who gathered for evening and weekend meetings and training sessions, and it included those SS men not belonging to the newly created armed units. Himmler, envisioning the General SS as a territorial militia, patterned it after the army's organizational structure, an arrangement also copied by the SA. He divided the General SS into Main Sectors (*Oberabschnitte*) corresponding to Military Corps Districts (*Wehrkreise*) throughout Germany and, in World War II, its occupied territories. SS Main Sectors were sub-divided into two to three districts (*Abschnitte*), each consisting of two to four regiments (*Standarten*). At its peak in 1939, the General SS consisted of about 250,000 men.[7]

General SS regiments included infantry and so-called "special units" – motorized regiments, communication and engineer battalions, various medical units, and an equestrian corps. "[W]ith its racial selection, ideological teaching, rigorously enforced marriage code, smart black uniform, and shiny jackboots," the General SS was, according to one historian, "the backbone and spiritual fountainhead of the pre-war SS."[8] But during World War II, the General SS dwindled in size and significance, serving mainly as a source for draftees into the German army and the Waffen SS.

The General SS remains one of the least studied SS components. There is no study analyzing the General SS.[9] The massive literature on the SS focuses mainly on SS police forces, the Waffen SS, and the concentration camp system. The purpose of this study is to provide a greater understanding of the General SS by analyzing one of its important elements: the Equestrian SS (SS-*Reiterei*), Himmler's mounted units dispersed throughout Germany.

The equestrian units (*Reiterstandarten*) were significant because they provided the SS, primarily an urban organization, with access to rural society and to the largely conservative landed gentry and aristocracy. Through the Equestrian SS Himmler penetrated the countryside and attracted numerous farmers to his organization. He likewise gained elite support. Himmler's mounted units naturally appealed to some members of the nobility, for equestrianism had long been regarded as a sport of the upper class. Proportionally there were more nobles in the Equestrian SS officer corps than in any other SS organization. As the organization matured, SS horsemen rode to victory in equestrian competitions throughout Germany and Europe. Equestrian SS successes significantly enhanced the social prestige of the SS. Triumphant SS jockeys afforded the organization an air of dignity, celebrity, and distinction.

The Equestrian SS also represented a unique component of the SS; it was the only SS branch acquitted at the Nuremberg trials despite being an integral part of the General SS. Hoping to complement its social function, Himmler conceived of the Equestrian SS as becoming an SS cavalry force of unquestioning political soldiers prepared to carry out all orders. The 1918-1919 unrest in Germany steadfastly remained in Himmler's (and Hitler's) memory. He thus regarded a mounted security force as essential for domestic stability.

Although another 1918 never occurred, World War II allowed Himmler to achieve his vision for his horsemen. Almost immediately after the outbreak of World War II, the SS established four Death's Head mounted police regiments (*Totenkopf-Reiterstandarten*) as an occupation force in Poland. These initial cavalry units multiplied as the war continued, using Equestrian SS personnel as cadre. During the war, SS horsemen willingly committed atrocities against civilians and soldiers. In particular, the SS Cavalry Brigade became a crucial part of Himmler's murder squadrons. It executed thousands of Jews in eastern Europe, and it was perhaps the first unit to carry out orders to shoot women and children. Thus, being the predecessor of the SS cavalry, the Equestrian SS deserved condemnation as a criminal organization at Nuremberg.

Despite the importance of the Equestrian SS, it is likewise ignored in literature on the SS. When mentioned by scholars, the Equestrian SS appears only as an especially pretentious and traditionally conservative SS organization. For example, German author Heinz Höhne's massive study *The Order of the Death's Head* mentions the Equestrian SS largely in passing; SS horsemen merited less than one page in a work of more than 650 pages. Höhne's study considers the equestrian units as exclusively elite formations designed solely to attract German aristocrats. His excessive reliance on a single Nuremberg Trial document limited his perspective. Its brief discussion also leaves the reader with the false impression that most SS members distrusted Himmler's horsemen.[10] This study, therefore, is designed to fill a gap in the literature by examining the organization, function, and leadership of the Equestrian SS.

CHAPTER ONE

The Equestrian SS: Origin, Structure, and Activities

At the beginning of the twentieth century, perhaps no sport captured the imagination of aristocrats and royalty as much as equestrian competitions. Charmed by the sport's grace and aspiring for membership in elite circles, social climbers joined jockey clubs and sometimes sacrificed fortunes on stables of prized race horses. Even cavalry regiments, whose members dressed in elegant and occasionally ornate uniforms, survived in numbers exceeding their limited usefulness in modern warfare.[1]

Germany has had a long and proud equestrian tradition although Nazi Germany is better known for its mechanized military machine rather than an army that relied on cavalry charges. During Hitler's rule, such Nazi formations as the SS, SA, and Hitler Youth attempted to preserve Germany's equestrian heritage. But for these organizations, horsemanship purportedly was not to be "the prerogative and affair of a propertied class, but a thing for all of those who from enthusiasm and love of horses profess to ride." A riding school in Munich founded for *Kraft Durch Freude*, the Nazi recreational organization for workers, prompted the party's official paper (*Völkischer Beobachter*) to exalt it for allowing "people of little means to participate in riding."[2]

Ideologically, Nazi propagandists regarded horsemanship as a means to remove social distinctions while serving as a *Wehrsport*, a martial sport with obvious implications. Equestrianism, they believed, had been too exclusive, generally restricted to army cavalry schools, titled individuals, and those who could afford to be trained by the masters of horsemanship. Nazi organizations like the SS broadened the sport's horizons by introducing some of the least privileged members of German society to horsemanship. Small farmers and blue bloods rode together in the Equestrian SS. Besides the sport's social significance, Himmler naturally expected it to provide training in horsemanship and cavalry techniques for an SS cavalry at his disposal.

The Equestrian SS began in 1930 with the Munich Equestrian Company. Gradually the SS developed additional mounted units throughout Germany and within a year the SS had organized riding companies in Silesia, Saxony, and in parts of northern Germany. Theoretically, wherever an SS infantry unit existed, an equestrian unit was organized. These units grew to be popular with the public as well as with wealthy rural families and businessmen.[3]

By 1939 the SS had deployed nineteen equestrian units consisting of 112 riding companies – 11,161 men in all. The organizational structure of the Equestrian SS largely mimicked the pattern of regular SS regiments. These units generally emerged from the various riding groups attached to SS foot regiments and ranged in size from the twelve-man riding squad (*Reiterschar*) and the forty-man riding battalion (*Reitertrupp*) to the 140-member equestrian company (*Reitersturm*), which also included a communications squad (*Nachrichtenschar*) of eight men with horses. (Only three companies could exist in any SS district.) As troop strength increased, these independent riding companies could apply to become equestrian regiments (*Reiterstandarten*). An equestrian regiment consisted of four to six companies with a communications battalion of thirty-six men and horses.[4]

The SS organized its equestrian units into areas corresponding to General SS sectors. Between 1933 and 1936 eight equestrian districts (*Reiterabschnitte*) appeared with regional equestrian leaders (*Oberabschnittreiterführer*) for each main sector. Each equestrian district contained at least one but no more than three equestrian regiments. The SS assigned the regional equestrian leader, with an adjutant and secretary, to the staff of each main sector to coordinate equestrian unit activities in his area. They generally selected leaders of individual units and forwarded to the chief equestrian leader all recommendations for promotions. Sometimes they cared for horses belonging to other SS units, particularly the SS Militarized Troops (*Verfugungstruppen*).[5]

As the Equestrian SS developed, it underwent several reorganizations (along with the General SS). Beginning in October 1936, Himmler eliminated the equestrian sectors altogether. Instead, in primary horse-breeding areas he appointed an equestrian inspector in the SS main sector (*Reitinspekteur in der Oberabschnitt*) to assist training and recruiting and to handle questions regarding breeds and breeding. Only SS main sectors *Nordost*, *Nordwest*, *West*, and *Nord* had an inspector, primarily because these areas contained a large number of SS horsemen. The Equestrian SS dominated these regions through successful recruiting. By 1939, these four main sectors contained nine of the SS's nineteen equestrian regiments and 5,317 men, nearly forty-eight percent of all SS horsemen.[6]

To direct his cavalry, Himmler appointed a chief equestrian leader (*Chefreiterführer*). As a member of Himmler's staff, the chief equestrian leader supervised all Equestrian SS activities. Issues involving the equestrian units went through his office before reaching Himmler. For the position, Himmler recruited Georg Skowronski, a horse enthusiast well known in equestrian circles. Himmler expected Skowronski to ensure that all mounted units embraced his desire for SS horsemen to compete with other SS men in displaying their devotion to Nazi ideology, SS duties, camaraderie, and loyalty. Skowronski failed to follow his own advice to his mounted officers. He was thrown out of the SS in 1938 after being convicted of misusing SS funds, excessively profiting from the sale of horses, selling unsuitable horses to the armed SS units, and spreading rumors that those units had been involved in illegitimate horse deals.[7]

In, 1935, the SS opened the first of three riding academies in the city of Forst – schools in Munich and Hamburg later opened – for Equestrian SS personnel to take month-long courses in riding and driving. An inspector of the SS riding schools, Christian Weber, supervised the schools while Wilhelm von Woikowski-Biedau, the inspector of the Equestrian SS, arranged for the enrollment of SS horsemen in training courses. In 1938, however, Himmler replaced von Woikowski-Biedau with Friedrich-Wilhelm Krüger, a devout Nazi and a seasoned SS leader.

Krüger, born May 8, 1894 in Strasbourg, was a World War I officer who joined the SS in 1930. He transferred to the SA to become head of military training. Himmler, however, allowed Krüger to retain his SS rank, and Krüger later returned the favor by reporting SA secrets to Himmler. Although he was an SA general, Krüger rejoined the SS in 1935, assigned to Himmler's personal staff. In 1936 he became inspector for border and watch guard units and in 1938, inspector of the Equestrian SS. He had not expected to be in charge of the Equestrian SS, nor did he want the position. He desired appointment as a main sector leader and, in a personal letter to Himmler, he suggested someone else would be better suited to handle the unified training program for the equestrian units. Reluctant at first, Krüger nevertheless attempted to enforce standardized training methods on all units.[8]

But the most important of all leaders were the commanders of individual units. Himmler placed great responsibility on his equestrian officers. All leaders, from regimental to platoon levels, had to complete equestrian training courses and master the practical and theoretical aspects of riding and cavalry instruction. An unyielding commitment to the Nazi worldview was essential because only precise ideological training created reliable political soldiers. And Himmler demanded that his horse-men train as soldiers. He instructed his leaders to act as commanders by maintaining a proper, martial appearance before their troops and by being proficient in military jargon.[9]

The leadership and staff of a typical equestrian regiment contained a variety of personnel and so-called specialists or directors (*Referenten*). The regiment leader relied on an adjutant and a secretary. A training director, an administrative leader with a secretary, a financial officer, a doctor and dentist, a veterinarian, an educational (ideological) instructor, a leader of "inner service," and personnel, press, athletic, welfare, and gas warfare specialists completed the regimental staff roster. It was often quite difficult to obtain qualified people to fill all of these posts, so individuals often performed two or more jobs within the regiment while it attempted to fill vacancies. The training leader frequently had to meet with all company leaders to ensure that SS horsemen received proper training. An equestrian company, on the other hand, sometimes contained only three men – the leader, the main troop leader, and an administrative officer – to run its affairs.[10]

To strengthen his cavalry, Himmler not only relied on equestrian officers but also required all SS regimental leaders (infantry) to support equestrian units when they were being organized. Equestrian leaders could request transfers for men with horses in other SS units as long as they lived in the area of the equestrian company or in one being organized. Theoretically, men had to be transferred to a riding unit when requested, and without exception. Himmler simply required that all transfers either own a horse or have one at their disposal so they could carry out their duties at any time. Despite this standard, in many units the number of SS riders exceeded the number of horses. But Himmler determined that if at any time a company could not mobilize seventy-five percent of its men on horseback, the unit would be immediately dissolved and members who owned horses would be divided among other equestrian units. The remaining men would be placed in an infantry unit, another special unit, or a reserve company.[11]

Infantry leaders often resented the preferential treatment afforded the equestrian units and occasionally refused to accommodate the requests of equestrian leaders; some simply attempted to transfer their least skilled members. In response, equestrian unit leaders returned all unsuitable personnel and sought the intervention of regional SS leaders when disputes occurred.[12]

While the SS regularly experienced some difficulty securing recruits, its greatest enrollment occurred shortly after Hitler became chancellor. In 1933 the Reich Ministry of the Interior issued a decree ordering all German rural riding associations (*Reitervereine*) to join either the SS or SA. This decree was part of the Nazi program of "coordination" (*Gleichschaltung*), the Nazification of Germany's social and political institutions. Refusal to join subjected the riding associations to dissolution, which would bar members from participating in equestrian tournaments. Most clubs joined the SA, but several in important horse-breeding regions – East Prussia, Holstein, Oldenburg, Hannover, and Westphalia – preferred the SS.[13]

Himmler overlooked normal SS standards in order to assimilate entire riding clubs, although SS doctors eliminated the truly undesirable. For the most part, the SS accepted applicants if they had a character reference, a horse (or one at their disposal), and no criminal record – except of course if an applicant had been arrested during Nazi agitation.

Limited background checks allowed men with unwanted political tendencies to enter SS ranks. In at least one instance, a communist joined the SS. These relaxed standards caused resentments among SS veterans and occasionally conflicts erupted with SS "old-fighters" (pre-1933 members), many of whom considered the horsemen as merely reactionary conservatives with no genuine dedication to Nazism. Indeed, in 1933 eleven horsemen were imprisoned in a concentration camp for refusing to accept the SS oath. In 1934, during the Röhm purge, Himmler had Anton Freiherr von Hohberg und Buchwald, an equestrian leader in East Prussia, shot in the smoking room of his estate for giving SS secrets to the army. Pulling the trigger was Erich von dem Bach-Zelewski, an SS district leader who, during World War II, became a notorious SS police leader. However, most SS horsemen accepted the SS creed and their membership responsibilities.[14]

Before achieving complete independence, SS equestrian units cooperated with the SA Equestrian Corps, and the SS copied many aspects of the Mounted SA. Ernst Röhm, commander of the SA, demanded mixed SA and SS equestrian units under the AW (*Ausbildungswesen*), the SA military training system, unless a special condition warranted the establishment of independent SS units (Himmler regularly discovered extenuating circumstances). Both cavalry corps shared an inspector of equestrian athletics (*Inspekteur des Reitsports*) who supervised the establishment of the SA and SS equestrian units to ensure a unified training regimen. He carried out the orders of the SA chief of military training (*Chef des Ausbildungswesens*) and conducted inspections to determine whether units had followed orders, received satisfactory training, and participated in tournaments.[15]

Since a sufficient number of horses available in a particular area rarely existed, the two groups divided territory throughout Germany. By decree, the strength of the Equestrian SS could not exceed ten percent of the Mounted SA – a significant recruiting advantage – and only the Equestrian SA or SS could exist in a locale. (While Himmler officially forbade SS recruiting in regions reserved for the SA, he blinked at numerous violations.) Theoretically, the SS regional equestrian leader and the SA regional leaders would meet to discuss dividing a territory and whether to transfer personnel. However, SS and SA district leaders and equestrian leaders often negotiated transfers. Proposals had to be submitted to the inspector of equestrian sports, who would then seek approval for the arrangement from the Supreme SA leadership. In some areas, the SA transferred entire units thereby increasing the number of men and horses to the point that SS companies could apply to become a regiment.[16]

Because a farmer's livelihood often depended on the health of his horse, many wondered whether their animals would be at risk if they joined the SS or SA. To appease those concerned, the SA, beginning in February 1934, offered low-cost horse insurance for SA and SS members. The insurance provided favorable benefits at a cost of only two to five *Reichsmarks* (RM) per year, depending on the horse's age. A policyholder received one-third of a horse's value if it were killed or had to be destroyed because of an accident, and two marks per day for fourteen days of treatment by a veterinarian for horses injured during SS or SA service. The insurance was a great success and soon the benefits improved dramatically. Within eight months, 60,000 horsemen bought policies. By December 1934, the insurance company had met all claims, paying out 106,217 RM. Some claims, however, raised suspicions among adjusters concerned with members "violating Nazi principles" by conspiring with veterinarians to exploit the system. The SA advised policy holders to keep claims as low as possible or face serious consequences.[17]

Fearing competition, several private insurance companies became angry and criticized what they called inferior policies offered by an organization practicing unfair competition. They sometimes refused to terminate the policies of horsemen who wished to rely solely on insurance offered by the SA. Some private insurance companies even rejected damage claims for horsemen who held SA policies. To correct the situation, the equestrian units compiled a list of grievances which induced the SA leadership to dissuade those companies "not at all in harmony with the spirit of National Socialism" from defrauding SA and SS members.[18]

Despite being originally aligned with the SA, SS equestrian units did achieve some degree of autonomy. Most equestrian units had been organized independently just before or shortly after the SS achieved official independence in 1934. Actually, several months before achieving autonomy, all SS equestrian units came under Himmler's direct control. The Equestrian SS, however, was much smaller than the SA Equestrian Corps; several SS equestrian units initially had been regiments in name only. The SS had not been as successful as the SA in securing recruits, but it did benefit from SA transfers.[19]

To provide a uniform basis for his independent cavalry, beginning in 1934 Himmler adopted a series of recruiting guidelines predictably and predominantly copied from the SA. In theory, the maximum age for new recruits with prior equestrian training was thirty-five. All other recruits could be no older than twenty-five. All candidates had to be examined by a racial specialist (*Rassereferent*), who determined whether they could receive an SS physical; Himmler desired only Nordic types to fill SS ranks. Men under 1.70 meters were supposed to be excluded. Unlike the situation with the rest of the SS, no admissions freeze for the equestrian units ever existed because Himmler recognized the difficulty in securing qualified horsemen. Recruiting remained a significant problem throughout the brief history of the Equestrian SS.[20]

Reorganizations

From 1930-1939 some 20,000 men passed through the ranks of the Equestrian SS. A lack of skilled personnel and a desire to expel opportunists and the unskilled inspired frequent reorganizations of mounted units. Between April 1935 and December 1936 the size of the Equestrian SS dropped by about twenty-five percent. In 1936, the SS simply dissolved some units or incorporated them into others, and preparations to establish additional units were curtailed. Some new arrangements seemed particularly odd and resulted because several regiments really had not met the strength requirements to be called a regiment. In Bavaria, for instance, Himmler combined Equestrian Regiment 17 in Bad Wörishofen with Regiment 15 in Munich. He attached Equestrian Regiment 24, a unit recently supplemented by the takeover of two SA companies, to Equestrian Regiment 14 in Karlsruhe for about three weeks in November before assigning it to the reorganized Equestrian Regiment 17 in Regensburg. Reorganizations occurred frequently in the equestrian units, and some regiments changed headquarters several times within a year.[21]

In SS Main Sector *Elbe*, Himmler combined regiments 16 and 22 into a reorganized Equestrian Regiment 16 headquartered in Dresden. With the reorganization, Regiment 16 totalled 756 men, about the required size for a regiment. The reorganization, however, posed problems. Most members of the consolidated unit were farmers, so about seventy percent of its horses were draft animals. With companies dispersed throughout the region – from seventy to 110 kilometers from Dresden – they rarely assembled as a group. The newly added companies from the former Equestrian Regiment 22 were even farther away from headquarters (110 to 170 kilometers). To complicate matters further, the unit briefly had no official leader because of the removal of its previous one for disciplinary reasons.[22]

The Equestrian SS also lost many men to the army once Hitler reintroduced the draft in 1935 (most of whom, not surprisingly, requested to serve in a cavalry regiment). Himmler warned his units to prepare for disruptions, and he stressed the need to recruit replacements from the SA and from those discharged from the army. He pointed equestrian leaders to the Hitler Youth as a reservoir for potential SS horsemen because many had already received ideological instruction and equestrian training, sometimes from the SS.[23]

Despite the need for more bodies, the Equestrian SS was becoming more selective. It relied vigorously on medical examinations and investigations into the racial backgrounds of horsemen. Previously, it had accepted some poor farmers who even relied on steers rather than horses to work their fields. Himmler, however, urged subordinates to recruit only horse owners or their sons. He no longer wanted to accept low-income members simply because they wished to ride. Even with stricter entrance standards, the SS established an equestrian regiment in Schwerin in 1937 and one in Vienna shortly after the union with Austria in 1938. This expansion returned the troop strength of the Equestrian SS (11,161) to about its 1935 level.[24]

Activities

Initially riding in tournaments was not heavily stressed, in part because so many recruits required ideological preparation as well as training in fundamentals. Himmler encouraged participation in tournaments only as long as a competitor's regular SS duties did not suffer. And he preferred team rather than individual participation so that high average scores could be achieved more easily. Only skilled horsemen could compete, for Himmler wanted only men guaranteed to project a favorable SS image. All participants had to get the approval of the company leader or, in the case of international tournaments, the blessing of the head equestrian leader. Even members of other SS units wishing to compete in tournaments needed the permission of the nearest equestrian company leader.[25]

Beginning in 1935, the Equestrian SS increasingly participated in competitions in Germany and abroad, garnering many championships and high placements. At tournaments, SS horsemen wore their uniforms with their ranks prominently displayed, whether they appeared as contestants or spectators. They rode as SS men, not as individuals, a reality Himmler believed the press would notice.[26]

SS jockeys were especially successful in show jumping and occasionally in dressage competitions, although they also won in other events, even racing. Himmler encouraged his units to organize tournaments with participation by the army, the SA, and the police. He wanted his cavalrymen to ride in as many equestrian competitions as possible. Within a short time Himmler's cavalry had become a triumphant sports organization, although in reality only a small minority of SS horsemen rode successfully for their regiments in tournaments.[27]

Himmler encouraged his jockeys not only to ride in tournaments but also to take an active role in equestrian events by setting up and tearing down obstacles and by serving in a judging or leadership capacity. SS leaders had to contact the organization holding the competition to confirm SS participation as judges or leaders because, except for major German equestrian tournaments, Himmler deterred SS jockeys from riding in any event organized and operated without SS influence. For that reason, he urged members to join private rural riding clubs and other organizations involved in horsemanship.[28]

Several prominent jockeys rode for the SS. In 1935, Günter Temme of East Prussia won the prestigious German Derby (*Deutsches Spring-Derby*) in Hamburg, and another East Prussian, Oskar Lengnick, won the Pardubice Steeplechase in Czechoslovakia, one of the world's toughest steeplechase races. In that year, the SS rode in its first international tournament, in Riga, emerging as the dominant team. East Prussian SS horsemen were the most successful of Himmler's riders and consistently led all other SS regions in tournament victories. Not surprisingly, the SS counted in its ranks the best horsemen from the former riding clubs there.

Most rural units, however, consisted primarily of farmers with plow horses. Yet Himmler, referring to the success of his East Prussians, expected similar success from the other equestrians. He declared that there were sufficient opportunity and resources available in all areas to be successful. Eberhard Freiherr von Künsberg, the leader of Equestrian Regiment 15 in Bavaria, told his unit that although it appeared that farm horses were unsuited for competitions, previous success had shown that one could win with those mounts.

Himmler's horsemen made great strides. Including firsts and placements, they totalled 544 victories in 1935, 904 in 1936, and 1,378 in 1937. They swept every major German equestrian championship in 1937, followed by 2,342 victories, including 551 first-place finishes, in 1938. Before World War II, SS horsemen won four of the last five German

Derby competitions in Hamburg. In early 1939, Friedrich-Wilhelm Krüger, Inspector of the Equestrian SS, sent a memorandum to all units congratulating them for their accomplishments, with special commendations going to the best horsemen: Temme, the spring jumping champion, Max Heidenreich, the three-day event champion, Carl Andreas, dressage champion, and August Nagel, cross-country riding champion.[29]

The Equestrian SS was by no means involved exclusively in athletic activities, as some members testified at Nuremberg and as some scholars have suggested. These units, as part of the General SS, trained as an SS cavalry and a mounted police force for emergency situations. They received paramilitary training, though perhaps limited and somewhat covert, and they learned about setting up roadblocks and barricades useful for police purposes; they often reported for barricade duty at Nazi functions. These instances do not implicate the Equestrian SS in any specific criminal activities, but they suggest that equestrian units were intended to have more than an athletic function.[30]

The SS attempted, often unsuccessfully, to keep the paramilitary aspects of the equestrian units secret, particularly before remilitarization. Memoranda discussed the importance of protecting SS documents stamped "Secret," especially those dealing with cavalry training. These papers had to be securely locked up with access available to only "truly reliable" men. Circulars reminded all horsemen that certain SS matters should not be discussed in public.[31]

The SS could hardly conceal all of its activities. During an event in Plankstadt, a small farming community in the demilitarized Rhineland, an SS riding company performed a demonstration using artillery. The local paper reported the event as allowing the public to view "a glimpse of the official training of the SS Reitertrupp Plankstadt." It described the artillery as being "ready to fire," giving the impression of a military display.[32]

When the report reached higher SS authorities, they wondered how damaging the information would be to foreign affairs. An ensuing investigation judged the article an exaggeration: The artillery piece was simply a dummy used occasionally by former rural riding clubs in Baden in their riding demonstrations. And the Equestrian SS had nothing to do with its publication. The equestrian leader had, in fact, warned the writer that no military aspects were to be reported. Nevertheless, Himmler formally reprimanded Dr. Fritz Hausamen, leader of Equestrian Regiment 13, for failing to follow orders – "it was his duty to avoid any appearance of military demonstrations." The SS, believing that the article contained treasonable views, had the Gestapo investigate its writer.[33]

Although SS horsemen acquired valuable skills, the army "officially" refused to recognize any military training of the Mounted SS. SS riders could acquire the horsemanship certificate (*Reiterscheine*), a license which allowed its holder to be placed in a cavalry regiment upon being drafted into the German army. After Hitler reintroduced the draft, the SS partly justified its paramilitary training as the preparatory training of future cavalrymen for the *Wehrmacht*. According to one report, SS horsemen had made favorable impressions on the army after being drafted. Still, the army often disregarded the certificate because mechanization had diminished the importance of maintaining large cavalry forces. At the outbreak of war in 1939, the army had only one remaining cavalry regiment. Nevertheless, the certificate provided the SS with an indication of the equestrian abilities of its members.[34]

The Equestrian SS also involved itself in a variety of other activities. Members organized hunts and tournaments and provided instruction in riding and driving to both SS and Nazi Party members, as well as to the German public. SS riders' regular obligations included parade duty, assistance at Nazi functions, and weekly duty rides often followed by inspections, discussions of official business, and sometimes ideological instruction. The Equestrian SS regularly participated in parades and as cordons at various German festivals and official Nazi Party functions. Himmler demanded that only those with a proper Nordic appearance who exhibited standards of professionalism be allowed to participate. He hoped not only to show proper respect for the occasion and guests present, but also to benefit recruiting.[35]

To cement bonds of friendship and mutual respect, the Equestrian SS regularly held social gatherings called "camaraderie evenings" (*Kameradschaftsabend*) for its units, for its patrons and sponsors (*Fördernde Mitglieder*), and for other Nazi formations. These units would gather for an evening of socializing – eating, drinking, and singing – and to listen to ideological or cultural presentations. Some equestrian leaders took their men to local businesses, especially those that supported the SS, to inspect how their fellow workers were enriching Germany.

Equestrian members were expected to take their commitment to their fellow (Aryan) citizens seriously. Hence, SS horsemen were active in Nazi welfare programs and in finding jobs for unemployed unit members. Equestrian unit leaders often posted job openings in their daily and weekly orders. They monitored unemployment in the ranks to find suitable jobs for unemployed horsemen. The SS or sometimes local businesses donated uniforms and other supplies to needy members. Individual units occasionally paid the SS expenses of their poorer members, for the SS tried to ensure that membership did not exacerbate one's economic status.[36]

Significantly and especially useful for the later defense at the Nuremberg Trials, the Equestrian SS captured the admiration of foreign diplomats. Equestrian Regiment 7 in Berlin, by far the largest of the mounted units, shared a distinct relationship with the German Foreign Office. The regiment merged diplomats and attachés from the Ministry of Intelligence and the Justice Department with numerous students, high-level civil servants, and members of Berlin's leading social circles (nobles and the financial elite). It was Himmler's most elegant and fashionable mounted formation. One member was Gustav Adolph von Halem, Chief of Protocol in the German Foreign Office, who became ambassador to Lisbon in early 1945. Prince Bernhard zu Lippe-Biesterfeld, the Dutch prince consort, also graced its ranks.[37]

Members of Equestrian Regiment 7 served as escorts and bodyguards for foreign diplomats and guests at Nazi celebrations and festivals, especially the Nuremberg rallies and the 1936 Olympic Games. Knowledge of foreign languages, the ability to communicate effectively, and social graces were as important as equestrian ability. Those proficient in foreign languages informed guests about Nazi Germany and defended National Socialism from disparagement. Sometimes cordial relations developed between escort and guest. Wolfgang Jasper, a member of an equestrian company attached to Regiment 7, escorted the Belgian ambassador, Vicomte d'Avignon, during 1936 fall festivals. Jasper made such a favorable impression that he was twice invited to the Belgian ambassador's home. Jasper, who also escorted the English and French ambassadors, testified at Nuremberg that he noticed no ill-will or unfriendly attitudes toward the SS from foreign guests.[38]

Paul Brantenaar, the regiment's commander and leader of an escort group, was especially sophisticated and refined. His knowledge of French and English allowed him to usher around guests of Berlin from many countries, and he frequently received gifts and honorary titles from foreign dignitaries. Himmler, Hitler, and officials in the German Foreign Office praised his service to the fatherland. His services were highly sought after, and not just by SS organizations. Brantenaar's SS career was not without complications. But when in early 1936 a Nazi Party court punished Brantenaar for concealing a previous lodge membership as well as business debts, Himmler personally intervened to protect his equestrian officer.[39]

The Equestrian SS of 1939 looked remarkably different from its initial formations. Its membership of successful jockeys, aristocrats, and businessmen gained the group an elite image even though most members were small farmers. Himmler displayed great affection for his mounted SS, appreciating the social prestige his organization gained from the elite cavalry troops. And, with limitations, the Equestrian SS had fulfilled Himmler's goal to involve rural society in his ever-expanding empire.

Institutionally, the Equestrian SS became a completely integrated component of the General SS, subordinate to the SS Main Office. And Himmler's horsemen trained to become true SS men: political soldiers who fulfill all obligations, expectations, and responsibilities as SS men. Like other SS components, the Equestrian SS had a paramilitary function. SS horsemen received pre-military training to prepare them for security and police duty. Many horsemen also trained with the Militarized SS Troops (*Verfügungstruppen*) as part of the broad SS "Police Reinforcement" program to provide a cadre of trained manpower for security and concentration camp duty in Death's Head units in the event of mobilization.

Although the ceremonial and athletic functions of the Equestrian SS brought rewards, Himmler's plans for domestic security and for the wartime expansion of the SS included a paramilitary role for his horsemen. To become dedicated political soldiers required an SS training regimen.

CHAPTER TWO

Training

Being an Equestrian SS horseman required significant sacrifice and commitment. Initially, the SS unrealistically expected men, some of whom had to drive, bicycle, ride, or walk several miles to meeting areas, to train and listen to ideological instruction for at least two hours during three nights a week and for four hours on Sundays. Himmler even suggested that SS members schedule their vacations when the SS was on break so that when activities resumed operations would proceed as scheduled. Himmler also preferred that his men not join other organizations because of the demanding SS schedule (exceptions being those groups involved in equestrianism). Obviously, great devotion was required because the men, after completing the day's labors and leaving their fields, would work for the SS. Many who quit, even in the late 1930s, cited as a reason a "loss of interest," their primary problem being the number of hours demanded each week.[1]

SS training programs were seasonal; ideological and theoretical instruction dominated the winter months but training in the field occurred in warm months. The men engaged in a variety of activities and drills as leaders prepared them to become an SS cavalry and trained gifted individuals to become superior jockeys. Some leaders required eighteen days of service each month. SS horsemen received instruction on many topics quite useful for farmers: horse breeds and breeding, anatomy, diseases, first aid, agricultural uses of horses, horse grooming, building makeshift stalls, proper feeding and drinking times, daily rations, and the effect of weight and temperature on animal performance. Other areas of instruction, while less practical for farming activities, furthered SS goals. SS riders practiced correct posture, jumping over natural obstacles, riding according to skill level, and cross country riding. The men learned how to guard stables and how to set up blockades and cordons for security duty. They also learned traffic regulations and practiced patrol duty and how to ride in parades. These exercises, drills, and activities remained fairly consistent until the outbreak of war.[2]

The SS eventually allowed modifications in its training schedule during harvest and planting times, and the number of days set aside each month for training declined. For the Mounted SS, the SS stopped establishing lengthy training schedules of several months and instead relied on a monthly training period which usually included eight or nine days of activities. Members active in agriculture no longer needed to apply for a long leave of absence. The SS agreed that sometimes agricultural work took precedence over SS duties, making it easier for farmers to be granted official leaves of absence. Successful jockeys likewise gained privileges. But SS horsemen could not completely neglect regular SS duties, for they too "had to live up to their obligations as SS men."[3]

Ideological Instruction

Within the entire framework of paramilitary training ideological instruction took precedence. Leaders devoted special attention to Nazi ideology during regular exercises and held ideological lectures to inculcate the Nazi worldview. All leaders were required to ensure that their horsemen joined the Nazi Party, a difficult task at times because the party occasionally froze admissions to keep from admitting opportunists. Through frequent lectures and presentations, SS horsemen received basically the same ideological training as members of SS infantry units.[4]

Each week the training program included ideological instruction, and commanders were sometimes responsible for carrying out instruction on a wide variety of National Socialist topics. Men learned the purpose and goals of the Nazi Party and the SS, the world views of both organizations, and the SS's relation to other party formations. They discovered the various components of the SS and other party formations. They were also expected to understand the importance of the black uniform and the requisite behavior of those who donned one. The uniform was for official gatherings only; regulations prohibited men from wearing the SS uniform at night clubs, carnivals, and similar places and events.

As part of ideological training, Himmler required all horsemen, especially those in urban units, to guard stables and to engage in menial tasks like cleaning stables and stalls, providing food and water to the horses, and caring for the saddlery. The latter activities would assist in breaking down social barriers and provide many with an awareness of the hard work farmers regularly engaged in.[5]

Men, including leaders, were required to adhere strictly to SS rules and regulations and devote themselves to becoming political soldiers for Hitler. SS riders received lessons on various SS requirements, such as the necessity to marry and have children and the importance of joining *Lebensborn*, the SS maternity organization which provided assistance to unwed mothers and their children. For Himmler, joining *Lebensborn* was the honorary duty of all bachelors and childless married couples. Equestrian leaders often reminded horsemen of penalties and punishments awaiting those who failed to meet their SS obligations.[6]

To assist commanders in every unit, the training division (*Schulungsabteilung*) in the SS Race and Settlement Office – the agency charged with maintaining purity in the ranks – selected education advisors responsible for indoctrination programs. In addition, regimental leaders established education leaders (*Schulungsleiter*) to deliver ideological lectures. These men, together with unit officers, generally attended preparatory indoctrination programs offered by the Race and Settlement Office. When no suitably trained personnel were available, the Nazi Party helped out.[7]

The units regularly received the SS *Leithefte*, the SS ideological journal which Himmler encouraged his jockeys to read. Lessons from the journal sometimes served as guides for presentations when education leaders were unavailable. Its contents were strictly for SS men, and all copies had to be protected and the contents held in strict confidence to keep outsiders from learning much about the organizations. Himmler also urged his horsemen to subscribe to and promote *Das Schwarze Korps*, the official SS newspaper. On occasion, the SS suggested appropriate books and movies, especially those emphasizing the party's position on key issues.[8]

Because SS ideology could be especially superficial – and downright foolish – boredom regularly trumped interest. And sessions tended to be redundant with a great deal of overlapping of themes. A shortage of so-called educators resulted in recurrent presentations by amateurs. Many SS horsemen, like SS members in general, quickly tired of indoctrination sessions, even when accompanied by a steady flow of beer and song. SS officials repeatedly admonished leaders to engage their audience with exciting lectures so that the message would not fall on deaf ears. Frequently it did and ideological presentations were scaled back generally to one weekday.[9]

Recurrent lectures on the so-called science of race were important educational programs to Himmler. After all, the peasant horsemen were paragons of Nazi ideology with its emphasis on a return to the soil. Himmler believed his jockeys needed to be taught the importance of race, not only racial eugenics, but racial antisemitism, by the racial expert in each unit. Racial purity was essential for advancement in the Equestrian

SS. Although he initially allowed many men of questionable desirability from the riding clubs to join the SS, he insisted that all officers submit hereditary papers to prove their Aryan roots. He also expected their wives to have a correct genetic background.[10]

Because there remained a suspicion among many regarding the reliability of SS horsemen, 1936 became a year of purification. The SS adopted stricter guidelines for promotions; candidates generally had to prove themselves ideologically sound. Accordingly, the SS determined to purge the ranks of the equestrian units of everyone not ideologically in tune with the "special struggle of the Schutzstaffel and the advancing struggle of the Equestrian SS." Only those who truly embraced the values of the period of struggle (before 1933) were the actual supporters of the movement and would remain on the "special and chosen team of the Führer." As the Equestrian SS learned, ideological training was the most important means for carrying out SS goals.[11]

A particularly thorny issue for ideological instructors was religion. Although Himmler wished otherwise, some SS members were regular churchgoers. Traditional beliefs and influences remained strong in many regions and attacks on religion could prompt unwanted responses among the faithful (especially from wives of SS riders). The SS directed education leaders to exercise great restraint when dealing with religious issues. Himmler forbade singing or playing music near churches out of respect for religious services; nor could men sing the anti-Jewish and anti-Catholic song *"Juden raus, Pabst hinaus."*[12]

Initially, the Equestrian SS reluctantly accepted many religious practices of its members. Some equestrian leaders sent Christmas greetings, told individual companies to organize their own Christmas celebrations, and encouraged members to give gifts to comrades less well off. Yet devout Nazis obeyed Himmler's directives and used the holiday season to instruct men to honor the old German festival of the winter solstice, not the birth of Christ. Among other things, ideological instructors discussed how the pagan festival influenced Christmas with the Christmas tree, the tree of eternal life from the traditional German celebration. But initially no major efforts were made to infringe upon religious beliefs and practices.[13]

The Equestrian SS in southern Germany included numerous Catholics, a denomination thoroughly despised by Nazis. While being anti-clerical in spirit, the SS hoped to avoid problems in the community or with the parents and wives of its members. Still, Himmler wanted the ranks cleansed of Catholic priests and members of Catholic organizations. He preferred to accept only "God believers" who had already left the church (atheists were intensely despised), but many southern, conservative, rural horsemen appear to have remained in the church, and many belonged to Catholic organizations.[14]

Eberhard Freiherr von Künsberg, a one-time leader of Equestrian Regiment 15 in Munich, remarked in a special order to his subordinate officers how predominant Catholicism was in Bavaria and among his riders. The Equestrian SS, he believed, would have a hard time getting members if it excluded men who belonged to Catholic organizations. Von Künsberg told his officers that instead of simply regarding these groups as enemies of Germany, they should "correct" the "false education" their members received from Catholic organizations. True SS men were those willing to "show their worthiness to be educated in the spirit of Adolf Hitler and all things German."[15]

Von Künsberg had an opportunity to discuss the Catholic issue in response to punishment inflicted upon one of his horsemen for refusing to fight. He penalized a recent recruit for – as usual —"damaging the image of the SS" by not defending himself in an "SS worthy" manner. Personal courage and determination, he declared, define SS men. The transgression, though, resulted in only a mild punishment because the young horseman had been only briefly in the SS, and his membership in a Catholic student group probably affected his behavior. As many realized, ideological indoctrination required some time to achieve its desired effect. But in the future, von Künsberg warned, SS members had better defend themselves or risk expulsion for cowardice: "The slightest attack must be repelled with great brutality. There should never be any other view in the SS."[16]

By late 1937 Himmler's purification program had dramatically reduced Catholic influence in equestrian units. In August of that year, the leader of Equestrian Regiment 17, another Bavarian unit which two months later merged with Regiment 15 in Munich, stated that no members of his unit belonged to Catholic organizations. It had to be comforting to SS leaders that in the birthplace of the Nazi movement (Munich), SS horsemen had fallen in line.

Predictably, Mounted SS members also received a significant amount of instruction on antisemitism. Like all SS members, they were expected to adhere to party and SS anti-Jewish principles. Visiting Jewish doctors and patronizing Jewish-owned businesses was not allowed. Members who acted otherwise, or who allowed their wives and children to do so, faced expulsion for "serious transgressions against National Socialist principles." Likewise, all purchases, whether made at a store or through a representative, had to come from pure Aryan firms. The Nazi Party and the SS dutifully supplied lists of all Jewish-owned businesses in their area along with guides to "acceptable" businesses.[17]

Nevertheless, at times the SS intervened to prevent members from engaging in antisemitic demonstrations in accordance with prevailing laws. Von Künsberg reiterated the Nazi decree against anti-Jewish disturbances. (At the time Göring, of all people, said opponents of Nazism were causing problems by harassing Jews under the guise of antisemitism.) He instructed his unit to halt such actions and to remove all "illegal" antisemitic signs such as the "tasteless placards" proclaiming, "Jews, enter town at your own risk," "Jews get out or otherwise...," "Jews will be hanged in the gallows," or caricaturing Jews being beaten or humiliated. These orders only occurred for superficial political reasons because antisemitism prevailed as an important theme during ideological training. After the Night of the Broken Glass (*Kristallnacht*), all equestrian units received circulars instructing members to turn over to the Gestapo Jewish goods seized in the uprising.[18]

Equestrian and Cavalry Training

Himmler's guidelines for the physical training of an SS cavalryman allowed him to master a variety of activities on horseback and on foot. Himmler wanted all horsemen to engage in challenging exercises as often as possible. Only beginners could practice basic riding techniques, and then for only short periods. But because of so many unskilled recruits, basic riding instruction occurred more than anticipated. Still, to prepare men for competition, riders rehearsed the fundamentals of horsemanship.

Cavalry training was the preferred method of instruction. On horseback, men practiced light trotting, galloping, and jumping over natural obstacles (such as fallen trees and especially trenches), and skill maneuvers (such as riding while holding three horses, one with the left hand, two with the right). SS riders rehearsed night marching and patrol riding to master rapid mounting and dismounting.[19]

Since cavalrymen could expect to dismount during operations, SS horsemen learned infantry fundamentals. They rehearsed by running with their horses for long stretches and by participating in regular infantry exercises like marching, rolling, and crawling. They practiced camouflage, disguise, shooting, map reading, and distance estimating. While SS training goals stressed the importance of creating "independent warriors," SS horsemen practiced as a unit to teach cooperation and camaraderie.[20]

To ensure proper training of his personnel, Himmler required all equestrian leaders to attend riding and driving courses. Only skilled horsemen and those who could benefit their unit after the training regimen were to be sent to these schools. In the early 1930s, SS horsemen generally took the *Rothkirch Kursus*, cavalry training courses taught by Edwin Graf Rothkirch, the former leader of the army's cavalry school (*Kavallerie-Schule Hannover*) riding team. Graf Rothkirch was one of the army's most successful jockeys and the author of *Gedanken über Ausbildung in der Reitergruppe*, a cavalry training manual used by individual units. Graf Rothkirch, however, trained SS horsemen for only a brief period; he retired in September 1934, after which the SS established its own riding academies. Facilities in Forst, Hamburg, and Munich (discussed in chapter four) provided a uniquely SS education.[21]

As a regular aspect of training, the SS organized several leadership meetings and two-day teaching conferences for equestrian officers during which they received instruction on such topics as how to carry out administrative tasks, conduct inspections, and mobilize units. They also learned proper command language, how to give and understand battle orders, and how to conduct war games. Leaders received specific instruction in cavalry operations during day and night, including getting oriented at night. After dark, exercises could concern the effect of light and noise on cavalry forces, setting up guard posts, and advancing maneuvers, surprise attacks, and dismounting to fight as an infantry unit. In essence, every equestrian leader had to be prepared to lead troops in all phases of battle.[22]

The average SS horseman trained at the company level. Leaders or training specialists essentially taught what they themselves had learned. Riders learned to understand and carry out orders, and they practiced war games as a mounted unit and as foot soldiers. They formed firing lines to practice shooting, studied battle strategy, learned how to use a compass for military applications, and how to estimate distance, evaluate terrain, read a map, and use camouflage. They practiced crawling and sneaking up on enemy positions, blocking off bridges, dispatch riding, reconnaissance activity, and patrol riding. Aspects of modern warfare were not neglected: Men learned how to respond to approaching motorized units and planes.[23]

Because the Equestrian SS would be used as a mounted police force in emergency situations, the SS regularly held mobilization exercises. These generally occurred at night to avoid conflict with farm work or other employment. Not surprisingly, rural units experienced the greatest difficulty in assembling their horsemen, although some units fared better than others.[24]

In part, this reflected the difficulty of training rural units, many of which were located far from the regiment's headquarters. It was likely that a company would be divided among several rural communities. These units consisted of farmers who worked grueling, physically demanding days in their fields. During harvesting, many farmers found it virtually impossible to follow SS training schedules. Some received permission to occasionally skip meetings.

In many units, initial mobilization exercises were rather comical. At times some men neglected to inform their fellow horsemen and, when designated informers were absent from home, a significant percentage of company members were unaware of an alarm. Also, orders often were not carried out properly. Some men appeared without their horses and other requisite materials, while others, when contacted, did not even know where to assemble.

When Equestrian Regiment 24 in SS Main Sector *Main* held several emergency mobilization exercises in 1936, its urban units generally took about an hour to gather at the alarm station; rural units usually needed about two hours to assemble, longer during bad weather. Company 2 consisted of four platoons of farmers dispersed in northeastern upper Franconia. Most lived in small towns and villages or on farms without telephones. Some farmers lived in houses without doorbells and nameplates. With few available automobiles, messengers frequently relied on trains to notify units, and designated individuals had to inform as many as eight comrades.[25]

Only with frequent mobilization exercises did conditions improve; most units reported significant progress by 1937. In February, Company 3 of Regiment 17 in Bavaria held a smoothly executed alarm exercise for its platoons. SS horsemen assembled quickly and were ready for further orders. Company 4 even held a successful emergency exercise in August during the harvesting of hops. The company leader praised the promptness of its horsemen, for it revealed, as he suggested, their pronounced understanding of their duty to the SS.[26]

By 1939, Himmler's cavalry was taking shape. The chronic absenteeism and ineffective training sessions had diminished appreciably. The prior practice of accepting substandard recruits ceased, the ranks were purged, and generally skilled personnel became Himmler's horsemen. And Friedrich-Wilhelm Krüger, inspector of the Equestrian SS, had begun assembling all equestrian unit leaders for advanced training courses. For the first time, commanders trained as a group, receiving special instruction essential for the standardized training of all equestrian units. The outbreak of war, of course, prevented this progression.

The goal of SS training – to create disciplined political soldiers militarily and ideologically committed to perform any task – remained incomplete but hardly a thorough failure. SS horsemen were part-time, amateur cavalrymen; the development of genuine political soldiers required a full-time assignment. And, like the regimens in most General SS components, the effectiveness of Equestrian SS training was diminished by a variety of other reasons: low budgets, time constraints, and poor leadership among them.[27]

But, because of regular indoctrination sessions, SS horsemen understood the purpose of the SS and their roles as defenders of Hitler and the Nazi movement. Even though ideological training was at times particularly superficial and haphazard and often conducted by amateurs, no rider could justifiably plead ignorance of the nature of the SS.

Even modestly successful paramilitary instruction enabled Himmler to assimilate a significant number of SS-trained farmers into his organization and thereby infiltrate the German countryside. Although an entire equestrian regiment undoubtedly could not have been mobilized immediately to execute difficult security operations, the Equestrian SS did serve as a pool of moderately prepared mounted personnel. It is therefore hardly surprising that SS cavalry units in World War II included many former Equestrian SS personnel.

CHAPTER THREE

The SS Riding Schools

To supplement its training program for Equestrian SS officers and to train men and horses of the Militarized SS Troops, the SS opened three riding schools: Riding School Forst (*Reitschule Forst*), the Remount Institute of the SS Main Office (*Remount Anstalt des SS Hauptamt*), and the SS Main Riding School (*Hauptreitschule*). With the opening of these schools Himmler expected to relieve the SS from having to send its men to schools run by the SA, the party, or the state. Here, he believed, men would receive a uniquely SS education. Although the schools mainly provided advanced training for Equestrian SS officers, men from a variety of SS organizations completed their courses. Young recruits and equestrian leaders received instruction in horse breeding and in practical and theoretical aspects of riding horses and carriage driving. Ideological instruction naturally complemented their training.

By constructing these schools, Himmler hoped to imitate the great institution of the German cavalry, the Hannover Cavalry School, whose purpose was to train officers and non-commissioned officers as riding instructors for army troops. Like men at the Hannover Cavalry School, Himmler's horsemen prepared to participate in equestrian competitions.

They also trained to acquire various certifications and honors, including the National Athletic Badge (*Reichsportabzeichen*) and the SA Athletic Badge (SA *Sportabzeichen*). These riding academies occasionally organized their own tournaments with international participation.[1]

To supervise these facilities, Himmler appointed Christian Weber as his inspector of the riding schools. Weber was a stout, beer-guzzling roughneck and practically Hitler's one-man bodyguard during his early days in Munich. Among his many passions were horses. He parlayed his connections into an impressive fortune, including stables for his ten race horses described by one observer as "a horse's paradise." He founded a successful international racing event, the Brown Ribbon of Germany (*Braune Band Deutschlands*), in Munich in 1934. Each year a special train from Berlin transported hundreds of guests for the week of festivities associated with the event. As inspector of the SS riding schools, he endeavored to secure a niche for SS horsemen in international equestrianism, but not excessively. He generally spent considerably more time entertaining Nazi bigwigs in Munich.[2]

Reitschule Forst

The first official SS equestrian academy opened on July 1, 1935. The Forst Riding School, a facility built with financial support from the Hansel Corporation, initially included a staff of twenty-eight. Its stables expanded from a collection of forty-five horses, including several worthy thoroughbreds, to eighty within two years. In month-long courses, participants trained in riding and driving, shooting, athletics, and ideology. Because the school emphasized advanced training methods, only Equestrian SS leaders or individuals who expected to become training personnel attended Forst.[3]

An average of twenty-five to thirty participants enrolled in these courses. The courses, crucial for preparing leaders of rural units, allowed them to be trained by experienced leaders. The school also placed great emphasis on producing successful tournament riders, and it provided the SS with its first victory in horse racing.[4]

Despite being an equestrian academy, the school served as an SS training center, not just as an Equestrian SS facility. The school broke in horses belonging to officers of the Militarized SS Troops. Men of the mounted and harnessed detachments of the Militarized SS trained alongside SS horsemen. The SS recognized no distinctions between Equestrian SS and non-Equestrian SS personnel.[5]

At first, Himmler appointed a seasoned cavalryman to run the school, but Wilhelm Gervers, a World War I cavalry veteran, received an honorary SS discharge to return to the army shortly after becoming the school's commander. His replacement was Hanns Mörschel, a devout Nazi with impressive credentials. A decorated World War I officer (Iron Cross First and Second Class), Mörschel served in the Free Corps in East Prussia and Schleswig-Holstein while commanding a police unit in Kiel. His colorful life also included a two-year stint farming in Argentina. He had openly supported the Nazis since 1931, becoming the first sponsoring patron of the SS (*Fördernde Mitglieder*) among the Kiel police force. His support of the party, which he joined in 1932, and the SS embroiled him in trouble with police authorities there. He endeavored to rid the force of Marxists; such actions led to poor evaluations and no promotions. He thereupon resigned from the police and joined the SS.[6]

Requesting assignment to work with an equestrian unit, Mörschel became a training specialist in SS Main Sector *Nord*, bringing to the SS needed skills as a horseman. He had commanded and trained mounted police units, he had successfully participated in equestrian events, and he had served as a judge at tournaments. An SS leader in 1934 characterized Mörschel as healthy, vigorous, and still one of the best tournament riders in Schleswig-Holstein, even though he was fifty-five years old. The SS soon named him equestrian leader of its *Rhein* sector because the region lacked experienced riding instructors. In June 1936, he became leader of the Forst Riding School until it closed in 1938. The aging equestrian successfully led the school through its training courses and personally rode to the school's first tournament victory.[7]

The Forst school had operated successfully, but after acquiring property in Hamburg, the SS closed it on February 15, 1938, ostensibly because its facilities no longer suited Himmler's increasing devotion to his armed SS units. A new equestrian school opened in Hamburg, initially called the Remount Institute of the SS Main Office (*Remontanstalt des SS-Hauptamtes*). The city of Hamburg donated to the SS a former stud farm, the *Traunche Gestüte*; Himmler envisioned it as a proper facility for mounts of the Militarized SS Troops. Instructors at Hamburg trained remounts and riding instructors for their unit's remount departments, provided advanced training for riding and driving personnel, and broke in the riding horses of armed SS unit commanders. All of these tasks were initially performed at Forst, but, in an effort to save money, the Hamburg school assumed the responsibilities. The Forst school essentially transferred its inventory to Hamburg.

The institute, however, did not neglect the Equestrian SS; Hamburg continued to offer cavalry training to its members. Beginning in September 1938, all equestrian units outside of East Prussia were expected to send personnel to the port city for five-week training courses. Hamburg provided accommodations and half the cost of meals; equestrian units paid for the other half, and SS Main Sectors covered travel expenses. Participants had to provide only their equipment and their clothing.[8]

Unfortunately for Mörschel, who expected the appointment, the SS selected someone else to command the school: Hans von Salviati. A former successful jockey for the army's cavalry school in Hannover, von Salviati had recently been discharged by the army and appointed to lead SS Equestrian Regiment 9 in Bremen. Himmler valued successful jockeys and instructors at the army's cavalry school. Von Salviati was one among several former professional cavalrymen recruited by the SS. Although von

Salviati had only recently put on an SS uniform, Himmler approved his selection to command the institute.[9]

The equestrian advisor at the SS Main Office, Wilhelm von Woikowski-Biedau, promoted von Salviati's appointment (and he suggested that Mörschel seek work in a private riding school). Feeling betrayed, Mörschel blamed rumors that he would quit Forst and leave the SS for having hurt his candidacy. He believed the SS sought to eliminate him because of his age, and he also believed (correctly) that a sort of conspiracy existed to use the Equestrian SS as a vehicle to recruit new blue bloods.[10]

An enraged Mörschel enlisted the aid of two powerful allies – August Heissmeyer, the head of the SS Main Office, and Oswald Pohl, the head of the SS Economic and Administrative Department. He asked them to intervene in the matter. To Pohl, Mörschel complained that while the "freshly arrived noble" might be a capable jockey, he appeared unqualified to lead a cavalry school and train SS personnel. He also asked Pohl whether, as rumored, the Equestrian SS was actively recruiting new nobles to become a preserve for the traditional German aristocracy.[11]

Believing Mörschel had been treated unfairly, Pohl and Heissmeyer supported his candidacy to lead the school. Pohl reminded Heissmeyer of Mörschel's leadership skills and of his support of the SS in Kiel, and he dismissed von Salviati's qualifications as being inferior to those of his close friend, Mörschel. But, despite the opposition of such powerful SS figures, von Salviati remained leader of the school (an appointment Himmler later regretted). The fifty-eight-year-old Mörschel took command of Equestrian Regiment 6 in Düsseldorf. Although shortly thereafter the thoroughly embittered equestrian leader requested an honorable discharge, he ultimately joined the staff of SS Main Sector *Nordsee* and eventually rose to the rank of brigadier-general of the SS and major-general of the Police.[12]

Pohl, meanwhile, remained concerned with the Hamburg institute. An investigation into its operations revealed a rather confusing situation within the Equestrian SS. No one claimed responsibility for the school, and the SS leadership office seemed unsure as to whether the school answered to the inspector of the equestrian SS, Friedreich-Wilhelm Krüger, or to the inspector of the SS riding schools, Weber. Pohl even wondered whether the SS actually needed a remount institute because of the increased mechanization of the armed SS units. The validity of the Hamburg school came into question.

Pohl contacted Heissmeyer concerning complaints from several SS offices charging the school with squandering funds and with not training horses. He regarded the facility as not only financially irresponsible but also as an incredible financial burden. His investigation revealed a poor state of affairs. After the school completely exhausted its first-year budget of 120,000 RM, it requested an increase to 150,000. But, he charged, in ten months of operations, it had held just three four-week courses which trained only seventy-eight armed SS and General SS members at a cost of about 1,500 RM per person. The state riding academy in Berlin, *Reichsfachschule für Reit-und Fahrwesen*, Pohl observed, charged only 300 RM per person for similar training. In fact, to save money equestrian unit commanders relied on Berlin rather than Hamburg for training. A mistaken Pohl declared that Hamburg had gone unused for months, nor could he recall hearing of any success by the school in tournaments. He therefore proposed closing the institute because he thought the SS could find better uses for 150,000 RM than to waste it on only fifteen horses and twenty-nine staff personnel in Hamburg.[13]

Heissmeyer brought the matter to the attention of Weber and Krüger, and asked whether they thought the school should be operated unchanged, with modifications, or be completely dissolved. Weber, avoiding responsibility, claimed that he had never intended to transfer the Forst school to Hamburg nor had he been involved in the arrangement he underscored. Had that been so, he would have found a more suitable place in central Germany for a training academy.

For Weber, the buildings in Hamburg hardly constituted a remount institute; the grounds lacked spaciousness, necessary enclosures, riding arenas, and stalls. He suggested naming the facility the Hamburg Riding School and restricting it to preparing only SS horsemen to participate in tournaments in northern Germany. The problems at the school, he said, stemmed, in part, from its horses, most of which had unsuitable temperaments. The armed SS units had requisitioned the school's best steeds, and the school's budget did not allow for purchases of seasoned replacements.

However, Weber declared, the school's mounts should not necessarily be regarded as insignificant, for the school had actually gotten rid of its many old, practically useless horses and eventually the school would buy more. In reality, Weber seemed more concerned with the SS Main Riding School in Munich and with establishing a breeding institute in Bavaria to develop prize-winning stallions than with activities in Hamburg.[14]

Still, Weber defended the school by claiming it had indeed fulfilled its assigned tasks completely. Contrary to Pohl's assertions, the school held not three but four training courses in 1938, Weber contended. Although the school used March to prepare for the upcoming 1938 training periods, it held courses in April, June, July, and August, and used September as a vacation period. Weber seemed unsure as to why the school held no courses in October and November, but he nonetheless praised von Salviati's dedication. SS jockeys there had ridden as champions in seven tournaments and placed in fifty events.

Weber claimed ignorance in regard to equestrian unit personnel training at the *Reichsfachschule* in Berlin, actions which he judged to have sabotaged the Hamburg school. Perhaps equestrian unit leaders thought the school trained only remounts, he wondered, for SS horsemen had regularly trained at Forst. But when Hamburg became a remount institute, all units generally stopped sending recruits. Even the SS Main Riding School in Munich suffered a reduction in the number of equestrian unit personnel sent there to be trained, Weber declared. He blamed Krüger for not using Hamburg since it had always been the task of the inspector of the equestrian SS to send men to the riding schools.[15]

Not surprisingly, Krüger viewed matters differently – he faulted Weber. Krüger regarded as excessive the travelling costs to Hamburg. Lacking a covered riding arena, which Krüger said Weber had not considered, meant that the school could not hold training courses in the winter – a loss of four to five months of training —and he gathered that an early fall frost had probably prevented the school from training horses and men in October and November 1938.

For these reasons, Krüger surmised, the Hamburg school could not legitimately be called a riding academy, for it simply did not offer the training he desired for his units. He placed little faith in the management of Hamburg, a reflection of what he perceived as poor leadership. For instance, although the school planned to conduct a training course in March 1939, officials informed equestrian units only eight days in advance. Bad weather and the lack of a covered arena forced the cancellation of the course anyway. Besides, Krüger revealed, Himmler had entrusted him personally with holding training programs for all equestrian unit leaders. He did not need to rely on Hamburg.[16]

Krüger flatly denied Weber's assertion that by sending equestrian unit personnel to train in Berlin he had sabotaged the Hamburg school. Because Hamburg held no courses during the fall and winter, he felt obligated to use the Berlin school. If given a choice, he would have gladly approved of free training for SS men. But he was unsure of what the school really offered. Since he had no jurisdiction over the school, and, as a result, no influence over it, he neither offered a proposal to enlarge its scope nor one to dissolve it entirely.[17]

Weber did agree that belt tightening was in order. Perhaps a budget reduction would teach administrators to be frugal. But closing the facility might be unwise, for the SS needed an institute to train SS horsemen and men of the armed SS units. Hamburg's previous training programs had proved that the school could handle these tasks faultlessly – or so Weber argued. The school indeed remained open, and during World War II it became a remount office for horses of the Waffen SS. The Bavarian, however, knew all too well that Himmler's true cavalry school was not in Hamburg but in southern Germany, in Munich, at the SS Main Riding School (*Hauptreitschule*). Young SS recruits would regularly train there as cavalrymen and ride as the official SS equestrian team.[18]

The SS *Hauptreitschule*

The most important SS riding academy was the splendid SS Main Riding School in Munich. Of its two riding arenas, one was perhaps the biggest, most modern in Germany. It had plush stables with room for sixty horses, an infirmary and veterinary hospital, and an apartment building with a large kitchen, dining room, large bathrooms with showers and baths, and a laundry room for all personnel and training course participants. Its riding arena was 100 meters long and 28 meters wide. Architect Karl Meitinger designed the academy, which was built by the Munich firm of Otto Scheidermaier. Construction began in October 1936 and the school opened in July 1937. The school became an SS showplace; numerous SS dignitaries, Nazi officials, and notable civilians visited the Munich academy. Its leader, Hermann Fegelein, was the single most important figure after Himmler in the history of the Equestrian SS. An unscrupulous and ambitious SS leader, he took full advantage of his position. Through his close friendship with Himmler, he eventually became a member of Hitler's inner circle in the Bunker during the final years of World War II.[19]

Fegelein was born October 30, 1906, in Ansbach to a Middle Franconian riding family. His father, Hans, an officer in a World War I cavalry regiment, owned a riding school in Munich where young Fegelein worked as a stable boy. The retired first lieutenant instilled in his son a love of horses and a passion for riding. After graduating from high school, he studied economics for four semesters in college (several historical accounts incorrectly call him illiterate). He also received military and police training. For about six months in 1924 and 1925 he served in an army cavalry regiment assigned to a machine gun detachment and later, 1927-1930, as an NCO and a police officer candidate in the Bavarian State Police. He taught various courses in horsemanship at his father's riding school which, since 1929, had been a meeting place for the Nazi Party. Fegelein joined the Nazi movement at an early age. In 1931 he provided riding lessons to members of the Nazi Student League, an organization of college students supportive of the party. In 1932 he joined the Nazi Party.[20]

Christian Weber introduced Fegelein to Himmler, and soon after the show rider joined the SS; his brother Waldemar joined later. Fegelein became leader of an equestrian company and the adjutant of Caspar Koenig, the equestrian leader of SS *Gruppe Süd*, which later became SS Main Sector *Süd*. He took various cavalry training courses and committed himself to the entire equestrian training of the SS. He quickly assumed leadership of Equestrian Regiment 15 in Munich and of Equestrian Sector V (*Süd*), a position he held until it was dissolved in 1936. Fegelein had found his calling, and, as an SS captain, was rapidly rising in the organization.[21]

With Weber, Fegelein founded the SS Main Riding School in Munich in 1935; in 1936 Himmler appointed him its commander. Fegelein, one of the SS's best tournament horsemen, held the Riding Sports Badge in gold and won numerous events, including the German Derby, Germany's most important jumping competition, and Weber's Brown Ribbon racing tournament. He even prepared equestrian events for the 1936 Berlin Olympics, although ultimately only army officers were allowed on Germany's equestrian team. The Hannover Cavalry School's monopoly perpetually frustrated Fegelein's ambitions.[22]

Fegelein hoped to turn his riding school into an equestrian institute that would surpass in achievements the Hannover school. The SS equestrian team he captained performed well in tournaments in Germany and throughout Europe. Munich, he imagined, would become the preeminent base for training SS participants in equestrian tournaments. The school specialized in four areas: jumping, dressage, driving, and racing, although its successes were predominantly in jumping competitions. Fegelein continually worked to upgrade the school's personnel and horses, and by 1939 the Munich school had assembled an impressive collection of talent, particularly in its show jumping stables. (His brother, Waldemar, also a successful jockey, joined the school as an instructor.)[23]

Günter Temme, one of Germany's most gifted jockeys and the best SS horseman, also joined the school's staff. An East Prussian equestrian, he gained significant fame and prestige for the SS through his numerous tournament victories. A cavalry officer in World War I, Temme was active in the Free Corps and the Steel Helmets (*Stahlhelm*). This early Nazi convert, like many SS horsemen, briefly served in the SA. After joining Equestrian Regiment 1 in East Prussia in 1934, he enjoyed immediate success in tournaments and this won Himmler's attention as well as his signature on promotion requests. He twice won the German Derby – the first jockey ever to ride flawlessly – and he also rode to victories at almost every major jumping tournament in Germany. The SS journal *Das Schwarze Korps* and the Nazi Party paper the *Völkischer Beobachter* recognized him as the most successful of all SS jockeys.[24]

Himmler rapidly promoted Temme and in 1936 transferred him to Equestrian Regiment 7 in Berlin, an outfit particularly noted for its upper-class traits. In fact, Temme frequently attended gatherings with army officers and German aristocrats. Furthermore, the "honor" his victories brought to the SS yielded special dispensations and privileges: in Berlin, Temme was often exempted from carrying out many regular SS duties. A pleased Fegelein finally secured Temme's services, and, in 1939 he rode for the SS Main Riding School.[25]

Fegelein also hoped to enlist former officers of the army's cavalry school to increase the legitimacy of his institute. One former successful jockey for the Hannover school, Hans von Salviati, had already taken over the SS riding school in Hamburg. But by 1939, Fegelein could count three former cavalrymen among his nine officers, including Martin von Barnekow, one of the army's best jockeys and also twice winner of the German Derby. From 1918-1930 he was a member of a cavalry regiment in the army. During this time he won numerous tournaments in Germany and abroad. He was the hero of the three-man German team that won the International Military Stakes in New York in 1928 and he was a gold medalist at the 1936 Berlin Olympics (while riding a horse later used by Temme). Von Barnekow had briefly been a member of Equestrian Regiment 7 in Berlin in 1934 but decided to renew his career in the army. After being discharged as a major in 1938, von Barnekow inquired about rejoining the SS. Fegelein was primarily concerned with von Barnekow's credentials as an instructor and, since the SS had infrequently purchased seasoned horses, his expertise in breaking in young, inexperienced steeds.[26]

Fegelein's impressive collection of talent demonstrated its abilities through numerous tournament victories. Although the army's team officially represented Germany in international "Nation's Cup" events, the SS gained a reputation in Europe for fielding formidable teams in other international meets. Fegelein always wrote to Himmler whenever the SS displayed its "superiority" through "embarrassing victories" over the army, such as in a Stuttgart tournament in 1939. After the event Fegelein declared Stuttgart to be important preliminary work for the Olympic preparations. He added, "The superiority of the SS was never before so great as in these days." Of perhaps twelve world-class horsemen in Germany, Fegelein later proclaimed, at least five wore the SS uniform.[27]

Fegelein viewed his position as similar to the official status granted to the Militarized SS units. His officers trained some of their personnel and wore grey military uniforms, although Himmler strictly forbade the wearing of uniforms beyond school grounds. Fegelein boasted that the ideological, military, and athletic training at his school was far superior to the training offered in Hannover. He trained men to lead troops, he boasted, while the cavalry school essentially prepared its officers to participate in tournaments.[28]

Fegelein's skills as a leader enabled the school not only to establish a strong reputation for fielding quality teams in athletic competitions but for providing sound cavalry training. Fegelein's academy even trained a young Yugoslav to become a cavalry officer. The representative of the General Chief of Staff of the Yugoslav army expressed an interest in having his son train in Germany. For political reasons, the Nazi Party and in particular Weber guided the future cavalryman to the SS school in Munich rather than to the army's cavalry school. Himmler naturally regarded the incident as an opportunity to cultivate beneficial relations between the Equestrian SS and the Yugoslav army while presenting a genuine alternative to the Hannover school.[29]

Gaining official status for the school became an obsession. Fegelein often reminded Himmler of the SS team's difficult struggle to gain its reputation. He wanted Himmler to negotiate with Hitler to secure complete equality between his equestrian academy and the Hannover Cavalry School (later designated the Army's Riding and Driving School). The army team was recognized as the official German team at equestrian events. A special concern of Fegelein's, it dominated the Olympic trials. Fegelein thought he should have made the 1936 Olympic team, a team restricted to army officers, and he wanted to ensure that SS jockeys competed in the upcoming games.

Most importantly, Fegelein wanted to protect what he privately considered to be his personal domain, for he knew that the precarious military situation in Europe in the late 1930s could destroy the school and its team. At any time the army could conscript his officers and Olympic candidates and his horses. His concern was warranted because equestrian units already had faced similar problems. Of the seven horses owned by the SS in Equestrian Regiment 17, all had been examined and registered with the army. The army could draft them immediately during an emergency. Indeed, by 1938, the regiment had already lost to the draft at least three SS-owned horses and a number of horses owned by members of the unit. The army had also conscripted several officers and non-commissioned officers, specialists, and men, including the regiment leader's adjutant and accountant, three company leaders, and several platoon leaders.[30]

Fegelein pointed to the Italian militia in his plea for Himmler's assistance. He emphasized the parity between the Italian militia and army officers and how they were regarded as absolute equals in Italy. Certainly, he thought, the SS Main Riding School could officially align itself to the Death's Head units to protect men from the draft, just like members of the Italian militia were beyond the Italian army's grasp. On one occasion, Christian Weber, the inspector of the SS riding schools, intervened to assist the Main Riding School. In 1938 the army's cavalry school declined to participate in an international Nation's Cup tournament in Nice which Germany had won in the previous two years. The Italian War Minister contacted Weber to solicit the participation of the SS riding school. An SS victory, Weber proclaimed, would offer an opportunity for Munich and Hannover to be regarded as equals. Fegelein's team, however, did not compete.[31]

To Himmler, Fegelein stressed that the foreign media had begun treating the SS and army teams as equals. More importantly, the *Fédération Internationale Équestre*, an organization led by SS Main Sector *Fulda-Werra* chieftain Josias Erbprinz zu Waldeck-Pyrmont, declared the terms SS leader and army officer (*Führer* and *Offizier*, respectively) to be identical. Tournaments in France and Poland had already complied by recognizing the SS Main Riding School's team as an official German delegation.[32]

Fegelein conceived of himself as a capable cavalry leader. During the Czechoslovakian Crisis in 1938, he pleaded with Himmler to name him leader of a fighting unit in case of mobilization and to reserve the school's horses and personnel for the SS. War between Germany and Czechoslovakia appeared imminent, and Fegelein wanted to ensure himself a military role. Himmler immediately intervened to keep Fegelein from being drafted by the army and initially planned to transfer him to SS Regiment *Germania* in the event of mobilization. Arrangements for the school remained incomplete. To Fegelein's (and Hitler's) disappointment, British Prime Minister Neville Chamberlain's appeasement policy at the Munich conference in September prevented war by allowing Germany to absorb the Sudetenland. Fegelein had to wait for another opportunity to fight for his country.[33]

Fegelein continued to be concerned with preventing the army from claiming his school's personnel and horses. Protecting them required delicate maneuvers to avoid angering the army. The men could not as a group be excluded from the draft, but Fegelein believed that individual exemptions could be obtained. To retain the school's horses, Himmler hoped to find a loophole in the army's requisitioning regulations to avoid having to attach the school to an armed unit. Munich owned about forty-five horses, most of them trained specifically for equestrianism and a few yet to be trained. Fegelein believed the horses were not really suited for active army service and would hardly fare well in battle. He did, however, believe they could be immediately used for police purposes such as patrol duty and surveillance.[34]

Fegelein became particularly distressed in spring 1939. He pestered Himmler with several letters pleading for him to remedy the situation. He told his *Reichsführer* that in case of mobilization the school could immediately activate a cavalry platoon. After all, Fegelein wrote, the men had been practicing their shooting and had received the requisite cavalry training – training that was superior to that offered in Hannover, he reiterated. After Himmler managed to protect the school's horses from conscription by reserving them for his armed SS units, Fegelein believed that the arrangement had thus affiliated the school with the armed SS. Surely, Fegelein pondered, a simple conversation with Hitler would resolve the matter. Himmler, however, instructed his impatient jockey Fegelein to expect a resolution only at a more favorable time. The auspicious moment occurred that summer. Himmler attached the SS Main Riding School to the Death's Head regiments to allow SS horsemen to be used for police purposes when actual warfare occurred. An SS cavalry became official.[35]

For a scattered group of mounted units, the SS riding schools offered an opportunity to provide SS horsemen with qualified instructors. The riding schools formed an integral component of Himmler's goal of having a permanent mounted SS counterpart to the army's cavalry school and mounted units. As at the army's facility, SS equestrian academies trained participants to excel on the tournament circuit and refined the cavalry skills of equestrian leaders.

All SS riding schools were integrated into the SS organization. Since the Hamburg and Munich schools had also trained men and horses of armed SS units, both institutes became important cavalry training centers after the outbreak of war. The Hamburg school became a remount institute for the Waffen SS, and the Munich academy became a depot for training replacements for SS cavalry forces in Poland. Fegelein created and took command of mounted SS Death's Head security forces in Poland, and most of his officers at the school joined him in the East.

The rise of the SS Main Riding School opened doors for its young leader. At equestrian events, Fegelein mixed with elites throughout Europe and with SS and Nazi notables. Himmler delighted in the victories of his SS jockeys and regularly congratulated Fegelein for his achievements. The two developed a close friendship, one that ultimately catapulted Fegelein to the apex of the Nazi hierarchy and survived until the final days of the Third Reich.

CHAPTER FOUR

Leadership and Financial Problems

Two consistent themes dominate the brief pre-war administrative history of the Equestrian SS: too few skilled personnel and too many financial problems. These difficulties largely reflected problems throughout the General SS system. Limited finances certainly contributed to the shortage of qualified cavalrymen. The SS had difficulty securing talented equestrian personnel to assume mostly honorary (unpaid) positions. Because most positions were unpaid and therefore generally unattractive to many, the SS at times had to rely on its old fighters to fill vacancies. The equestrian units, like engineer, communications, and motor detachments, never became part of state-paid troops. Squadrons such as equestrian medical detachments (*Sanitätstruppe*) consistently suffered from a shortage of qualified personnel and often had to be dissolved.

The SS looked within its own ranks, to the army, the business community, and the SA for capable instructors. Some former army cavalry officers joined the SS, and the business community lent a few instructors with equestrian skills. Occasionally SA horsemen left to become SS equestrian leaders. Some leaders assumed control over a unit before acquiring proper credentials, and because qualified replacements could not be found, the indiscretions of a few resulted in only light punishments.

Participation in the Equestrian SS required a significant sacrifice of time, and it put a tremendous strain especially on leaders. Although the SS tried to pay leaders a salary sufficient to keep them from seeking full-time employment elsewhere, SS funds were in short supply. Many worked full-time outside of the SS and had to pay for their own supplies, for telephone bills, and for gasoline for their cars or motorcycles to travel long distances.[1]

With the rapid expansion of the Equestrian SS after 1933, especially with the inclusion of poorly prepared or completely untrained individuals from rural riding clubs, the limited number of riding and cavalry instructors posed immediate problems. Naturally Himmler expected his equestrian units to recruit skilled personnel, but his insistence that they penetrate as many rural areas as possible initially meant that standards had to be kept low and farmers, largely untrained, had to be accepted. SS main sectors often had limited funds available to hire specialists to train their unskilled horsemen and, at times, appealed to their superiors to help compensate riding instructors. Not all requests for support were answered, but, in late 1934, the SS secured the services of two equestrian-trained former police sergeants, one being Hanns Mörschel, who later became leader of the Forst Riding School. SS Main Office officials said they would soon provide two additional instructors but insisted that main sectors would have to pay their salaries.[2]

Himmler also expected riders to train at SS riding schools and at the SS officers training academy, the *SS-Führerschule Bad Tölz*. Courses at these academies were specifically designated for equestrian leaders and skilled horsemen under age twenty-five. Early on, SS officials regularly berated equestrian leaders for sending too few participants or for sending too many unsuitable men, including beginners who had difficulty mounting a horse. Academy personnel also complained of SS participants who arrived without necessary supplies. In time, unit commanders corrected these problems but initially equestrian units had difficultly finding acceptable men for the lengthy training courses. Most of the men who qualified for training to become instructors or equestrian leaders often had other employment obligations. Often they needed to remain on their farms.[3]

Some equestrian leaders neglected their administrative tasks. Commanders of small equestrian detachments were regularly criticized for poor managerial skills. Some failed to fill out forms properly and missed deadlines; some failed to follow proper channels and did not comply precisely with training mandates. Higher SS leaders often complained of continually reminding equestrian leaders concerning proper administrative procedures. Individuals in violation often received reprimands and warnings that future violations could get them expelled from the SS. Part of the problem lay with the inability of the SS to hire full-time administrators to handle the paperwork. But a major reason was the enormous amount of paperwork generated by the SS. Leaders and members overburdened by their full-time jobs outside of the SS predictably neglected their obligations to the organization.[4]

In addition to a lack of specialists, the Equestrian SS suffered from acute financial problems. Several units exceeded their budgets, thereby forcing members to pay maintenance expenses. Units seldom received money to purchase horses, and some went years before acquiring their own mounts. To alleviate the problem, SS horsemen tried several money-raising plans. Some horsemen canvassed for donations and solicited funds from patrons. Most horse purchases resulted from these contributions. Although financial sponsors provided needed assistance, in many regions donations rarely covered expenses. Major contributors were few, and, at times, some units were barred from collecting donations.

Financially vulnerable regiments sometimes sought creative ways to raise funds. Members of Equestrian Regiment 15 in Munich thought they had found a solution by selling surplus fodder donated by local farmers to feed SS horses. Outraged farmers, some of whom refused to make further donations, forced the immediate termination of the practice.[5]

Not surprisingly, riding lessons were a popular fund-raising activity, and several units established riding businesses to provide lessons to the public and party members. These businesses proved quite profitable and allowed units to buy additional horses while simultaneously abetting recruiting. Some regiments earned enough money to rent stalls and arenas as lesson sites and to hire specialists to assist in training and in caring for horses. But lessons were no panacea. They failed to eliminate all debts, and they raised suspicions that riding businesses were private concerns enriching unit leaders. Hans Floto, leader of Equestrian Regiment 13, was expelled by the SS for "handling funds in an improper manner." Floto said that his immediate superiors knew about the riding business, supported it, and refused to audit the regiment upon request. The business, profitable at first, enabled Floto to purchase three horses for the regiment.[6]

During an SS investigation, Floto always maintained that the enterprise was strictly an SS affair. He used business funds only to hire specialists, buy horses, recruit financially secure members, and to allow his men to participate in tournaments. The regiment started the business only to relieve financial pressures – the considerable financial burden to less-well-off members who had to pay for horse care and maintenance, he declared. The city of Mannheim allowed the SS free use of an arena and stables where Floto had total supervision over the business.[7]

What bothered SS officials was Floto's prior personal financial difficulties, his apparent misuse of funds to pay expenses, and his shoddy bookkeeping methods. Haphazard withdrawal of used funds ultimately left the business in debt, although Floto said he spent funds only to pay legitimate business expenses; he claimed he spent a considerable amount of his own money on the business. Although the SS could not find any instance in which Floto personally profited from the venture, Oswald Pohl, SS chief of administration, suggested the equestrian leader be discharged immediately for improperly handling SS funds. Floto had continued the riding business after its contract had expired, and it remained in debt.[8]

As a replacement, the SS chose one of its old fighters, Rudolf Freiherr von Geyr. Von Geyr joined the SS in 1929 holding positions in Main Sector *Rhein*; he lead a motor company and an infantry battalion. His good leadership skills and military training, in the army and in the SS, allowed for a smooth transition to an equestrian unit. In this instance, the SS found a suitable equestrian regiment leader within its ranks, and von Geyr remained official commander of Equestrian Regiment 13 until 1943.[9]

Dr. Fritz Hausamen, leader of Equestrian Regiment 14 in Karlsruhe and whose actions frequently came under scrutiny, also encountered difficulty with his riding businesses. A decorated World War I veteran, Hausamen became a veterinarian and animal breeder in Baden and Karlsruhe after the war. His Nazi Party activity began in Baden in 1930 when he became a rural propagandist. After joining the SS in 1931, he soon became leader of a motor unit. In 1933 he became an equestrian leader and a horse breeding expert in the Reich Food Estate. He almost singlehandedly established and enlarged the Equestrian SS in Baden to the point that it compared favorably with units in major breeding areas. He canvassed for donations, the funding source for most of his unit's horse purchases. Hausamen became a valuable link between the Equestrian SS and the farming community, and thus a man of importance to Himmler. However, his reputation as a drunkard increasingly created problems for him, as did his activities in organizations outside of the SS.

Hausamen's drinking problem on one occasion caused him to attack a party member at a nightclub. A drunken Hausamen saw a Nazi comrade inappropriately dressed and exhibiting what he believed was behavior unbecoming to a National Socialist when he supposedly performed jazz steps to waltzes. When Hausamen confronted the man, they exchanged words and then blows. Hausamen acted solely in self-defense, or so he claimed. A Nazi Party court accused him of damaging the party image by causing the fight at an official SS function, but the court merely reprimanded him because he was too valuable to the Nazi movement and the SS. He remained in his post because the Equestrian SS needed an expert veterinarian, animal breeder, recruiter, and instructor.[10]

Eventually his superiors found his behavior unbearable. SS Main Sector *Südwest* said it could no longer tolerate his drinking problem, for it had led to a lack of "energetic leadership" and a "terrible state of affairs" in his equestrian regiment. Hans Prützmann, a Nazi old fighter and the main sector leader, condemned SS riding schools in Baden as purely commercial enterprises. SS horsemen rode infrequently, and Hausamen neglected the regular training of his unit by excessively emphasizing private lessons. Instead, other Nazi formations and private citizens used the horses for a fee. Hausamen even allowed the League of German Girls (*Bund Deutscher Mädel*) and other women to use SS facilities, which led to "unpleasant rumors in Karlsruhe" about SS members flirting with the young females. Furthermore, during a surprise audit, the main sector leader discovered that Hausamen had filed false reports to disguise the actual debt of his unit. With Hausamen too distracted by his other activities in Baden to lead the equestrian units properly, Prützmann recommended a transfer. Eventually the SS transferred him, but he remained in the SS because of his knowledge, skills, and rural connections.[11]

Although the riding lessons and SS sponsors provided needed financial support, winnings from tournament prize money were an essential funding source for equestrian regiments. But in July 1938, Himmler had a change of heart. He wanted all equestrian units to transfer prize money won with SS-owned horses to the National Socialist People's Welfare Organization (*Nationalsozialistische Volkswohlfahrt*), the Nazi charitable organization for families, especially women and children. Each SS main sector had to report to Himmler the amount of prize money won each month.

Himmler based his decision on his belief that the army and the SA renounced their prize money, but he obviously understood the beneficial political implications of supporting one of Hitler's prized programs. Himmler, however, had only a slight understanding of the situation. Only the army cavalry school (Hannover), not the entire army, and only the jumping stables of the Supreme SA Leadership renounced prize money. Beginning in 1935, the cavalry school decided to award its prize money to the next placing finisher, provided he was a German citizen who rode for a private stable. The SA adopted the same policy in 1937.[12]

Almost immediately the decree created anxiety in the Equestrian SS and among main sector chieftains. Concerned equestrian leaders wondered how they would finance their units, and SS main sector leaders worried about having to increase their financial support of equestrian detachments in their regions. Prützmann – then leader of SS Main Sector *Nordwest* – wrote to Himmler imploring him to change the order. The decree probably signalled the demise of the Equestrian SS, Prützmann wrote, for it needed the prize money to participate in tournaments and for training and supplies. Equestrian regiments had little money available for tournaments, and SS horsemen had previously experienced difficulty raising money, he declared.

Prützmann commended the army and the SA for supporting horsemanship in Germany by giving prize money to private clubs and small stables. Their benevolence allowed German citizens to compete and preserve horsemanship and horse breeding throughout Germany. However, the state supported the army and the SA financially, thereby permitting the two groups to behave so charitably. Prützmann asked Himmler to alter his order to allow equestrian units to keep their prize money and require only the SS Main Riding School to follow the lead of the army and the SA's jumping stables.[13]

August Heissmeyer, boss of the SS Main Office, also advised Himmler to reconsider his decree. Heissmeyer described to Himmler how the Equestrian SS in SS Main Sector *Nordost*, the most financially successful of the equestrian units, had used its winnings to support its horses and to com-

pete favorably with the army and the SA. The units were self-supporting
financially, but the new order created potential problems. Although the
riding inspector in the SS main sector paid for an instructor to train young
recruits, the renouncing of prize money would harm the prominence of
the East Prussian SS horsemen and their ability to pay for a recently constructed riding arena and stables. They would spend about sixty percent
of the prize money to send participants to tournaments before factoring in
fodder, straw, and grooming costs. Heissmeyer told Himmler that the SA
was becoming insignificant because of the increasing success SS horsemen were experiencing; the loss of prize money would jeopardize everything thus far gained. Heissmeyer asked Himmler to allow equestrian
units to keep sufficient funds to cover tournament costs. What remained
could then be transferred.[14]

Surprisingly, Himmler's order went largely unenforced for several
months while higher SS officials pleaded with him for a change of policy.
Prützmann neither reported, nor transferred, prize money won by units in
Main Sector *Nordwest* and the Hamburg Remount Institute. The SS Main
Riding School prepared to transfer its prize money but was unsure of
where to send it. Friedrich-Wilhelm Krüger, inspector of the Equestrian
SS, implored Himmler to rescind the order and told his equestrian units
to keep their prize money pending a clarification. Himmler, preoccupied
with pressing national concerns in the late 1930s, requested Krüger to
send him yet another statement concerning prize money won by the army
and the SS. Krüger reaffirmed that only the army's cavalry school and the
stables of the Supreme SA Leadership renounced their prize money.[15]

In March 1939, Himmler finally decided that, as with the army's
cavalry school, all prize money won by the SS Main Riding School would
be given to the next placing contestant, but only if he rode for a private
stable. Prize money won by members on SS-owned horses would be transferred without exception to the People's Welfare Organization. The personal staff of the *Reichsführer-SS* would reimburse all transferred funds,

and a special fund would reimburse the SS Main Riding School. However, Himmler, modifying his original decision, allowed SS members riding privately owned horses to keep all of their prize money. As long as SS jockeys continued to win events, as they increasingly did, Himmler funded the units.[16]

Regardless of its difficulties, the Equestrian SS had become an integral part of the General SS. Although it appears that the equestrian units at times were mismanaged, poorly led, and underfunded, so were many General SS units. Tournament success, however, allowed some units to finance essential activities. The Equestrian SS survived and generally matured as skilled and dedicated personnel joined its ranks. Himmler had his private cavalry and at minimal cost.

CHAPTER FIVE

Conflicts and Problems with Other Organizations

Although many equestrian units consisted primarily of farmers and agricultural workers who rode work horses best suited for plowing, horsemanship tended to be an upper-class activity. The Equestrian SS, not just the Berlin regiment, contained a significant number of nobles. The presence of aristocrats, together with the fashionable Berlin regiment and the general association of horses and horsemanship with society's upper strata, gave the Equestrian SS an elitist image. Indeed, there was a certain "snob-appeal" which prompted one historian to claim that "atmosphere, tone, and views were like the former cavalry regiments of the army."[1]

This alone could cause problems and conflict between SS riders and regular SS foot soldiers, but other mounted SS activities also tended to foster resentment. Because equestrian unit members cared for the unit's horses, or their own, and farmed their fields, they were sometimes exempted from such activities as public parades, barricade duty, and responsibilities at Nazi functions. This led to grumbling among SS "old fighters" who considered the mounted SS reactionary, Masonic, and elitist, and not a genuine National Socialist organization. Whether quarrels involving the Equestrian SS with other SS organizations evidenced the

remarkable degree of suspicion of SS jockeys remains open to speculation. The SS system was rife with rivalries and turf wars.

A particular problem arose in Bavaria between Equestrian Regiment
15, led by an aristocrat, Eberhard Freiherr von Künsberg, and SS Regiment 31, a regular foot detachment. The conflict concerned authority,
recruiting, and elitism. Von Künsberg, the son of a police leader, as a
child received a traditional classical education. Because his parents died
during his adolescence, von Künsberg had to work his way through the
University of Munich law school as a construction worker and common
agricultural laborer. Good grades earned him stipends and fee reductions.
The allure of Nazism appealed to the young, impressionable von Künsberg,
who from 1921 to 1923 belonged to a Hitler Youth brigade called
Jungsturm Adolf Hitler. He joined the Nazi Party in 1929 while a law
student in Munich, becoming active in student politics as a Nazi student
leader. In that same year he joined the SS as member 1,552 and soon
became an officer in the SS main office.[2]

His Equestrian SS career began in 1933 as a platoon leader. The following year he became the adjutant to Hermann Fegelein, equestrian leader
of main sector *Süd* and Equestrian Regiment 15. Later that year, von
Künsberg became leader of Equestrian Regiment 15 in Regensburg. During his tenure, his weekly orders regularly counseled his troops to dedi-
cate themselves to the SS. A devout Nazi, he consistently reminded his
men of what was expected of political soldiers. The SS, wrote von
Künsburg to his men, "is the community from which we fulfill our duty
to the Führer and the people." Equestrian units were important parts of
the SS, for their rural roots allowed the organization "to implement the
ideas of Adolf Hitler."[3]

Von Kunsberg's tenure as an equestrian leader was not without conflict. Although he generally received good evaluations as an equestrian
leader, his superiors occasionally warned him about not following proper
administrative channels and once admonished him for an insult directed

at a spectator during a parade of his unit. The SS also reprimanded him for contacting the army, an SS violation. Von Künsberg had been attempting to establish a mounted police force to ensure that the army could not requisition the men and horses of his unit.[4]

His actions aroused the suspicion of Reinhard Heydrich, the head of the SD, the SS security service. An ensuing investigation revealed several unsettling conditions within the Regensburg regiment and tarnished its leader's image. The unit was seriously in debt despite having received a considerable donation from the Nazi Party leadership in Bavaria. Von Künsberg's regiment owned no horses and its financial situation raised fears of some higher SS officials about future disruptions in the unit. Von Künsberg, the report disclosed, may have had private debts, was rarely at his post, and habitually took expensive trips because of his connections with high party officials in several cities. In his defense, chief equestrian leader Georg Skowronski argued that, although he deserved being watched, he nevertheless remained a competent, industrious SS leader and an absolutely reliable National Socialist.[5]

SD investigators cited von Künsberg for causing problems between the Equestrian SS and other SS offices and Nazi formations. He had illegally recruited members from the Motor SA and accepted students who had not fulfilled their compulsory school attendance requirement. His main dilemma, however, involved a quarrel over territory, recruiting, and authority with SS Regiment 31, an infantry unit in Bavaria.[6]

Von Künsberg complained to his superiors of violations by the infantry regiment. Recruiting suffered, he said, because the foot regiment refused to allow members who owned horses, including a badly needed veterinarian, to transfer to the Equestrian SS. Evidently his subordinates had heard a rumor that the infantry commander, Emil Frels, had announced at a leadership gathering his supremacy over all SS units in the region and his intent to dissolve equestrian and motorized formations. Later, some SS foot soldiers, referring to the elite character of the SS cavalry, supposedly commented sarcastically, "Now you'll have to remove your spurs."[7]

Frels charged von Künsberg with inappropriately draining the infantry regiment to strengthen his own unit. And SS horsemen, Frels complained, were not genuine SS men but pretentious status seekers who felt superior to regular SS infantrymen. He had always believed in camaraderie and cooperation, not competition, and so he had always been willing to help the equestrian units. The district SS leader concurred. Von Künsberg's recruiting from SS foot regiments strained relations and, as specified in the earlier SD report, others had heard of complaints about the equestrian leader from men in various organizations, including Hitler Youth leaders.[8]

Friedrich Jeckeln, SS Main Sector leader in Bavaria, cited Frels for being less than truthful and prone to exaggeration. In a matter involving the transfer of the veterinarian, the doctor apparently feared repercussions if he initiated a transfer request, preferring to allow von Künsberg and his subordinates to handle the matter. The infantry leader, realizing the difficulty in replacing specialists, falsely accused his comrade of transferring the veterinarian against his will.

The SS disciplined Frels and von Künsberg remained in his post. The SS, of course, expected cordial relations among its units and von Künsberg at least officially complied. He advised his subordinates to contact infantry units to organize a joint, camaraderie evening get-together. He later wrote to his apparently apprehensive horsemen to disregard the gossip of "jealous groups and people" who spread rumors that equestrian units would be dissolved.[9]

Within a year, von Künsberg resigned his post to complete his law studies in Berlin. He became an officer in the Nazi Party and worked in its foreign office. But he remained affiliated with the Equestrian SS and in 1938 joined the staff of the inspector of the SS riding schools. Himmler was clearly pleased to have members with such important connections.

In fact von Künsberg had quite a remarkable career as a party official. He associated with Alfred Rosenberg, the Nazi Party's ideologist, and Joachim von Ribbentrop, Hitler's foreign minister. Von Künsberg became a diplomatic minister in the Foreign Ministry, and, after the outbreak of war, an art plunderer in France and the Soviet Union.[10]

By no means were the complaints of the Equestrian SS limited to SS infantry units. Editors of the SS journal, *Das Schwarze Korps*, hinted that many SS riders hardly seemed devoted to the movement. In their second issue, editors encouraged the horsemen to become dedicated SS men, arguing that:

> in the first place they have to cultivate the National Socialist spirit, that is, all the virtues, all the qualities that the SS has cultivated in the long years of its existence and by which it has proven itself: loyalty to the *Führer*, readiness to obey, discipline, readiness for action, obedience, love of the Fatherland, love of the ancestral earth, and love of the home and hearth.[11]

This concern was not entirely unwarranted. In the fall of 1935 an SS main sector leader, questioning the convictions of SS horsemen in Silesia, recommended assembling them for intense ideological instruction. In 1937, during an investigation of an equestrian leader accused of defrauding the Reich's Food Estate, the Nazi agricultural agency, the SS court announced that the proceedings had confirmed the findings of the court's previous probes into the Equestrian SS. Equestrian leaders, it judged, frequently lacked the honesty and the kind of behavior expected of National Socialists and SS officers when working with the public. The ruling, however, spoke to the inappropriate actions of a few horsemen rather than to a general rejection of Nazi ideology by SS riders.[12]

Regardless, the Equestrian SS was hardly unique in receiving criticism of its supposedly deficient ideological commitment. Education officers of the Race and Settlement department, the office involved in guaranteeing SS racial purity, consistently deplored the indifference toward ideology among members of the General SS. In truth, many officers of the Militarized SS Troops also seemed more concerned with attending the army's beer hall gatherings than with listening to SS ideological presentations. In January 1939, the head of the SS Educational Office complained about the limited effect of SS ideological training: "Boredom with these...[ideological]... subjects is gradually becoming noticeable among the men and so instruction has been extended to cover the basic concepts of National Socialist ideology."[13]

Not surprisingly, competition between the Mounted SS and its main rival in recruiting, the SA Equestrian Corps, led to disputes. But, before discussing the friction between the two groups, a brief history of the Mounted SA seems appropriate. In 1930 the SA established equestrian units modelled after the army's cavalry units and rural riding clubs. All horses in the units had to be either privately owned or the property of the SA (no rental horses were allowed) to ensure that the organization had access to them at all times. The SA, however, did allow for certain concessions. Men interested in joining could be admitted even if they did not have access to a horse. These formations, designated reserve equestrian units, did not receive official recognition.[14]

The SA enthusiastically developed mounted companies consisting of squadrons and platoons of varying strengths, each under the immediate control of the company leader. Once a sufficient number of companies had been established, the *Obergruppe*, the main territorial division of the SA, could petition the Supreme Commander of the SA (*Oberste SA Führung*) to combine them into a regiment (*Standarte*). Equestrian regiments were subordinate to the various SA administrative units, *Gruppen*, *Obergruppen*, *Brigaden* or *Standarten,* in the area and worked closely with the office of inspector of equestrian sports (*Inspekteur des Reitsport*). The inspector dealt directly with equestrian leaders concerning equestrian matters. However, company leaders had authority over the lower mounted units.[15]

The SA and SS Equestrian corps had similar organizational structures. Both initially deployed companies, consisting of at least twenty persons, later grouped together as regiments. But the SS was allowed to establish at most only three companies in each SS District. The SA had by far a larger number of equestrian units. In SA *Gruppe Westmark* in 1934, for example, SA Equestrian Regiment 52 comprised 3,600 men divided into forty-seven companies scattered across the region. Most of them had strengths under 100 men, some had as few as thirty. The leader of the regiment remarked how difficult it was for all detachments to coordinate activities. To improve efficiency, the SA created additional equestrian regiments with fewer companies and organized them into Provincial Riding Groups (Riding Group Bavaria, for example).[16]

Although the SA naturally preferred experienced and talented horse owners, in agricultural communities it accepted men who could provide their own mounts. In 1933 a dramatic increase in membership occurred after the SA discontinued the requirement of private horse ownership. Each *Gruppe* was faced with supporting the establishment of equestrian units by providing riding facilities.[17]

To increase membership, SA units absorbed former members of the riding formations of the student riding groups and the Steel Helmet, the nationalist ex-servicemen's organization incorporated into the SA in 1933. More importantly, thousands of potential members were found in the public riding associations dispersed throughout rural Germany. The SA was primarily behind the decision to incorporate Germany's equestrian associations into the Nazi formations. In the middle of 1933 Ernst Röhm and the Ministry of the Interior met with the leader of the rural riding associations to discuss their transfer into either the party or the SA. Nazi officials decided that the associations could join either the SS or the SA. Both groups assimilated entire riding clubs, but most clubs enlisted in the SA.[18]

In 1935 the SA Equestrian Corps' strength totalled about 88,000 men compared to about 12,000 for the SS. During the following year, the Mounted SA became associated with a new organization, the National Socialist Equestrian Corps. It included non SA and SS members aged eighteen to twenty interested in acquiring a riding certificate and serving in a mounted or harnessed army detachment. With its own administration, it remained theoretically distinct from the SA but answerable to its leadership. Nazi leaders at first expected it to coordinate equestrian training for the SA, SS, and Hitler Youth to prepare men for the army. Ultimately it became an exclusively SA organization.[19]

By 1939 there were approximately 200,000 members of the Mounted SA. Like the Equestrian SS members, most SA riders were farmers, many of whom did not own a horse. Over eighty percent of the Mounted SA members were farmers, and in horse breeding areas over 95 percent. A significant number of nobles could also be found in the ranks of SA horsemen. The Mounted SA organized hunts and tournaments, and it provided riding lessons and equestrian cavalry training as well as instruction in breeding and anatomy and in diseases of horses.[20]

Until 1934, the Equestrian SA and the Equestrian SS maintained close ties. Both initially used similar terminology, and SS horsemen remained subordinate to the SA leadership. The SA chief of paramilitary training, Friedrich-Wilhelm Krüger, in guidelines for training men and leaders, stressed the importance of marksmanship and emphasized riding and cavalry training. However, he also insisted that all equestrian units, including the SS, receive proper ideological instruction, which at that time meant imbuing all horsemen with the "spirit of the SA."[21]

Men sometimes trained together and coordinated activities. After the incorporation of the rural riding clubs, the SA transferred men and entire units to the SS. But tensions regularly surfaced because the two tried to out-recruit each other. At times the SA refused to transfer certain units requested by the SS and instead offered substitutes, usually its recently established units. The SA also refused to transfer riders whenever it re-garded the SS as sufficiently strong.

The SS preferred to examine transfers medically to exclude the in-sufficiently Nordic and those who failed to meet the physical require-ments of membership. On one occasion, in July 1934, the SS scheduled medical examinations for members of the SA in the rustic communities of Mensfelden and Kirberg and notified the responsible SA leaders. None of the men appeared on the day of the examination. The SA equestrian leader had strict orders not to comply with any SS orders. His superiors further decreed that anyone involved in cooperating with the SS would be punished and no longer remain a stormtrooper. This quarrel occurred just after the Röhm purge and perhaps reflected the increased hostility and tension between the two organizations.[22]

The Equestrian SA's earlier start enabled it to penetrate the country-side before its SS counterpart, and despite proscriptions to the contrary, both organizations recruited vigorously, often in the same rural areas. In 1937 the SS deployed an equestrian unit in the city of Schwerin in Mecklenburg, an area dominated by the Mounted SA. The SA had al-ready deployed two equestrian units there, with plans to build a third, and it resisted SS attempts to establish its own regiment. But the SS success-fully outmaneuvered the SA essentially because farmers were interested in learning to ride, and because many of them ultimately rejected the poor, inadequate SA training. Men deserted the SA in droves.[23]

The Mounted SA had controlled Mecklenburg since 1933 by absorb-ing all German riding clubs. But in 1935-1936 many men quit. Farmers wanting to learn to ride rejected the "other services" offered by the SA, and the SA also had a noticeable lack of riding instructors and specialists. Men often had to walk over twenty kilometers to riding lessons. In some instances horses were ridden to death; deep-seated distrust of the SA arose. Farmers became suspicious and reluctant to surrender their horses to ei-ther the SA or SS. Indeed, a horse was a precious investment, and the livelihood of many farmers and equestrian unit members depended on the well-being of their animals.[24]

In discussions with the SS, the SA repeatedly insisted that it controlled the Mecklenburg area and that the SS was forbidden to recruit or establish an equestrian corps. Tossing aside these warnings, the SS gradually gained the trust of the local farmers and deployed an equestrian regiment in Schwerin. Penetration into Mecklenburg was a significant advance for the Equestrian SS. Mecklenburgers generally enjoyed equestrianism, and the SS considered it a favorable horse-breeding region. But SA officers interfered with SS recruiting efforts. They harassed and attempted to "demoralize" SS recruits, especially those who wished to transfer from the Mounted SA. SA horsemen who wanted to join the SS were not allowed to do so and were threatened with disciplinary proceedings.

The SS promised to train recruits by using only specialists and qualified riding instructors with at least twelve years of experience. No longer would farmers have to walk long distances with their horses to riding lessons. In one instance an instructor travelled by bicycle and motorcycle to several areas in one morning to provide riding lessons. However, as the new SS horsemen discovered, the SS increasingly emphasized "other services," namely ideological instruction. But no exodus occurred as previously when they belonged to the SA.[25]

Himmler frequently stressed to all SS departments the need to maintain favorable relations with other party formations, a mandate equestrian leaders were responsible for keeping. Ironically, Eberhard von Künsberg of Equestrian Regiment 15 was one who regularly admonished his men to support and respect other Nazi organizations. During an SA athletic competition in 1935, the SS, along with the army and the police, refused to salute the SA flag. Von Künsburg quickly reminded his horsemen that the SA flags were "flags of the movement" and should therefore be held in high esteem. (Earlier von Künsberg had admonished his men for attacking disrespectful civilians who did not greet the SS flag during marches.)[26]

Later, persistent quarrels among local SS leaders, the SA, and the Hitler Youth – usually concerning turf battles over recruiting – moved von Künsberg to demand that these matters be settled immediately to reduce the damage to the prestige and appearance of the SS. There appears to have been significant discord between several Nazi groups. He ordered his subordinate officers to settle promptly all disputes and declared that the leaders of the units would be held responsible for any ill-will between SS and party formations.[27]

The SS and SA equestrian corps did, on occasion, cooperate and compete on friendly terms. Both, at times, provided a measure of respect for the other's territorial domain. In 1938, Erwin Selck, the leader of Company 2 of Equestrian Regiment 10 in SS Main Sector *Fulda-Werra*, was tempted to recruit in SA territory. His unit faced a drastic shortage of men and horses as a result of the draft and a recent reorganization within the SS. Ultimately he refused to consider accepting more than a handful of men and horses, for he wanted no problems with the Equestrian SA, especially since its leaders had honored agreements in the region and had not intruded on Equestrian SS territory.[28]

Each organization held tournaments and invited the other to participate and they sometimes borrowed each other's equipment. It quickly became obvious that what the SS lacked in numbers, it more than compensated for with talent. By the late 1930s the SS could easily argue that it had the most talented equestrian corps among the Nazi formations.

An interesting contest between SA and SS jockeys occurred at the short-lived National Socialist Competitive Games in 1938. Administered by the SA, these military sports competitions in Nuremberg in 1937 and 1938 during the Reich Party Congresses purportedly fostered healthy camaraderie between the participants: the SA, the SS, the army, the police, the Hitler Youth, the Reich Labor Service, National Socialist Motor Corps, and the National Socialist Aviators Corps.

The SS dutifully participated in the equestrian events and fielded what team captain Hermann Fegelein judged its best team. The army and police declined to take part, leaving the SA and SS as the only partici-pants. Furthermore, the SA changed procedures at the last minute. No advanced speed and endurance test would occur as planned, only a mod-erately difficult one so that more favorable results could be obtained.[29]

Fegelein investigated the event and determined that the course in-deed fulfilled requirements for an advanced race. As a result, he decided to field a team of the most experienced horses and jockeys of the SS Main Riding School. Being more concerned with upcoming Olympic prepara-tions, he did, however, request modifications to reduce the risk of injury to men and horses. Although the SA denied the request, it soon began altering rules to its advantage. The SA did not allow SS judges, not even as auxiliaries, and did not follow weight and time requirements. Fegelein also discovered that the SA had changed obstacles at night, after the SS had completed its rides, to make jumps easier for its own jockeys.[30]

Fegelein considered the entire competition a farce. The SS had no role in either constructing the courses or in judging, nor did he see any athletic value in an equestrian competition closed to the public and with-out army and police riders. He confronted SA leaders to discuss his com-plaints only to be assured that the SA meant no harm and wanted only mutually beneficial relations with the Equestrian SS. The SA leadership invited Fegelein to dine at their table at the closing dinner as an indica-tion of their commitment to camaraderie. Unimpressed by the gesture, he nevertheless attended.[31]

Fegelein dismissed SA jockeys as amateurs. Although he complained about their actions, his main concern was with the absence of army jock-eys. By that time, he began focusing his contempt on the main rival to his ambitions: the Cavalry School Hannover. Fegelein relished competitions against jockeys from the Hannover school. Eventually, he imagined, both schools would officially become equals.

The army's cavalry school reigned as the official German equestrian team, a privilege Fegelein found particularly unpleasant. Despite his contempt for the army, Fegelein hoped a compromise could be reached. He wanted to field mixed teams composed of army and SS personnel in international events to gain recognition for his school as an official German organization. He corresponded with Major Harold Momm, an exceptional jockey and leader of the army's show jumping stables since 1936, asking for SS participation on the German national team at equestrian events. Despite Fegelein's frequently derisive comments about the inferior quality of the Hannover school and the diminishing talent of its riders, the army fielded a strong team and dominated international events under Momm's leadership; his team brought home thirty Nation's Cup Prizes to Germany. As a participant, Momm set an international record by using the same horse to win nineteen of those awards.[32]

Fegelein also asked the German Olympic Committee to address the issue of mixed teams. The committee agreed that in the future —while offering no precise date – the German team would consist of both SS and army jockeys, the group with the most members having the privilege of selecting the team captain. In a display of diplomatic posturing, the committee's general secretary lamented the competition and strained relations between Munich and Hannover and hoped that the two schools would unite to create a team that everyone would support. He told Fegelein to expect a letter from Momm proposing a mixed team for an upcoming tournament in Rome and pledged to help Fegelein purchase horses. The committee also agreed to hold two Olympic equestrian trials in Munich.[33]

Fegelein had not originally intended to compete in Rome, fearing the expenditures might harm the school's finances and thus its chances of purchasing good breeds. However, the possibility of participating on a unified German team changed his mind. Momm contacted Fegelein, saying how pleased he was to learn that the SS was strengthening the German representation by going to Rome. But instead Momm planned to set up a mixed team for another tournament in Italy, not the one in Rome. This would be the beginning of a beneficial, cooperative effort to make the German team the strongest in the world, he announced, and he looked forward to meeting with Fegelein to discuss these prospects to (of all things) "continue the good relations between Munich and Hannover."[34]

The ever cynical and now completely frustrated Fegelein again contacted Himmler concerning the decisions of the Olympic Committee and Major Momm. He believed Momm's kindness was hardly genuine, for he had promised to include SS horsemen on the team only under pressure from the Olympic Committee. Momm had been promising co-participation for over a year, Fegelein said, yet each time the army found a reason to avoid the matter. Fegelein had no reason to believe that things would change without an order establishing equality between the SS and the army. Himmler admonished Fegelein to accept whatever Momm offered because he had no plans to discuss the matter further with Hitler.[35]

Two additional events increased Fegelein's hostility toward the army: an encounter with the army's mustering commission and a failed horse purchase. During a mustering (a type of military examination) of the troops of the SS Main Riding School, three members of the school visited the appropriate military district to be inspected by the Wehrmacht. Fegelein had already received his examination by a doctor in an SS infantry regiment which he regarded as sufficient. However, he received a notice from the police for violating an order, but dutifully, he said, reported to the military district officer. Fegelein was brought before a mustering commission which he sarcastically described as "an old major, an old staff doctor, and some secretaries."

Fegelein told Himmler that while he reported in uniform and displayed proper courtesy, the army did not reciprocate. He expected some deference for being known throughout Munich as the leader of the SS Main Riding School. Instead, he learned he would be punished with a fine. Fegelein notified Himmler of the rude and disrespectful treatment he received. One officer supposedly told the jockey that he was probably not especially important to the SS, otherwise he would have already been assigned to an armed unit. Surely such behavior was intolerable and reflected just how unequal things were between the two cavalry schools, he thought.[36]

Fegelein's frustration increased after a botched deal to buy horses from the Frau Glahn Stables. The famous German stables had previously been led by two SS horsemen, the deceased Axel Holst and Günter Temme. In Fegelein's mind, a verbal agreement to purchase three horses had been reached, with the right of first refusal. Since none of the horses had recently won tournaments, he considered the price excessive and needed to talk to Himmler about the deal. Before anything was resolved, Frau Glahn sold the horses to the army. Fegelein deplored her behavior and reminded Himmler of how Holst had died riding one of her horses (Temme had also suffered numerous injuries while riding Glahn's mounts). These were the machinations of Momm, he claimed. He knew of the agreement but because he feared competing against the SS – Momm suffered from an anxiety psychosis – he bought the horses to prevent the SS from becoming invincible Fegelein wrote. Although Fegelein initially wanted to buy from Frau Glahn the horse Temme had ridden to victory at the German Derby in Hamburg, he conveniently changed his mind. He professed to Himmler that, unlike the army, the SS really did not need to purchase mature, experienced horses because it had been successfully training all of its young thoroughbreds.[37]

SS horsemen never did participate on the German national team. Fegelein had the opportunity to talk to Momm in Hamburg at the German Derby in 1939 to address the issue again. (His brother Waldemar won the event.) Momm said he suggested to the army High Command that two SS jockeys be put on the team competing in Switzerland but the army refused. Fegelein's ears heard only lies. Supposedly his subordinate, Martin von Barnekow, a former army cavalrymen, listened while the army's leadership expressed its intention to prevent the SS from joining the national team. The army, von Barnekow added, announced its main competitors as no longer the French, the Polish, or the Italians, but only the "black riders." Nevertheless, Himmler, preoccupied with more pressing matters, told Fegelein to let the issue rest. As a concession to soothe Fegelein's wounded ego, Himmler gave his school a substantial sum – 50,000 RM – to buy horses. Two months later Germany was at war, and Fegelein began recruiting members for a mounted SS occupation force.[38]

Not surprisingly, Momm's opinion of Fegelein and SS equestrian abilities was hardly favorable. Fegelein's SS Main Riding School had its opportunity to gain notice in 1938 at an event in Bucharest, Momm recalled in his memoirs, but SS horsemen left the Rumanian capital empty-handed, completely unsuccessful in international competition. Although Fegelein dreamed of international success and made great efforts to purchase talented horses, Momm considered the SS jockey an inconsequential figure in the equestrian world and one who never understood that great horses did not make outstanding jockeys; neither did talented thoroughbreds ridden by experienced horsemen constitute a successful team (a criticism of the Equestrian SS's blatant attempts to acquire Germany's best civilian horsemen and former Hannover cavalrymen). SS riders displayed their ineffectiveness against quality competition in Bucharest, Momm wrote; Germany deserved only the best to represent it in international competitions he insisted.[39]

Momm's criticism of the SS equestrian team seems shortsighted and based in part on his animosity towards the SS and Fegelein. The Bucharest tournament was the first Nation's Cup event for Himmler's horsemen, and SS jockeys lost only to teams that had recently won or would win a Nation's Cup in 1938 and 1939 (including teams that had defeated Germany in several tournaments). The SS equestrian team was still in its infancy – the SS Main Riding School was less than a year old at the time – yet increasingly SS horsemen began to triumph in international tournaments. By the summer of 1939, Fegelein's school had attracted several talented jockeys. The team Fegelein led in the summer of 1939 had improved vastly with the addition of Martin von Barnekow, Günter Temme, and another recently successful SS horseman, Otto Meisterknecht. With Himmler's financial support, the SS Main Riding School was becoming not just a rival but a legitimate alternative to the army's cavalry school. Momm had reason to be concerned about the emergence of the SS team.

In a larger sense, though, the Equestrian SS's conflicts with the army, the SA, and other SS units reflected general patterns in Germany after the Nazi takeover. The Nazi system itself was rife with conflicts, rivalries, jealousies, and turf wars. Within the SS, some disgruntled SS "old fighters" (early supporters) probably sincerely regarded SS horsemen as reactionary conservatives rather than genuine political soldiers. Still, clashes resulted often over pedestrian issues involving recruiting and questions of authority. The rivalry with the Mounted SA was largely unavoidable because both organizations shared similar ambitions. But again, the disputes also mirrored the general animosity between the SS and the SA.

CHAPTER SIX

Case Study: Equestrian Regiment 10

An examination of a specific equestrian unit offers a view of the Equestrian SS from the bottom up and sheds light on the function and struggles of Himmler's cavalry. The relatively abundant source material on Equestrian Regiment 10 – more than on any other mounted unit – allows a study of the Equestrian SS in microcosm. Although each equestrian regiment confronted unique challenges, many experiences of Equestrian Regiment 10 were encountered by other units.

The regiment was organized on March 15, 1935, headquartered first in Frankfurt am Main, then in Koblenz in SS Main Sector *Rhein* in central Germany. After a reorganization of the SS, the unit transferred to Arolsen in January 1937 in a new SS main sector, *Fulda-Werra*.[1] The regiment's extensive area of operations covered a region of considerable diversity in central Germany. Both thinly populated rural areas and heavily peopled cities reflected a region where subsistence agriculture and small-scale artisan crafts co-existed with heavy industry. The Nazis found considerable support here during Hitler's political ascent.[2]

The regiment began with the establishment of equestrian units attached to infantry regiments. The SS also began organizing small riding groups in several communities by accepting anyone who had access to a horse. By 1933, three independent equestrian companies had emerged, and, because the number of men who wished to join the SS had been consistently increasing, negotiations opened with the SA to gain the region for the SS.

There appeared to be a strong general desire among the men to serve in the Equestrian SS. The units, however, had tremendous difficulties following SS training schedules. Most of the men were farmers with draft horses. During an inspection, chief equestrian leader Georg Skowronski noticed variations in horse breeds and member skills, and ridiculously advised leaders to encourage their men – small farmers – to purchase thoroughbreds or perhaps to trade their plow horses for one to promote an élan for group participation in tournaments. He also complained of too many horsemen with long hair and below proper height, suggesting that short candidates would no longer be accepted since they tended to be especially upset when kicked out. He did, however, express his pleasure upon discovering the absence, through discharges, of most older, overweight men who were no longer able to mount and dismount.[3]

Because there were no specialists in the small platoons, the main sector equestrian leader or his adjutant had to travel frequently to provide basic training sessions. As a remedy, Skowronski suggested that all officers and men who had successfully completed courses at equestrian academies be promoted immediately so they could command units or at least be trainers. He also urged equestrian leaders to contact squad leaders of an infantry unit to practice exercises under combat conditions. According to Skowronski, this would give equestrian units a clear notion of acting as a group prepared to do battle on horseback or dismounted as infantrymen. (Horsemen were not only supposed to constitute an impeccable mounted unit, but also expected to show that they could be "horsemen on foot" in the manner of infantrymen.)[4]

During the summer of 1934, the SS and SA completed arrangements to transfer three SA companies. Furthermore, there appeared to be continued interest among many SA horsemen in joining the SS. Several reports indicated that farmers and members of rural riding clubs taken over by the SA quit, or, in some instances, refused to join because they wished to ride for the SS. In some areas, farmers refused to join the SA while a significant number of SA horsemen became completely frustrated with SA equestrian leadership, creating dissension and conflict in the units.[5]

To gain some of these recruits, the SS relied on a prominent connection. In Dorsheim in central Germany, an SA riding group had ceased all activity because local farmers refused to allow the SA to continue using their horses. The unit, composed of transfers from a regular SA foot regiment, was willing to ride but it distrusted Nazi paramilitary formations. The accountant of SS Equestrian Company 5 of the *Rhein* sector blamed in part "the thick-headedness of some farmers," those who refused to allow anyone the use of their horses, for creating problems; he intervened to secure the men and horses, but all attempts had failed. Fortunately for the SS, the mayor of Dorsheim interceded on its behalf. In a show of support, the mayor negotiated with the farmers and secured the use of their horses for the SS. An SS veterinarian judged the mounts the best in the unit.[6]

While the Equestrian SS increased its membership, its units hardly constituted an elite force. Most members were farmers too busy to attend all meetings and training sessions. The men of the Oberursel company were scattered across communities about fifteen kilometers apart. They worked their own fields often without any help. Despite their dedication and enthusiasm "for the cause," they often missed meetings. Scheduling four days of service each week was impractical and impossible during planting and harvesting seasons.[7]

The SS encountered serious dilemmas. Many horsemen were beyond SS age requirements, but without them there would be insufficient numbers to carry out any activities. And, it was feared, discharges probably would cause younger members to leave.

Training sessions likewise revealed substantial differences in the equestrian skills of troops and the significant variations among units. Some were especially talented and well-trained, but numerous novices prevented group training, mounted group exercises, and night marches. Problems arose with basic military matters, such as conduct in the ranks and a true understanding of Nazi ideology. Erwin Selck, commander of Equestrian Company 2 in Oberursel, suggested altering the training schedule to allow for specialists to meet with each group. Leaders of the smaller units could then work intensively to improve the equestrian ability of the men by spring 1935. Only then would many units have the ability to begin regular group exercises.[8]

The leader of Equestrian Company 4 in Niederneisen, Wilhelm Stotz, expressed similar concerns regarding his unit's ability to function according to SS guidelines. The unit was an SA transfer with only limited training. Many men were simple farmers who barely possessed basic riding ability. Conducting exercises on horseback during the week was futile because the horses were busy working in the fields. Most members of Company 4, like those in other rural units, were small farmers who could devote little time to the SS. Some simply did not show up for exercises whether they were excused or not. Only on Sunday afternoons could training occur on horseback. Still, some horsemen could attend to certain agricultural obligations only on Sunday and thus rarely appeared. Weeknight training, when it occurred, did not begin until 9 o'clock because the men worked late in their fields. Part of the planned activities was often shortened or eliminated. Group services were rarely held because local mounted units were too small (some had only four or five members) to fulfill the purpose of the training program. Stotz reported his personal decision to reduce the number of days of service to three, including Sunday, reserving one weeknight for a group meeting. Although it was an improvement, the schedule still did not completely solve attendance problems. The weekly meeting day had become basically useless because too few individuals attended.[9]

His men were losing interest, because too many exercises were carried out on foot. A show ride or something similar would be beneficial, he thought, but the men generally had few equestrian skills, not having had an opportunity to be trained on horseback. As a certain discontent was setting in, Stotz lamented how a shortage of recruits required him to keep people above the maximum age limit. Still, it was difficult to assess the precise level of indifference because most riders had come from rural riding clubs where members met only one weekday and on Sunday.[10]

Also, according to Stotz, the possibility existed that the financially burdened unit might face dissolution. It could not recruit financial sponsors because those it would have preferred already were supporting SS infantry units. Even inactive members of the former riding associations would not support the SS because they were supporting other organizations, especially the Mounted SA. Only scheduling changes would prevent his unit from dissolving and thereby forcing members to join other formations. After all, he insisted, he could not compel the horsemen to remain because they belonged to the free farming community.[11]

Some members of small units grew frustrated with various SS requirements and not just with schedule. They complained about having made new purchases, such as uniforms, and grumbled about other sacrifices. Some farmers wondered whether the SS truly understood the demands of farming. Those who had left generally did so because the SS required too many days for training, and because they had to travel too far to attend meetings. More would quit if the schedule did not change, leaders predicted.

Several volunteer firemen became disgruntled and chose to leave the SS. To disguise their genuine disaffection, they used as a pretext a decree by Minister of Interior Wilhelm Frick requiring all volunteer firemen to seek discharges from the SS or SA to prevent a reduction in their training in the fire brigades. Other fireman resisted leaving: "We swore to the Führer...to guarantee the safety of the Third Reich. We did not buy uniforms to have them eaten by moths."[12]

One by one company commanders requested a change in the number of days set aside for SS duty, with additional allowances during harvesting. One suggested training on foot or on motorcycle because horses used in harvesting and plantings were usually worn out by day's end. Still, Hermann Burk, the leader of Equestrian Company 1 in Frankfurt and simultaneously leader of all equestrian companies in the *Rhein* region, told his superiors 90 percent of the men were active in agriculture, yet despite almost sixteen hours of strenuous daily labor, most still were interested in serving in the SS. But they were simply too fatigued when they reported for training. He recommended having service only on one night a week and on Sundays during harvest periods. Fearing a massive flight, the SS relented and modified its schedule.[13]

With these unimpressive units, in November 1934, August Heissmeyer, the leader of the *Rhein* main sector, proposed the establishment of an equestrian regiment in his domain. By that time, the units had their own building in Frankfurt, each company had its own office and a financial administrative officer, and each squadron had an instruction room, training material, and a sandbox for practicing military maneuvers.[14]

Heissmeyer initially anticipated Hermann Burk becoming the regiment's commander because he had been working with each mounted company for some time. Himmler, of course, preferred only academy-trained leaders for equestrian regiments, and Burk was one of only a few horsemen in the region to have completed the Rothkirch cavalry course. Another was Oskar Hix, the adjutant to the regional equestrian commander of the *Rhein* sector. Hix frequently travelled by car to provide cavalry training to equestrian detachments dispersed throughout the region. He taught both cavalry and infantry courses, inspected troops, instructed unit leaders in how to handle administrative tasks, and even delivered ideological lectures. Hix arranged transfers from the SA and rural riding clubs, talked with farmers about joining, or at least allowing the SS to use their horses, and he concluded horse purchases.[15]

What his horsemen really needed, Himmler believed, was an experienced SS leader and jockey who could mold them into true SS men. He chose Caspar Koenig, a long-time Nazi who previously was equestrian leader of Main Sector *Rhein*. Burk became his director of training and Hix remained as adjutant.

The regiment fell well below Himmler's expectations: its strength represented an insufficient number of officers, enlisted men, and horses. According to guidelines established by Himmler, an equestrian regiment had to consist of at least five companies, each with five officers and 140 men with horses for a total of twenty-five officers and 700 men. Yet the actual strength of the unit was 386 men with 389 available horses, although there existed sixty additional candidates prepared to join the ranks. In December the number of men increased to 440, but with no corresponding increase in the number of horses. During the bureaucratic process of becoming a cavalry regiment, recruiting slowed and the unit actually decreased in size, perhaps inconsequentially, to 437 men by March 1935. Despite having just over half of the required number of men, several of whom did not own a horse or have one at their disposal, the SS consolidated the mounted companies into an equestrian regiment.[16]

Equestrian Regiment 10 faced significant recruiting problems throughout its existence, especially after the reintroduction of the draft in 1936. Later, such requirements as recruiting for the armed SS further reduced the pool from which it could select new members. And SS horsemen who filled the ranks of police reinforcements for the Death's Head units certainly aggravated the mounted regiment's manpower shortages.

Two crucial factors kept the strength of Equestrian Regiment 10 below SS averages for a mounted regiment. The Mounted SA practically monopolized the region and established equestrian units before the SS could respond in kind. Furthermore, insufficient interest by prospective members in riding and stronger inclinations for membership in motorized units in central Germany added an almost insurmountable barrier to successful recruiting.[17]

With a limited pool of men from which to choose, recruiters could not always be selective in identifying possible candidates for admission. One case in point concerned candidates in Dillenberg. Medical examinations found about 80 percent of them unsuitable for SS service. The recruits were intended to strengthen an undermanned mounted platoon in Herborn, but the unit was dissolved; its members transferred to an infantry regiment.[18]

Manpower shortages reached a near crisis level with the overall reorganization of the SS after the incorporation of the Rhineland. The creation of Main Sector *Fulda-Werra* in January 1937 and the inclusion of Equestrian Regiment 10 in the region resulted in a reorganization of the regiment. The SS divided the regiment into two parts; three companies fell within the boundaries of *Fulda-Werra*, while the other three remained with Main Sector *Rhein* to be absorbed by Equestrian Regiment 13.[19]

Hence Equestrian Regiment 10 lost almost 50 percent of its horsemen after the reorganization. It no longer contained six companies but three: two in Frankfurt and one in Oberursel. It lost companies in Niederniessen, Bingerbrück, and Saint Katharinen as well as a platoon in Wiesbaden. Its strength in December 1936, the month before the reorganization, was 345 men with 25 candidates, but by January 1937, it had declined to a mere 180 men, hardly the size of a respectable cavalry regiment.[20]

To rebuild the unit, Prince Waldeck-Pyrmont suggested a temporary solution: extend the age to thirty-five for one year. He justified the proposed policy change as an absolute necessity and a reflection of reality; many young Germans did not own a horse nor did they have money to rent one. The request was denied, however. One might expect the prince to have a significant influence on the Equestrian SS in his main sector because he was a leading member of an important equestrian organization, the *Fédération Internationale Équestre*. But he seemed to have had little effect on the development of Equestrian Regiment 10.[21]

Equestrian leaders sometimes acknowledged the futility of their recruiting efforts. Erwin Selck, leader of Company 2 in Oberursel, complained that he could accept only men who owned horses because his unit suffered acutely from a lack of horses. He no longer agreed to accept non-horse-owners because it had become impossible to provide equestrian training to a large number of people. He lamented the fact that the SA had penetrated the region before the SS, but ultimately he felt compelled to avoid recruiting in regions controlled by the Mounted SA, it having honored previous agreements.[22]

Regimental leaders thus increasingly looked to strengthen their ranks with transfers from SS infantry units, especially horse owners in detachments in areas isolated from unit headquarters. In such areas as Langen where, according to exaggerated reports, there was supposedly "considerable interest" in riding, a few men from foot units intended to transfer to a unit attached to Company 1. Farming was a prominent occupation in the region, and so Equestrian SS leaders expected to gain a foothold, because infantry units had not really made an impression and some former members of SA riding units had expressed interest in riding for the SS. Still, the core of the unit came from SS infantry formations.[23]

Despite its dilemmas, in 1937, the regiment made plans to establish a fourth mounted company in Thuringia, a region without equestrian units. With headquarters in Gotha, the SS prepared to organize additional platoons in Erfurt, Eisenach, and Nordhausen. Dr. Hans Ullrich, serving with SS District 27 as an adviser on riding matters, was expected to lead the new unit. Ullrich also held an important position as General Director of an insurance company, the *Gothaer Lebensversicherungs A.G.* Expected to provide the cadre for the unit were members of a former equestrian unit in Eisenach, reassigned to SS Infantry Regiment 14. Reportedly, enough interested SS men with horses and experienced Hitler Youth riders would allow the company to mount between fifty and sixty members almost immediately.[24]

The plan collapsed. Ullrich, preoccupied by his job and by honorary positions that required him to travel throughout Germany and abroad, expressed his aversion to commanding the unit. The SS was wasting its time attempting to establish a mounted company, he claimed, because the SA had already enlisted men interested in horsemanship. However, SA mounted units had hardly made a favorable public impression. Although the best riders in the region wore SA uniforms, SA units were generally poorly trained and had few quality horses. Consequently, the Mounted SA rarely appeared in public. As far as the SS was concerned, Ullrich declared, only a few platoons could be organized at best. He instead urged the establishment of an SS equestrian club (*Reitsportgemeinschaft*) to allow mounted recruits in Thuringia to participate in small tournaments.[25]

Dr. Fritz-Herbert Wolff, co-founder and administrative officer of a dissolved equestrian company in Erfurt, took a similar position. In a lengthy report, he described the limited interest in riding in Thuringia. Although the region once provided the army's cavalry school with a few outstanding mounts and was home to an equestrian school to train cavalry and horse-drawn transport formations, central Germany was becoming increasingly motorized; the Equestrian SS could probably enlist only a few men, he believed. Thuringia simply lacked young, horse-owning Germans. Wolff's former Erfurt company consisted of old horses of limited ability; the company could mount only six men on horseback for parades. Nor was the unit especially integrated into the SS community. Friction, rather than a spirit of camaraderie, existed between SS mounted and infantry formations.[26]

Since Thuringia was not a major breeding region, appropriate conditions required to establish equestrian units did not exist. Especially lacking were talented and knowledgeable cavalry leaders, and SA horsemen showed no interest in transferring. Like Ullrich, Wolff suggested that the SS concentrate on establishing an SS equestrian team to enable those interested in horsemanship, including members of SS infantry regiments, to ride for the black corps in tournaments. Perhaps the men could train on Sundays, and maybe a few could be sent to the riding school in Gotha if funds became available. As a result of these two unfavorable reports, *Fulda-Werra* canceled plans to establish the equestrian company and instead organized an equestrian tournament club, the SS-*Turniergemeinschaft*, in Gotha and Erfurt.[27]

However, during the recruiting process modest progress occurred. SS mounted platoons formed in Eisenach in 1937 and in Nordhausen in 1938 through transfers from SS infantry units and the Hitler Youth. Even with the support of community leaders in Eisenach, the unit remained well below manpower expectations. The Nordhausen platoon had been organized without an administrative structure because it consisted largely of students preparing for examinations to receive their high school certificates.[28]

In Nordhausen, initially, normal SS training was impractical because the students were too busy. Most had no income, relied on their parents for spending money, and could hardly afford SS dues. Paying for equestrian training was unthinkable. The unit did, however, have potential financial patrons. But donations had to be budgeted, and the unit had no one to record the amounts. The solution, a staff member thought, was to use an invalid to collect donations regularly. In return he could keep six percent.[29]

The tedious process of strengthening the Nordhausen platoon took several months before the commander of Infantry Regiment 67 agreed to cooperate in the transfer of some of his men. Needing a leader, the mounted unit also asked that an experienced, over-age cavalryman be allowed to join. Evidently the request was denied, and a few months later the SS transferred a member of an infantry unit to command the platoon. Thanks to a significant donation, the unit began to prosper and even held a successful tournament in its first year of existence.[30]

No such results occurred in Giessen, an area the SS thought provided favorable recruiting conditions. Home to a riding institute and the University of Giessen's veterinary medical school, the city had a significant number of riding instructors and veterinary students. Already one member of the school's faculty, a veterinarian, rode for the SS in Company 1, and a few other instructors at the university formerly belonged to an equestrian unit. Plans to establish the unit did not begin until January 1938. One would expect such an important center to have prompted earlier recruiting efforts. But finding few men interested in joining the SS, recruiters left empty-handed. No SS mounted unit could be organized.[31]

One of the equestrian regiment's greatest recruiting failures occurred in Marburg/Lahn. In December 1938, Marburg became the focal point as a base for a mounted company. Marburg had actually been targeted four years earlier. A quixotic report in 1934 concluded that a small mounted unit already there would be the foundation of not just an equestrian company but of a mounted regiment. The unit, called SS School Marburg, began as a twenty-man mounted detachment attached to Infantry Regiment 35 in SS Main Sector *Rhein*. It was established with the support of a local pharmacy affiliated with the University of Marburg. The doctor of Company 2 of the infantry regiment arranged with a local pharmacy for the use of its horses. The pharmacy not only lent horses to the SS but also provided equipment and accommodations for men and horses; the SS really covered only fodder costs. The SS, clearly benefitting from this relationship, wanted to keep its connections with the pharmacy. When an equestrian leader delayed exchanging horses at the pharmacy's request, the infantry regiment intervened to settle a dispute which potentially could have dissolved the mounted unit. The regiment's doctor intervened to pacify the pharmacy, while its commander decided that it would be in the best interest of the SS to select another leader for its equestrian unit.[32]

The Marburg unit was intended to be the nucleus of a future equestrian regiment, supposedly because many individuals in the vicinity were interested in joining a mounted SS unit. The Equestrian SA had already established a foothold in the area by taking over the riding clubs, but some SA horsemen apparently wished to transfer to the SS. An equestrian official estimated that he could quickly enlist about sixty horsemen with mounts under the leadership of three officers. But for four years all attempts to increase the size of the unit failed miserably because of a lack of interest among the local population; the Marburg unit remained only a mounted platoon. The number of transfers from SS infantry units and the SA was inconsequential. By the outbreak of World War II, the Marburg platoon had less than thirty members.[33]

In addition to its recruiting difficulties, Equestrian Regiment 10 suffered from significant administrative problems. Reorganization, frequent personnel changes, the draft, time constraints, and limited funds to hire skilled individuals naturally resulted in difficulties in properly administering units. Admonishment and, if required, punishment resulted from poor administrative practices as the SS sought to ensure that unit leaders and staff members properly followed procedures. Mounted companies had difficulty acquiring accountants and, after the regiment's medical detachment was dissolved, doctors to examine recruits.

Generally the main problem resulted from a reliance on volunteers with full-time civilian jobs. Company 6 in Saint Katharinen entrusted the manager of a grain and fodder supply store to handle its bookkeeping. Already overburdened by his job, the accountant was unable to find time to record SS dues and extra fees required of non-party members. The company, which transferred from the SA, included mostly sons of poor small farmers, forty-three of whom were non-party members. Many often had difficulty paying SS dues, and reportedly only one could afford the additional fee required of non-party members. Company records needed updating, but when the accountant requested assistance with bookkeeping, no one else could handle the workload.[34]

The regiment's medical detachment had difficulty finding a suitable member to handle its correspondence. It appointed a former Hitler Youth member with no business training to manage the paperwork. Because the young horseman was completing his formal education, he could work only from 7:00 to 8:00 in the morning and after 8:00 at night. He often made careless errors and had problems getting materials mailed on time. Although he had not been trained for the position, he was assigned because no one else could, or, most likely, wanted to do the work.[35]

Criticism of slipshod administrative practices aroused the anger of one company leader. Wilhelm Schweizer, a full-time *Reichsarbeitsrichter*, a judge involved in adjudicating labor disputes, commanded Equestrian Company 2 in Frankfurt. He often found himself overburdened with SS obligations. On one occasion, he angrily responded to criticism of his leadership ability, especially when the company missed a deadline for filing athletic and welfare reports. In a letter to Ludwig Lang, leader of Equestrian Regiment 10, Schweizer asserted that, although overburdened by judicial obligations, he had enthusiastically volunteered his time to the SS. Attending the theater and having a private life became impossible once he became commander. He not only led the company but was its ideological instructor and was solely responsible for raising about 1500 RM for his company. His attention to leadership obligations left little time for riding and sports. He always performed his duties admirably, he stated, generally with little assistance and without paid co-workers.[36]

Schweizer blamed his subordinates, especially his bookkeeper, for paperwork problems. He had inherited irresponsible co-workers whom he could not control when he assumed command, he charged, because the SS refused to expel incompetent staff members. He brazenly urged that all threats of punishment be stopped and blame for mistakes be appropriately directed. Because of his private occupation, Schweizer was not dependent on the SS for a career, so he could be somewhat stern when dealing with his immediate equestrian superiors. However, he really had no desire to be dismissed from the SS.[37]

Schweizer's complaint reflected the inherent difficulty associated with relying on volunteers to handle administrative obligations. At times, the volume of correspondence could be overwhelming, but SS companies simply had no funds to hire competent personnel. The immediate problems, therefore, were financial. The regiment had insufficient funds to ensure that subordinate units functioned properly because the General SS system of operations was inherently flawed. The SS did not provide the resources to allow General SS units to fulfill Himmler's expectations.

Equestrian Regiment 10 therefore relied significantly on wealthy patrons for financial support. It benefitted from two wealthy benefactors in its ranks. One, Dr. Erwin Selck, commander of Company 2 in Oberursel since March 1934, occasionally donated money to purchase and care for horses and to support tournament participation. In December 1937 Selck gave the regiment an impressive endowment: 5,000 RM to maintain a *Turnierstall*, an official tournament team, and 2,400 RM to buy a horse. The regiment, having few horses of its own, frequently used rentals. It had attempted to rectify the situation but could afford to buy only older horses generally unsuited to successful tournament competition. Selck had his own stables and wanted the regiment to be successful in tournaments. Regiment leaders, when looking to acquire horses, knew Selck could provide money to buy experienced horses, and his contributions certainly yielded benefits. The regiment's tournament victories dramatically increased in 1938.[38]

Selck also wanted to assist less-well-off members of his unit. For Christmas in 1937 he provided the regiment with 1,000 RM to use toward bonuses and gifts for needy comrades. He intended the donation to serve as the foundation of a welfare fund. Part of the money was awarded to the regiment's horse groomer whose uniform had been worn ragged. Although the General SS prided itself on providing assistance to needy members, Equestrian Regiment 10 hardly received a similar contribution from Main Sector *Fulda-Werra*. The regiment relied more on Selck than the main sector to assist members financially in need.[39]

Another wealthy member of the regiment, Dr. Georg Kranzlein, a chemist and the unit's director of gas warfare, also helped defray some costs of tournament participation. In 1937 he made an interesting purchase: 300 gas masks for the SS. His inspiration came, he claimed, from an understanding of the dangers of gas warfare. Kranzlein did not neglect his SS comrades in infantry formations. He donated 200 gas masks to the equestrian regiment, the remaining 100 going to SS Infantry Regiment 2 in Frankfurt.[40]

The Commanders

Equestrian Regiment 10 had four different commanders during its existence, all of whom served most of their pre-war SS years with the mounted units. Two had previously been SA members and only one was without World War I experience. The unit's first two leaders, Caspar Koenig and Carl von Pichl, began their SS careers outside of the Equestrian SS; the former joined an SS infantry unit and the latter enlisted in an SS motor unit. Both men later held staff positions in the General SS. Its third leader, Ludwig Lang, was expelled from the SS after commanding the regiment for only a few months. When World War II broke out, commander Rolf Becher joined the SS cavalry in Poland.

Its first commander, Caspar Koenig, was an experienced old fighter and an early Nazi Party member. After serving in World War I, Koenig enlisted in a Free Corps unit in 1919, and he joined the Nazi Party in 1921 while serving in the SA (1921 to 1923.) He joined the SS in 1931, enlisting with an infantry regiment in Munich. By 1932 he had organized and commanded a cavalry troop attached to the regiment. His commanding officers praised his leadership skills and character and recommended him for leadership of an equestrian company.[41] In 1933 he took command of the Munich equestrian company and later that year became equestrian leader of SS *Gruppe Süd* (later renamed SS *Oberabschnitt Süd*).[42]

Koenig spent almost his entire pre-war SS service career as an equestrian officer. A riding accident in 1934 and the actions of head equestrian leader Georg Skowronski, however, nearly derailed his equestrian career. An injured Koenig requested a reassignment. His interest in the science of race and eugenics, he thought, suited him for a transfer to the Race and Settlement Office. Nazi Party leaders in Munich offered him a position for his extensive service to the movement.[43]

Actually the behavior of chief equestrian leader Georg Skowronski weighed more on Koenig's mind than the injury. Skowronski had been urging main sector equestrian leaders to solicit donations for his office. Koenig, a former soldier, felt obligated to abide by a superior's request; otherwise, he suspected, his SS career could be in jeopardy. On one occasion, Skowronski used money donated by I.G. Farben to buy two automobiles. Koenig, uncomfortable with raising money for Skowronski, discussed his dilemma with August Heissmeyer, the *Rhein* main sector leader. Heissmeyer admired Koenig's leadership and commitment to the SS and blamed the entire matter on Skowronski's abuse of power and SS funds. The main sector leader voided Koenig's transfer request because the SS could hardly afford to lose a skilled cavalry commander. He also lectured Skowronski about his improper behavior (Not surprisingly, Heissmeyer later became a strong voice calling for dismissal of the head equestrian leader). The main sector confiscated the two cars.[44]

Koenig remained *Rhein* main sector equestrian leader when he assumed command of Equestrian Regiment 10; thus he held both posts simultaneously. Unfortunately, his SS officer file contains no correspondence concerning his tenure as regimental leader. His command, apparently meeting with favor by his superiors, proceeded without incident. In February 1936 he transferred to become equestrian leader of Main Sector *Südwest* and head of Equestrian Sector VI. He took command of Equestrian Regiment 13 in November 1936, then transferred in January 1937 to lead Equestrian Regiment 14. He received a favorable evaluation from Friedrich-Wilhelm Krüger, inspector of the Equestrian SS, at the equestrian leadership training course in February and March 1939, but was transferred four months later to SS Death's Head Regiment 7. His commanders there, however, became thoroughly dissatisfied with the former equestrian leader.[45]

Scheduled to take officer training courses at the SS Officer School in Munich/Dachau, Koenig refused to appear, citing high blood pressure and tonsillitis as reasons. He submitted official medical statements verifying his condition. One Death's Head officer complained of Koenig's extended absence. He was therefore transferred again, this time to SS District 16 in Magdeburg as a staff leader. He fully expected the position to lead to an appointment as leader of a main sector, but World War II halted his General SS career. Koenig became a reserve officer in the Waffen SS.[46]

After the fall of Poland, his friend Heissmeyer at the SS Main Office attempted to transfer him to the recently created Death's Head Cavalry Regiment commanded by Hermann Fegelein. Fegelein, who knew Koenig and who constantly strengthened his troops, found no use for the former SS horseman. Koenig did, however, end up in the Waffen SS. He fought with several units, among them SS Death's Head Regiment 10 and the *Leibstandarte Adolf Hitler*.[47]

Information on Koenig's two immediate successors, Carl von Pichl and Ludwig Lang is, at best, sparse. However, both appear to have had difficulty handling the regiment's reorganization. Few men were added to the regiment, and the unit found minimal tournament success. The Equestrian SS barely maintained a presence in the main sector.

Austrian-born von Pichl, another World War I veteran, joined the SS in the spring of 1932 as a motorized unit leader in Linz and Vienna after being an active Nazi Party member in Austria. In 1935, von Pichl took a position with SS Main Sector *Mitte*. That year, Skowronski arranged for him to travel to Hungary – he was fluent in Hungarian – to buy horses for the SS, but von Pichl was arrested and detained for two days in Czechoslovakia on his return trip to Germany. Czechoslovakian authorities apparently questioned him about his Nazi Party membership, causing the SS to send a complaint to the German Foreign Office.[48]

In April 1936 the SS selected von Pichl, because of his leadership skills and sound knowledge of horses, to replace Koenig as commander of Equestrian Regiment 10. The main sector even lent him money to buy a horse. Von Pichl commanded from April 1936 to April 1937 during the transfer of the unit's headquarters from Koblenz in Main Sector *Rhein* to Arolsen in *Fulda-Werra*. Like Koenig, he held regimental command while serving as main sector equestrian leader. He was well respected and evaluated as a good riding instructor by the leader of *Fulda-Werra*, Prince Waldeck-Pyrmont. Von Pichl then became an equestrian specialist with Main Sector *Rhein*, and in May 1937 he became leader of Equestrian Regiment 15, a post he held throughout World War II; later that year he accepted another position, inspector of equestrian affairs in Main Sector *Süd*. Von Pichl remained leader of Equestrian Regiment 15 despite being judged unsuitable for a leadership position by Equestrian SS inspector Krüger.[49]

Ludwig Lang, who replaced von Pichl, led the regiment from May to December 1937 when he was stripped of rank and expelled from the SS for violating procedures and concealing his indebtedness. Documents in his personnel file do not reveal Lang's specific infractions and provide only a few details about the equestrian leader. Like several other SS equestrian leaders, he was a World War I veteran who served throughout the war in a cavalry regiment. His dismissal as commander elevated his adjutant, Rolf Becher.[50]

Experienced and athletically gifted, Becher assumed command on January 1, 1938, and became the regiment's last official leader. Becher, a Sudeten German born in 1906 to a factory owner, enrolled for a time in business school, then in an art academy. However, in the late 1920s he decided to turn his hobby and true passion, horsemanship, into a profession. He became a riding instructor and an active tournament contestant, specializing in show jumping and cross country riding. A German citizen since 1928, Becher joined the Nazi Party in 1932 and the SA in the following year, surprisingly as a member of an SS motor unit in Dresden. Later, in 1933, he became an adjutant in SA Reitercorps 33 in Dresden. In 1934 he transferred to the *Ausbildungswesen*, the SA military training program, as a platoon leader and riding instructor at the SA cavalry school in Gotha.[51]

Frequent quarrels with the school's commander over proper equestrian training methods prompted Becher's transfer to Berlin. He became a staff member of the head of SA military training, Friedrich-Wilhelm Krüger, who later became inspector of the Equestrian SS, until the *Ausbildungswesen* was dissolved in 1935. After a few weeks of unemployment, Becher joined the SS as director of training and athletics for Equestrian Sector VII in Düsseldorf. Shortly thereafter, in September 1936 he became training director for Equestrian Regiment 6 in Düsseldorf.[52]

Becher possessed a sound theoretical and practical knowledge of horsemanship, attributes Himmler expected of equestrian leaders.[53] He had taken the Rothkirch cavalry training course and had trained SA and SS horsemen at the SA riding school in Gotha. He had also co-authored a training manual used by Equestrian SS leaders. Becher's skills made an immediate impression on Heinz Offermann, leader of Equestrian Regiment 6. Offermann praised him as a devoted riding instructor who meticulously supervised the entire training of the regiment and ensured that all companies properly followed training techniques. Offermann credited Becher with dramatically improving the equestrian skills of unit members; the regiment, he said, owed its success in tournaments to his teaching methods. But Becher's abilities were not restricted to the riding arena; he was also a qualified infantry instructor.[54]

Despite the high opinion of his talents, Becher was not immediately selected to become an equestrian regimental leader. Perhaps this resulted

in part from his opinions, often openly expressed, which may have alien-
ated some who could have aided his career. In January 1937, after being
removed as director of training, he had no official position in the SS. But
for several months the equestrian inspector of Main Sector West paid him
to continue providing training in the main sector. In June, however, the
SS transferred him to Equestrian Regiment 10 to become Ludwig Lang's
adjutant. Becher's previous work in the region as a member of the SA
seemed advantageous. Recognizing Becher's credentials, Hermann
Fegelein lured him to Munich as an instructor at the SS Main Riding
School. An official transfer occurred in November, but Lang's dismissal
cleared the way for Becher to remain in Arolsen, this time as commander
of the regiment.[55]

Becher, who took considerable interest in improving the equestrian
skills of his unit, proved to be a capable commander. Within a year, about
100 new members joined his regiment, increasing its strength to 289.
Although Equestrian Regiment 10 was the smallest of the SS equestrian
regiments when he took over, only six other equestrian regiments had
won more tournament events by the end of his first year in charge. In
1937, the regiment had not won a single event, but under Becher's leadership it achieved tournament success. Becher, not surprisinglgy, was
among the unit's most successful riders, the SS's third best in cross country events. He participated in as many tournaments as possible (generally
in central Germany) and maintained good relations with the SA, the army,
the police, and private rural riding clubs, all competitors he invited to
tournaments conducted by his unit.[56]

Tournament participation could be expensive, so the regiment frequently relied on prize money to defray costs. Although a special fund
existed to cover travelling expenses, Becher's winnings covered most of
his participation costs. Sometimes, if the regiment fared poorly in a tournament, it had to assume a significant loss. When Himmler issued the
1938 order to send all prize money to the Nazi welfare agency, Becher

was perplexed and concerned. He called the order devastating for the further development of the Equestrian SS and wondered how he would participate in tournaments. For an SS tournament in Nordhausen in October 1938, Becher had intended to use previous tournament earnings to cover expenses (which he calculated to be about 450 RM) for the regiment's tournament team.[57]

Fortunately for him, a wealthy patron financed the tournament. Still he told *Fulda-Werra* that he could not participate in future events without using prize money. Although Equestrian SS inspector Friedrich-Wilhelm Krüger allowed Becher to use prize money to participate, Himmler's decision took precedence. The *Reichsführer* SS did, however, reimburse the regiment for most of its expenses.[58]

Becher, seemingly satisfied, looked forward to a productive year ahead. Krüger, in fact, relied on Becher, his former SA cavalry instructor, to help lead the equestrian leadership training program in February and March 1939 designed to standardize training in all equestrian units. *Reitergedanken*, the book Becher co-authored, would serve as the basis for the entire training of the mounted units. He appeared to be one of the rising officers in the Equestrian SS.[59]

The unexpected death of Becher's best steed in 1939 destroyed his hopes for numerous victories on the tournament circuit and ended his chances for gaining recognition as the best SS cross country rider. The tournament team was left with only two horses. While Becher continually sought to find a suitable replacement, he had to cancel plans to participate in a major international tournament in Vienna. Thereafter, the amount of prize money earned and number of tournament victories declined. As war approached, he expected to be drafted into the army, but Hermann Fegelein kept an interest in his talents. Instead of being drafted by the army, he joined Fegelein in the SS cavalry in Poland.[60]

Equestrian Regiment 10, hardly an elite SS mounted unit, continually suffered from manpower shortages and administrative problems –

organizational difficulties faced by most General SS formations. Although organized in 1935, the unit did not become a real presence in central Germany until in 1938, the year Rolf Becher became commander. Clearly, however, central Germany provided few favorable preconditions for the Equestrian SS. The Mounted SA predominated and enlisted most young German males interested in horsemanship. Even under the regional leadership of SS main sector leader Prince Waldeck-Pyrmont, an aristocrat active in horsemanship in Europe, Equestrian Regiment 10 was an obscure presence in central Germany. Naturally, it would take some time before the SS could gain a strong foothold in the region.

Furthermore, as Robert John Shalka's study of the General SS in *Fulda-Werra* reveals, in central Germany there was hardly a rush to join the SS. The limited success of Equestrian SS recruiters therefore reflected a general indifference among the population to enlist in the Black Corps. In this regard, perhaps Equestrian Regiment 10 should be viewed differently. With the deck stacked against it, the success of Becher's regiment in tournaments seems somewhat respectable. Moreover, the appointment of Becher, an experienced, talented commander, provided the Equestrian SS in *Fulda-Werra* with a legitimate opportunity to flourish and outshine the vastly larger Mounted SA.[61]

CHAPTER SEVEN

Das Schwarze Korps and the Equestrian SS

The SS journal, *Das Schwarze Korps* (The Black Corps), was an extraordinarily popular publication that eventually became Germany's second largest weekly paper. The publication, which began in February 1935, disseminated information and propaganda to SS members and the general public. It had 750,000 subscribers by March 1944 and was posted in public places throughout Germany. A close relationship existed between its editorial staff and the SS leadership, and the paper remained somewhat independent of the restrictions placed on other publications.[1]

Equestrian SS members were expected to read the publication to reinforce their ideological indoctrination, and to promote the weekly throughout the homeland. During a subscription drive in late 1935, Eberhard von Künsberg, commander of Equestrian Regiment 15, told his horsemen:

> No other newspaper has to such a degree grasped the essence of our struggle and no other newspaper is in a position to bring truth to light . . . . Therefore, the press of our struggle deserves the farthest-reaching promotion and dissemination in order to enlighten the public about the goals of the SS.[2]

As previously mentioned, von Künsberg had been especially concerned with inculcating his largely Catholic equestrian regiment with SS ideology.

Das Schwarze Korps played a prominent role in publicizing Equestrian SS activities and its function and in presenting mounted units to the rest of the SS. Articles on the SS equestrian units appeared regularly in the paper, beginning with its first issue. The editorial staff depicted the mounted SS as an integral SS component which, through tournament victories, increased the prestige and respectability of the SS. More importantly, the paper proclaimed, the Equestrian SS, because of its ties to the countryside, represented the fulfillment of Nazi and SS rural ideology which glorified the German peasant.

"Blood and Soil" was the chief slogan of Nazi rural propaganda. According to the theory, the peasant (*Bauer*) was the cornerstone of Germany and the only one who could produce the food, on German soil, necessary to nourish and strengthen the German people and to assure Germany's existence as a healthy nation. The peasant was more than just a farmer – he had ancestral ties to the land, and he placed family and community above everything, especially financial gain. This distinguished him from the agriculturalist (*Landwirt*). An agriculturalist, and any other food producer in general, farmed solely for profit. Therefore, the history of the German people was a history of the peasant; the agriculturalist appeared only after the introduction of a monetary system.[3]

Himmler, important to Nazi rural propaganda, became involved in rural issues as an agronomy student in the early 1920s. In 1924 he wrote several articles for rural newspapers and campaigned for the National Socialist Freedom Party in rural Lower Bavaria. In 1925 he became deputy Reich propaganda chief and assisted in formulating Nazi rural propaganda. Himmler, like Hitler, believed that Germany's existence as a healthy *Volk* (nation, race, or people) depended on a return to the soil. Himmler glorified the peasantry, maintaining that "the peasant was the source of all that was good, pure, strong, and beautiful" and that a rural population had to be the foundation of the new Germany.[4]

Himmler even considered himself to be a peasant and attempted un-successfully to become a poultry farmer. Ironically, much of Himmler's and the Nazi Party's rural propaganda was delivered to urban audiences, the SS being primarily an urban organization.[5] Himmler wanted the SS connected to the farming community as closely as possible; therefore, he assigned farming specialists (*Bauernreferenten*) to all units. But for Himmler and the editorial staff of *Das Schwarze Korps*, the SS eques-trian units, composed largely of farmers, was the true link between the urban SS and the peasant community.[6]

The editor of *Das Schwarze Korps* was Günter d'Alquen, a close friend of Himmler. An early and passionate supporter of Nazism, D'Alquen had previously worked on the official Nazi Party newspaper, the *Völkischer Beobachter*. However, he found the paper to be too conservative and be-came dissatisfied with what he considered static coverage of party events and policy. He intended *Das Schwarze Korps* to be a radical loyal oppo-sition weekly read not only by SS and Party members but by all Ger-mans.[7] He understood the public's appetite for sensationalism and thus deftly interspersed articles promoting Nazi and SS propaganda with en-tertaining pictures, editorial cartoons, and scandal-mongering exposés.[8]

D'Alquen and his editorial staff introduced the Equestrian SS in the paper's second issue. While admonishing the horsemen to become de-voted SS warriors, the editors used political and military imagery (and romantic, pious platitudes) to explain the importance of the equestrian units. One article claimed that the units served to revive Germany's cav-alry tradition which was lost because of the drastic demobilization of the German army after World War I. It referred to equestrian units as a peas-ant cavalry, and stressed that these "sons of peasants," who "placed them-selves in voluntary service of the movement," honored their fatherland by helping to recreate Germany's cavalry tradition.[9]

The paper emphasized that SS horsemen were important because they affirmed Himmler's rural ideology. According to *Das Schwarze Korps*, the SS had "in racial respects . . . the best representatives from the ancestral peasant farms (*Bauernhöfen*)" who were involved each day in difficult farm work, labor that made them physically fit and athletically adept. Not surprisingly, the *Völkischer Beobachter* praised the farming community for having the proper attributes to preserve Germany's cavalry tradition. Riding was not simply for pleasure, the paper declared, for it was also a physically demanding sport. Farmers rose early and went to bed late and thus understood hard work. Their experience with and knowledge of horses made them better suited to become cavalrymen than city boys, the paper declared.[10]

This rural theme appeared in several articles on the Equestrian SS. Editors portrayed SS horsemen as genuine SS members, but *Das Schwarze Korps* reminded riders to accept SS ideology:

> From the inspired horsemen must dedicated *Staffelmann* be made. In the first place they have, therefore, to cultivate the National Socialist spirit. That is, all the virtues, all the qualities that the SS had cultivated in the long years of its existence and by which it has proven itself: loyalty to the Führer, readiness to obey and discipline, readiness for action and obedience, love of the Fatherland, love of the ancestral earth, and love of home and hearth. As long as an SS horseman mounts a horse, he cultivates the spirit of camaraderie, which Germany's sons in the World War cultivated to such a significant extent.[11]

Even Himmler remarked to the Equestrian SS that ideology must be taken seriously. At a tournament in Munich, he told SS horsemen to be true SS men and to be National Socialist soldiers at all tournaments. Covering the event, the SS journal declared that SS horsemen understood the importance of political ideology, for they had been taught from the beginning the importance of Nazi ideology as well as the importance of physical and athletic achievements. The paper applauded SS horsemen for proudly proclaiming the SS creed and singing the SS loyalty song, "When everyone else becomes disloyal, we will still remain loyal" (*Wenn Alle Untreu Werden, So Bleiben Wir Doch Treu*), after an exclusive Equestrian SS tournament in Munich in 1935 for the "Reichsführer-SS Equestrian Prize."[12]

The ideological significance of the Equestrian SS remained a consistent theme in the SS weekly. It announced that at an equestrian leadership conference in October 1935, SS leader Erich von dem Bach-Zelewski and a representative from the Race and Settlement Office had spoken on "blood and soil" and the importance of the SS and the Equestrian SS as protectors of this concept. Head equestrian leader Georg Skowronski stated that SS horsemen considered themselves above all as SS men, and that equestrian training was not simply carried out for athletic reasons. He said his goal was "to train strong and determined warriors and ready- for-action activists as carriers of our idea and movement." Skowronski further said that the Equestrian SS, "because of its ties to the land and peasants, . . . [was] . . . going to be the first organization to reach the racial goal that the *Reichsführer* SS had established."[13] At a leadership conference in 1936, equestrian regiment leaders again heard that it was their duty as SS men to carry out the ideological struggle everywhere and to be examples of dedicated National Socialists and SS comrades.[14]

Numerous articles on the equestrian units dealt with their successes at competitions in Germany and abroad. SS horsemen consistently triumphed in tournaments, and *Das Schwarze Korps* used these events to showcase SS talent. The paper declared that with the development of the Equestrian SS, it was hard to imagine a tournament without SS jockeys. *Das Schwarze Korps* constantly stressed SS horsemen's success against numerous entrants and staunch competition, especially the SA Equestrian Corps and the army cavalry members. It placed SS riders among the most successful of SS athletes.[15]

Not surprisingly, the rural theme appeared in several of these articles. According to the paper, equestrian events united rural and urban SS units. While discussing a 1935 tournament at the University of Munich's riding school, the paper declared that the Bavarian Equestrian SS worked closely with the various Nazi peasant leaders (some of whom were SS horsemen), thereby uniting rural farmers with urban athletic competitions. Repeatedly, *Das Schwarze Korps* portrayed SS riders as farmers who left the countryside to participate in urban events, and as peasants who dropped their plows to compete for the glory of the SS. SS horsemen were victorious, articles stressed, not because they rode special breeds or bought horses at exorbitant prices, but because of their dedication, superior knowledge of horses, equestrian ability, and rigid work ethic. SS riders often rode farm horses and breeds not specifically fit for equestrian competitions. Sometimes an SS "peasant" triumphed on his draft horse, the paper announced proudly.[16]

This view of the Equestrian SS as peasant cavalry complemented Himmler's ideology concerning the necessity of sports. Himmler believed that sports instilled discipline, and so he compelled SS members to participate regularly in athletics. The SS emphasized combative sports and especially those requiring skills beneficial in wartime, such as motorcycling, auto racing, and horsemanship. After a Munich tournament in 1936, *Das Schwarze Korps* declared, "Through its achievements, the mounted SS displayed the new military spirit in our nation."[17] *Das Schwarze Korps* also implied occasionally that equestrian units had functions in addition to tournament participation. In 1939, Friedrich-Wilhelm Krüger, inspector of the Equestrian SS, informed equestrian unit leaders that "horsemanship is a military sport, and knowledge of horses is a service to the fatherland."[18] SS horsemen did not simply represent the SS at equestrian competitions; they were also engaged in an important duty valuable for preservation of Germany's greatness. Through their service in the SS they became disciplined, chivalric soldiers.

Das Schwarze Korps romantically portrayed several SS horsemen as gallant knights. One example was Axel Holst of Equestrian Regiment 7 in Berlin. According to one article, Holst was a "knight in shining armor" and the embodiment of a dedicated SS man. Holst, a Swede by birth, emigrated to Germany during World War I.[19] He achieved fame for his victories in national and international tournaments, becoming one of Germany's best riders.[20] But in January 1935, Holst was crushed to death after his horse fell on him at a tournament in Berlin. *Das Schwarze Korps* referred to him as possibly the world's best jockey and stated that he "was not interested in becoming an SS leader, but simply an SS man." It also called him a "shining example for all young SS men." The SS honored Holst at subsequent equestrian tournaments and Equestrian SS leadership conferences.[21]

Das Schwarze Korps also focused on the importance of SS riding schools. According to the paper, the SS, with the opening of the Forst Riding School, was perpetuating Germany's cavalry tradition. Hanns Mörschel, the school's leader, earned praise as a proven and well-qualified instructor, an example to all SS men, and a gifted athlete who, despite his advancing age, continued to participate in all activities. In 1937, at age fifty-seven, he won three first prizes in carriage driving.[22]

The SS Main Riding School in Munich, the paper proclaimed, was the best SS riding school with "probably the biggest and most modern riding arena of its kind in Germany." The paper admired Fegelein's institute as an architectural beauty with luxurious sleeping accommodations, a marvelous balcony, and large windows that "let in light, sun, and air." The school, the paper reported, successfully participated in tournaments and gained an impressive reputation in equestrian circles. It especially noted victories by members of the school in international tournaments, and it duly mentioned it whenever the school successfully competed against members of the army's cavalry school.[23]

The school knew how to train horses properly, according to the newspaper. The horse Hermann Fegelein rode in winning the 1937 German Derby in Hamburg was a former farm animal purchased at a bargain. Furthermore, the school trained SS men in how to care for horses properly and in how to prevent unnecessary deaths on the battlefield. Most importantly, it trained riders to compete for the SS and not for personal glory. *Das Schwarze Korps* declared that "SS horsemen, like all SS athletes, ride not for trophies, nor for ribbons, nor for other superficial recognitions. They ride not for themselves, but for their uniform, for the Staffel, for all of us."[24]

Individual equestrian units established riding schools on a much smaller scale. A riding company of Equestrian Regiment 7 built a riding school in Berlin after two years of community work. It had to clear woods, level the ground, and install electricity, plumbing, and a sewerage system. An article on the school implied that a spirit of community and comradeship, reflecting exemplary National Socialist behavior, had developed among horsemen who helped to construct the training facility.[25]

Das Schwarze Korps also reported on an equestrian company in Leipzig which built an arena and stalls available to both the SS and the public. The company, like most equestrian units, had suffered from a shortage of riding horses. The unit had recently purchased additional animals but was unable to find a suitable location to shelter them. After some time, its leaders found an abandoned barn where members could work in their spare time to upgrade the facility. They repaired the structure, built stables, and constructed one of the better riding arenas in central Germany, according to the newspaper.[26]

The school trained individual SS members and housed members' horses and those belonging to the company. According to the publication, the equestrian company cultivated the true spirit of National Socialism – its facilities were available to the public, and the working class was especially invited to participate. Riding was not just for the upper classes, the newspaper emphasized, for it was now possible for each "worker" in the SS to participate in equestrian sports. *Das Schwarze Korps* declared: "That is the socialism that we in Germany want to have. No egalitarianism, no taking from others to give to some, but cooperation to eliminate existing social barriers."[27]

The importance of Equestrian Regiment 7 in Berlin in providing escorts and bodyguards for foreign diplomats and prominent guests at Nazi celebrations received publicity in the SS journal. It portrayed SS horsemen as knowledgeable and elegant escorts who impressed their hosts, especially Benito Mussolini. SS horsemen had to prepare thoroughly for their roles, for anyone who performed unprofessionally would be reprimanded. The journal regarded the members of the Berlin regiment as important SS ambassadors who, because of their knowledge of foreign languages, informed diplomats and others about Nazi Germany and presented the SS as something other than a band of unsophisticated Teutonic warriors.[28]

After the outbreak of war in September 1939, *Das Schwarze Korps* continued to report on Equestrian SS activities; however, the focus changed to activities of Waffen SS cavalry units. Often forthrightly, the paper presented highly favorable reports of SS cavalrymen. *Das Schwarze Korps* reported that mounted police regiments established in Poland consisted of Equestrian SS members, including several of the SS's best tournament riders. The journal described their activities and reported that they were not just maintaining safety and order but also serving the local population by bringing in harvests and arresting field thieves. The weekly also reported on mounted police units and the Jewish Question. It declared, "Our SS horsemen are entrusted with the Jews who are finally enlisted in positive work, which primarily consists of cleaning up operations and road construction."[29]

As the war ensued, *Das Schwarze Korps* compared SS cavalrymen to the gallant German knights who fought against Attila the Hun and "saved" Europe from the Mongols. SS horsemen were now protecting Europe from Bolshevism and reviving the German cavalry spirit. Although mechanization reduced the importance of the horse in wartime, the paper claimed that cavalry units were crucial to the German war effort. It described reconnaissance activities of the units and their successful battles with Soviet forces and resistance fighters. The East, with its wide, open plains, according to the paper, was the natural element of a cavalryman, but horses were also important in areas with difficult terrain such as waterways and swamps. An article describing the terrible conditions affecting the SS cavalry during its operations in the Pripet Marshes in 1942 mentioned swarms of mosquitoes plaguing the men and horses sinking knee deep in the swamp. Besides day and night battles on horseback and on foot, the men often had to search for food for themselves and feed for their animals. The mounted units, having to cross thirty-five rivers, even used captured Soviet gunboats to form an improvised navy.[30]

The cavalry leader, Hermann Fegelein, gained fame in several articles. Calling him a "daredevil" and one of the Waffen SS's best leaders despite his relatively young age, the journal proclaimed Fegelein as personally responsible for directing and deciding battles; his unit performed superhuman feats against much stronger Soviet forces. In listing his numerous military honors, the journal credited the courageous Fegelein for regularly appearing at the front to fight alongside his men.[31]

To the end, Himmler's horsemen graced the pages of *Das Schwarze Korps*. The Equestrian SS received considerable attention in the SS journal; it publicized Equestrian SS activities and regularly focused on its ties to rural Germany. Writers attempted to show that these units were crucial to the SS because they linked the urban SS with the German countryside and were thus ensuring the return of Germany's new elite, the SS, to its roots. The paper, which sometimes admonished SS horsemen to become devoted National Socialists, maintained that they were genuine SS men who understood the importance of ideology. *Das Schwarze Korps* also portrayed the Equestrian SS as a peasant cavalry and therefore the fulfill-ment of Nazi and SS rural propaganda. During World War II the paper described the valiant military spirit of the horsemen by depicting them as "gallant knights" who tirelessly fought barbarians on the eastern front.

CHAPTER EIGHT

A Social Profile of the Equestrian Officer Corps

Heinrich Himmler continually expressed his intention to transform the SS into Nazi Germany's new aristocracy. On one occasion Himmler mentioned his desire to create a racial and political elite during a meeting with representatives of Germany's traditionally privileged class. The meeting, held in Munich shortly after Hitler became chancellor, included senior military officers, estate owners, scholars, and industrialists who heard the SS leader stress that the state required a nobility and that the SS would serve as such for Nazi Germany. Himmler emphasized the need to link the National Socialist Revolution with Germany's established traditions, thereby providing the SS with "genuine military tradition, the distinctive outlook, bearing and breeding of the German nobility, the knowledge, ability, and creative efficiency of the industrialists, and the profundity of German scholarship." Many in attendance seemed pleasantly surprised by Himmler's open invitation to support the Nazi movement; almost everyone present enlisted in the SS.[1]

Himmler's invitation to prospective members met with favor among many of Germany's traditional elites. Himmler even gained Nazi Party assistance in his appeal to the elites, for it was shortly after the meeting that the Reich Ministry of the Interior issued a decree ordering German equestrian associations to join either the SS or SA. As a result, the state aided the SS in gaining entree into the conservative German countryside and helped Himmler to realize part of his agenda outlined during his meeting with German notables – "the bearing and breeding of the German nobility."[2]

A distinctive characteristic of the Equestrian SS was the number of nobles in its ranks, especially in the leadership corps. In comparison to the General SS and the German population, nobles were over-represented in the equestrian corps, particularly in its leadership. The percentage of noble officers in the equestrian units was 3.5 percent and among its leadership 20.3 percent, compared to only 2 percent in the General SS and only 0.5 percent among the German population.[3] Most Equestrian SS nobles joined the SS after Hitler's "seizure of power" in January 1933, yet a significant number, 32 percent, became SS members before Hitler became chancellor and before any riding club to which they may have belonged was ordered to join the SS or SA. Most nobles also joined the Nazi Party during the early 1930s. Twelve percent joined the party before February 1930 and 44 percent by March 1933. Obviously, many equestrian nobles became genuine supporters of the Nazi movement, having been attracted to SS ideology before the seizure of power. These nobles were also characteristic of the Nazi movement's attraction to young Germans. The average age of Equestrian SS nobles in 1938 was 38, the same as that of the General SS membership.[4]

One devoted young noble was Hans Karl von Treichel, who joined both the SS and the Nazi Party before January 1933. Treichel, a World War I and Free Corps veteran, was the son of an estate owner and cavalry officer. After the war, he studied agriculture in Heidelberg and Göttingen, eventually leasing and farming land. In time he bought an estate and, though constantly in financial difficulties, was able to retain the property after it was put up for auction. In February 1932, he joined the SS and the

Nazi Party and began to devote a great deal of time to the movement; this resulted in his expulsion from a fencing fraternity. Two years later he became an equestrian unit leader.[5]

Although not financially strong, von Treichel devoted considerable resources and attention to the party and to the SS. During the period of struggle (1920-1933), he spent approximately 1,000 RM on the movement, 500 in connection with a visit to his estate by Hitler and his escorts. He served the SS in an honorary (unpaid) capacity and provided an official room on his estate to his equestrian unit. He paid all utilities and often fed the unit's adjutant and administrative officer. However, for failing to attend an official leadership conference, Himmler demoted him to a subordinate position for one year. Von Treichel unsuccessfully claimed that he was ill at the time and that neither he nor the unit had money available to fund his trip to the conference. In 1936 Treichel became director of equestrian training in Berlin, dying shortly thereafter of kidney failure. Upon hearing of his death, his wife committed suicide, thereby orphaning three children.[6]

German nobles joined the SS for reasons other than ideology. The elegant black uniform attracted recruits, many of whom believed it enhanced their social prestige. Some wanted to express their loyalty to the state, particularly after the Nazi party temporarily stopped accepting members in May 1933. Others liked the career opportunities, the camaraderie, the SS's elite appeal, and, of course, the opportunity to continue to participate in sports.[7]

However, not all equestrian nobles were devoted National Socialists, for 16 percent never joined the party; most in this group joined the SS after 1933. Such was the case with Hans von Salviati, a World War I and Free Corps veteran, who served in an army cavalry regiment in 1920 until he was discharged in 1925 as a lieutenant. He studied horsebreeding and agriculture in East Prussia and became a successful tournament rider. From 1934 to 1936 he served in the Army's Hannover Cavalry School as a member of Germany's official equestrian team, which was quite successful in international competitions. After leaving the army, von Salviati joined the SS and immediately became leader of Equestrian Regiment 9 in Bremen. His equestrian training and abilities allowed him, in 1938, to assume command of the Hamburg Remount Institute and to become head of Himmler's Remount Office (in charge of training cavalry and officer mounts). Clearly an opportunist, von Salviati became the subject of rumors by fellow Equestrian SS comrades at the Hamburg school who questioned his political beliefs. An investigation revealed that von Salviati had made little attempt to join the Nazi Party, that he probably had a poor Nazi worldview, and that he had not fully recognized the importance of the Jewish Question. An SS court demanded that von Salviati try to join the party when it next accepted members.[8]

Von Salviati neglected the warning. He joined the army during the war, serving mainly as an adjutant to Field Marshall Gerd von Rundstedt in Paris. As German military successes began to decline, he recorded in his diary his disillusionment with both the Nazi regime and the Army High Command. The Gestapo confiscated the diary after the July 1944 assassination attempt on Hitler and used it as evidence against von Salviati. The SD, the SS Security Service, arrested him as a "dyed-in-the-wool" enemy of National Socialism and so Himmler banished him from the SS, turned him over to the People's Court, but then had him shot. Himmler also ordered SD chief Ernst Kaltenbrunner to investigate others whose names appeared in Salviati's diary.[9]

Like the nobility, most equestrian officers joined the SS after January 1933. But as Table 1 indicates, a far greater number of equestrian regiment leaders (43 percent) joined before the seizure of power than did their subordinates (22 percent). This trend was especially true concerning membership in the Nazi party. Most leaders who joined the Nazi party – 70.7 percent – did so before or shortly after Hitler became chancellor (Table 2). Only about 41 percent of the officers could claim this, yet both tables suggest that Nazi ideology had indeed proved attractive to many equestrians.[10]

Table 1
Date of Entry into the SS

	Equestrian Leaders	Equestrian Officers	Equestrian Nobles
Before Jan. 1933	43.0	22.0	32.0
After Jan. 1933	57.0	78.0	68.0
Total	100.0	100.0	100.0
Number of Cases in Sample	58	73	25

Table 2
Date of Entry into the Nazi Party

	Equestrian Leaders	Equestrian Officers	Equestrian Nobles
Before Feb. 1930	22.4	6.9	12.0
Before March 1933	48.3	34.2	44.0
After March 1933	19.0	46.6	28.0
Did Not Join	10.3	12.3	16.0
Total	100.0	100.0	100.0
Number of Cases in Sample	58	73	25

Scholars have noted the youthful aspects of the Nazi movement and its attraction to young German males. Herbert Ziegler in his study concluded that "the SS leadership, like the membership of the NSDAP and the SA, was much younger than could be expected from the age distribu-

tion of the male population at large."[11] The Equestrian SS, both its leadership and officer corps, conformed to this general pattern as shown in Table
3. However, in comparison to Ziegler's figures for his study of the SS
Death's Head Units (SS-TV), SS Militarized Troops (SS-VT), and General SS, leadership ages and membership tended, on average, to be higher.
In 1938, the average ages for members of the SS-TV, SS-VT and General
SS were 21, 23, and 29, respectively. The average age of the equestrian
unit members was 40.[12] The age disparity between the SS-TV and SS-VT
and the equestrian units was undoubtedly because armed units required
young recruits. The age of the equestrian leadership also tended to be
much higher than that of the SS-TV and SS-VT. In 1938, the average age
of an equestrian regimental leader was 41, while SS-TV and SS-VT average ages were 31 and 29. But the leadership of the General SS, with an
average age of 38, was similar in age to the equestrian leaders.[13] However, this was not the case concerning the age distribution at the time of
joining the SS. Recruits who eventually became equestrian leaders tended
to be much older than those in other General SS positions. Almost 50
percent of General SS leaders were age 30 or under upon joining compared to about 30 percent of the equestrian leaders. Also, more than 25
percent of equestrian leaders were age 41 or older when they joined. Consequently, a majority, approximately 64 percent, probably participated in
World War I (58 percent for the membership).[14]

On the whole, equestrian unit age structure differed somewhat from
that of the General SS, the Nazi Party, the SA, and the national population. It was, in comparison to the population, under-represented in the
age 61 and older category but over-represented in this same category in
comparison to the General SS. Surprisingly there were several SS riders
still active in their sixties. SS Corporal Ihrke (first name unknown), born
April 9, 1875, was a World War I veteran and former stormtrooper who
joined the Nazi Party in 1930. *Das Schwarze Korps* praised him for his
Nazi agitation and frequent arrests as a member of the SA. One arrest

Table 3

Age Distribution of SS leadership in 1938 compared to membership of Nazi Party, SA Leadership, and German Male Population

Age Groups	Equestrian Leaders	Equestrian Officers	General SS	Nazi Party	SA	SA Leaders	Population	Nobles
30 or less	13.3	23.8	19.6	37.6	36.2	26.1	34.6	19.1
31-40	37.8	34.4	47.2	27.9	31.0	30.4	21.3	57.1
41-50	37.8	29.8	27.0	19.6	24.5	31.1	15.8	14.3
51-60	11.1	7.5	5.4	11.2	5.8	8.1	14.1	9.5
over 60	0.0	4.5	0.8	3.7	2.5	4.3	14.2	0.0
	100.0	100.0	100.0	100.0	100.0	100.0	100.0	
Total Number	45	67	853	2,493,800	161	326	23,736,188	21

Source: Except for equestrian unit leaders and equestrian officer, Ziegler, *Nazi Germany's New Aristocracy*, 65.

Table 4

Age Distribution of the SS Leadership at the Time of Joining the SS

Age Groups	Equestrian Units	General SS
30 or younger	30.8	48.0
31-40	43.6	37.2
41-50	23.1	12.5
51-60	2.5	2.3
60 and over	0.0	0.0
	100.0	100.0
Total Number of Cases	39	788

Source: Figures for the General SS come from Ziegler, *Nazi Germany's New Aristocracy*, p. 73.

resulted from his wearing the outlawed Nazi uniform, sarcastically re-ferred to in the paper as the "state threatening" yellow pants. He joined the SS in 1933, serving as a blacksmith in Equestrian Regiment 7 in Ber-lin; he continued to ride cross country and steeplechase past the age of sixty.[15]

Important to any social analysis of Nazism is an assessment of the occupational structure and educational achievement of its support base. Various scholars have concluded that the lower middle class represented the primary support for the Nazi Party, even though it also received sup-port from various other groups in German society. The SS "secured re-cruits – though in varying proportions – from the juste milieu of German bourgeois society." Ziegler further argues, "SS leaders come from quite different social backgrounds . . . [which] . . . hardly conforms to the usual picture of lower middle-class Germans flocking to the banners of Na-tional Socialism."[16] Equestrian Regiment leaders (see Table 5) certainly came from the various economic and social groups in Germany. Doctors and lawyers rubbed elbows with bricklayers, and even aristocrats were at times led by former "social inferiors." But, unlike in the General SS, the lower middle class was over-represented. More than 52 percent of equestrian leaders belonged to this social group. The upper middle class was vastly over-represented in comparison to the SA, the Nazi Party, and the national population, and the lower class was under-represented in comparison to the population.[17] Thus, the occupational structure of the equestrian leadership was atypical of that of the General SS in Ziegler's study and reaffirms earlier findings of lower middle-class support.

In the educational sphere the achievement of equestrian leaders appears to be somewhat less impressive than that of their General SS comrades, who were, in general, better educated than the German population. In 1938 over 24 percent of General SS leaders had received a college degree compared to about 7 percent of equestrian leaders. Roughly 29 percent of equestrian leaders had, however, received a high school diploma (*Abitur*) or had attended a university. Regardless, SS ideology did not emphasize or value education.[18]

Equestrian leadership tended to reflect other aspects of SS ideology. About 98 percent of leaders were married and 76 percent had children. Seventy-three percent of the God-believing leaders had left the church, although one Catholic, Hanns von Wolff of Equestrian Regiment 6 in Düsseldorf, left the SS for the army for religious reasons.[19] Many had served in World War I and had supplemented their military experience in the various paramilitary forces, such as Free Corps (23.2 percent), Steel Helmet (7 percent) and SA (14 percent). About 40 percent served in the army between the wars. During World War II, 20 percent served in the army at one time or another and 35 percent served in the Waffen SS.[20]

Equestrian Officer Profiles

One of the most prominent equestrian leaders, Rudiger Wilhelm von Woikowski-Biedau, was born in Leipzig in 1888; he was one of the oldest equestrian officers. After joining the SS in May 1933, he immediately

Table 5

Occupational Structure of SS leadership, Nazi Party Membership SA Leadership, and the German Population

Occupational Groups	SS Equestrian Unit Leaders in 1938	General SS in 1938	SA Leaders in 1935	Nazi Party in 1938	Population in 1933
Lower Class	21.1	26.7	13.3	33.2	54.5
Lower Middle Class	52.6	42.7	72.0	57.8	42.7
Upper Middle Class	26.3	30.6	12.3	9.0	2.8
Total	100.0	100.0	97.6	100.0	100.0
Number Cases	45	853	952	234	27,047,899

Sources: In this study the lower class includes skilled and unskilled workers and enlisted military personnel. The lower middle class includes independent craftsmen, farmers, small businessmen, salaried employees, civil servants, and non-academic professionals. The upper middle class includes managers, higher civil servants, professionals, students, entrepreneurs and officers. Table and data are taken from Ziegler, *Nazi Germany's New Aristocracy*, 104. SA Leaders column does not total 100% because Ziegler omitted Mathilde Jamin's category of *mithelfende Familienangehörige*. Mathilde Jamin, *Zwischen den Klassen: Zur Sozialstruktur der SA Führerrshaft* (Wuppertal: Peter Hammer, 1984), 194-95.

Table 6

Highest Level of Educational Attainment of SS Leadership in 1938

Educational Level	Equestrian Units	General SS
Primary School	26.2	37.0
Middle School	11.9	4.2
Secondary School	21.4	22.9
Secondary School with Abitur	16.7	4.3
University	11.9	5.3
University with Degree	7.1	24.4
Other	4.8	1.9
Percent Total	100.0	100.0
Total Number of Cases	42	816

Source: General SS figures are from Herbert Ziegler, *Nazi Germany's New Aristocracy*, 115.

began recruiting members and establishing mounted units for what would become Equestrian Regiment 16 in Dresden. The following year he took command of Equestrian Regiment 11 in Breslau and simultaneously served as main sector equestrian leader in SS Main Sector *Nord*. In 1936 he assumed a recently created position, equestrian inspector in Main Sector *Nordwest*, and two years later he replaced Georg Skowronski as chief equestrian leader (*Chefreiterführer*). His career in the SS, however, covered more than just Equestrian SS matters. In 1938, Himmler named him head of the horse purchasing commission, a position affiliated with the armed SS units (both the *Verfügungstruppen* and the *Totenkopfverbänden*). Von Woikowski-Biedau had to locate suitable horses for the armed SS units and for the *Ordnungspolizei*, Germany's regular, uniformed policemen.[21]

Like many equestrian leaders, von Woikowski-Biedau became embroiled in controversies and violated SS regulations. He benefitted, however, from his friendship with two important SS officials: Werner Lorenz, head of SS Main Sector *Nord*, and August Heissmeyer, head of the SS Main Office (*Hauptamt*). When the SS court asked that the cavalry leader be thrown out, Lorenz and Heissmeyer protected him. Von Woikowski-Biedau emerged from a lengthy SS investigation with only a severe reprimand, despite revelations that he had violated several rules.[22]

The SS investigation into his misuse of funds began in 1936. The court suspected him of having strong Catholic views and of having fraudulently obtained two tickets to London that were to be raffled off to raise money for the Equestrian SS. But the main difficulties arose from his financial operations as main sector equestrian leader in Hamburg. Investigations discovered that the Equestrian SS in Main Sector *Nord* had maintained a *Schwarze Kasse*, an illegal, off-budget account, although SS regulations prohibited such funds. The Equestrian SS also falsely billed and overcharged the Reich Food Estate to cover expenses for an equestrian display during one of its agricultural exhibitions. This was done, the SS court stated, with von Woikowski-Biedau's approval and the help of his two assistants, adjutant Bernard Massury and administrative leader Ernst Kölln.[23]

The court described von Woikowski-Biedau as a devout Catholic and a self-interested swindler for taking tickets to London intended for a fundraiser. (His "deceptive ways" were reprehensible "Jewish business practices", according to the court.) It deplored his attempts to defraud the Reich Food Estate, especially since the SS and the Reich Food Estate had good relations and SS members held several high positions in the organization. The court concluded:

> This investigation ... confirmed the previous experience of the SS Court. That is, leaders of the Equestrian SS frequently do not possess the honesty and attitude expected of National Socialists and SS officers when carrying out and handling their business affairs.

Certainly we want SS officers to meet the public to promote the SS and thereby gain financial advantages. But this advantage must be achieved through honest methods.[24]

The court demanded that equestrian leaders behave decently and honestly to develop a sense of trust with the public and with all organizations. It recommended that Massury and Kölln be stripped of only one rank because they had simply followed orders. The court urged that von Woikowski-Biedau be stripped of rank and banished from the SS for life.[25]

The cavalry leader defended his actions and enlisted support from his superiors. He dismissed his supposed Catholic beliefs as simply inaccurate rantings from his lunatic sister-in-law, an artist who once belonged to a cloister. He said she was of unsound mind and could not be trusted, and a German court later concluded the same thing. As for the tickets to London, the equestrian leader stated that the auction had never taken place, so he offered to buy them for 40 RM but paid 10 RM and innocently forgot to pay the balance.[26]

Concerning the more serious allegations, von Woikowski-Biedau claimed that the secret account had existed before his appointment. Furthermore, he remembered ordering Kölln to dissolve it in December 1935. He also denied submitting false bills and defrauding anyone. SS horsemen cared for their horses and paid all of their expenses, so he charged the Reich Food Estate accordingly, all of which supported Equestrian Regiment 4 in Hamburg. Georg Skowronski, chief equestrian leader at that time, suggested charging the organization more (which the SA did, even though it had fewer horses at the event).[27]

Von Woikowski-Biedau's connections, Lorenz, and Heissmeyer, suggested that he be given only a severe reprimand. After all, they declared, he had acted only out of concern for the financial condition of his units because he never enriched himself, and there was no proof that he approved the sending of false bills to the Reich Food Estate. Lorenz said the organization was not really harmed; it received a bill, examined it, and agreed to pay it. Its leaders complained only after learning of the SS investigation. Besides, Lorenz declared, von Woikowski-Biedau always had performed his duties faultlessly and was viewed favorably by all formations, including the army. Lorenz wondered whether the SS could really afford to lose yet another equestrian leader.[28]

Himmler initially approved his subordinates' wishes and gave the SS horseman only a strong reprimand. But a letter to the *Reichsführer* from the Nazi Party's treasurer suggested the case be re-examined. Himmler, not wishing to appear excessively lenient toward an SS official who had taken advantage of a party organization, decided to strip his cavalry leader of rank and dismiss him from the SS. The intervention of Lorenz and Heissmeyer again saved their comrade. Himmler finally agreed to strip him of two SS ranks, reducing his rank from colonel to major, and to remove him from working with the Equestrian SS. (Massury and Kölln each lost one rank.) However, the punishment appears to have gone unenforced. Documents in his personnel file refer to him continually as SS Colonel von Woikowski-Biedau, his rank prior to demotion, after which he remained active in the Equestrian SS and became equestrian inspector in Main Sector *Nordwest*. Too old to serve in the military, he commanded Equestrian Regiment 9 during World War II.[29]

Although von Woikowski-Biedau occasionally violated SS principles, as an aristocrat he represented the bearing and breeding of the social class Himmler expected his cavalry to embrace. Because the upper classes dominated the world of horsemanship, the Equestrian SS obviously contained numerous officers who, at least superficially, could project an image of respectability. But equestrian officer Peter Wexel, a drunkard and a brute, had none of the social graces associated with international equestrianism.

Wexel, a World War I veteran who later served in the Free Corps, joined the Nazi movement in 1923 and quickly gained a reputation for fighting communists in Düsseldorf. He probably transferred from the SA to the SS in 1930. In 1934 he became leader of Equestrian Regiment 6 in Düsseldorf; the following year he took command of Equestrian Regiment 22 in Halle. His thick SS officer file, however, does not document his skills as a cavalryman but rather his disreputable behavior as an SS officer. Several SS evaluations described Wexel as distrustful and easily offended, and also as a man of great physical strength but of limited intelligence.[30]

A host of problems eventually led to Wexel's dismissal. On several occasions, including official SS functions, he fought with SS members and with members of the public, and he complained about the black shirts to non-SS members. He owed money to several people, including a woman he had lived with for some time. After their parting, she successfully sued him for expenses (rent, food, clothing) she had incurred while they lived together. The SS removed Wexel as an equestrian leader and unsuccessfully attempted to appoint him to a less prominent SS office. Eventually he was discharged, but the SS found employment for him in the German Labor Front (*Deutsche Arbeitsfront*), the Nazi labor organization, inasmuch as he was an early supporter of the Nazi movement.[31]

Similarly, Oswald Herde had an unflattering tenure in the Equestrian SS. A World War I veteran, Herde worked on his father's farm before joining the SS in 1933. He helped organize the original Equestrian Regiment 12 in upper Silesia, he commanded it, and later he became an equestrian training specialist in Main Sector *Südost*. Herde, however, became the target of an investigation that resulted in his dismissal from the SS. Amazingly, Herde committed several transgressions of SS regulations during his tenure as an equestrian officer. He spread rumors about other SS members, criticized the SD, complained publicly about the entry fee (to resounding applause) at an official SS function, and tried to get another SS officer to award him a riding medal without having taken the required examinations.[32]

Herde received only warnings and light punishments for his misbehavior. He actually left the SS to return to his father's farm and asked to be placed in a reserve SS unit. When he requested a return to full-time active duty, the SS discovered a more serious violation of SS regulations: He had used SD stationery and had falsified the signature of a superior. (The investigation also revealed Herde to be somewhat of an exhibitionist; he exposed himself to a neighbor and enjoyed sexual intercourse in his apartment while the window and curtains were open.) Although SS Main Sector *Südost* recommended that Herde be arrested and imprisoned in a concentration camp, Himmler decided only to strip him of rank and banish him from the SS. Later, Herde unsuccessfully attempted to rejoin the organization.[33]

Erdmann Skudlarek, a World War I and Free Corps veteran who fought in the border war against Poland in 1919, replaced Herde. Skudlarek joined the Nazi Party and the SS in 1931 and within a year assumed command of an SS motor company; shortly thereafter he became commander of an infantry battalion. In October 1935 he became leader of Herde's former Silesian unit, Equestrian Regiment 12. The Equestrian SS in Silesia was overwhelmingly rural; ninety-nine percent of SS horsemen were either farmers or agricultural workers. They had been poorly trained, especially in ideology. Most could regularly attend SS training sessions only during the winter. Skudlarek also found the unit almost financially ruined, and the main sector could not afford to send him and the leader of Equestrian Regiment 11 to train at the Forst Riding School.[34]

Skudlarek had good leadership and administrative abilities, but little experience as a cavalry leader. The SS did, however, send him to complete cavalry training courses at Forst. The head of SS Main Sector *Südost* and equestrian unit leaders blamed much of the problems in Silesia on Hyazinth Graf von Strachwitz, the leader of SS Cavalry Sector III. Von Strachwitz had supposedly selected equestrian leaders carelessly and had completely neglected his units. As a result, the cavalry sector had to be completely reorganized. In 1936, after the reorganization and merging of Equestrian Regiment 12 into Equestrian Regiment 11, the SS transferred Skudlarek to command Equestrian Regiment 3 in East Prussia. Although he joined the Equestrian SS without prior cavalry experience, he proved to be a capable commander and SS officer. Like many equestrian leaders, Skudlarek served in various SS branches. In 1938 he ended his SS equestrian service career to take another SS position: investigative officer in Main Sector *Nord*. When World War II broke out, he joined the Higher SS and Police Leader North (*Höhere SS und Polizeiführer Nord*).[35]

Unlike Skudlarek, Jacob Wein, adjutant and later leader of Equestrian Regiment 12 in Schwerin (its numerical designation came from the dissolved Silesian mounted regiment), brought to the SS cavalry experience and skills as a communications squadron leader. Although his twelve years in an army cavalry regiment (1919-1931) earned him only the rank of sergeant, he received commendations as an excellent horseman and riding instructor. After being discharged, he became a civil servant in Mannheim who handled secret directives. He joined the SA in November 1932 and helped to establish and lead communications units. Because his skills satisfied superiors, he earned their trust as a communications expert.[36]

In June 1936 Wein wrote to Himmler to request a transfer from the SA to an SS equestrian unit. Wein expressed a strong desire to be a professional soldier and his general love for equestrianism. He told Himmler of his repeated but unsuccessful attempts to join an equestrian unit in *Nordboden*, the only one in that region, and asked that his intentions be kept confidential to avoid problems with the SA. The SS found Wein especially suited to command an equestrian unit and dispatched him to Mecklenburg to lead a new mounted regiment. SS recruiters there had assured recruits, especially former SA horsemen, that the recently formed Equestrian Regiment 12 in Schwerin would be commanded by an experienced cavalryman. In 1937, the SS secured for Wein a transfer and a one-year leave of absence from his civil service position so that he could join the Equestrian SS in Schwerin; he also received a guarantee that he could resume his previous job.[37]

Wein's experience and leadership ability certainly benefitted the recently formed equestrian regiment in Schwerin. He helped to strengthen the Mecklenburg unit and even established a riding and driving school to train regimental personnel. He obviously enjoyed his position and newfound status. In 1938 he requested another one-year leave of absence to remain with the SS, but Himmler refused his request. By that time the SS had discovered unpleasant facts about him. Wein owed money to another SS member. He had borrowed money from a bank to buy a horse by using an SS veterinarian as a cosigner. He then immediately sold the horse without repaying the loan. After the veterinarian complained to the SS about owing money to the bank, an investigation ensued. The SS discovered that Wein was not as trustworthy as a previous SA evaluation had stated. During the investigation Wein attempted to use contributions to the equestrian regiment to pay off his loan and to hire a lawyer to defend him during SS judicial proceedings. Himmler stripped the cavalryman of his rank and banished him from the SS, a judgement that could harm his civil service appointment.[38]

Wein, however, defensively claimed that he had spent a significant amount of his own money on SS-related activities. Because his equestrian regiment had neither money nor a car, he had to pay for most of his official travel expenses. He incurred moving expenses because the headquarters of the regiment changed several times, and, since he lived away from his family, he incurred debts travelling to his home. Wein, declaring himself and his family financially ruined, asked the SS for 2000 RM, which he calculated as his actual expenses during his service. Although Wein did not receive payment for his expenses, the SS altered his punishment. Out of concern for his family, the SS simply discharged the horseman and paid for his moving expenses to return home. The SS also repaid the bank loan.[39]

Wein's successor, Karl Struve, also served twelve years in an army cavalry regiment before joining the SS (1933). In 1934 Struve became the training director for Equestrian Regiment 5 in Pomerania. Within a year he became adjutant and then unit commander. He helped the regiment develop talented jockeys to compete in tournament competitions. Struve himself won several dressage events. In 1938 he assumed leadership of Equestrian Regiment 12 in Schwerin. An evaluation characterized him as a reliable Nazi who, nevertheless, needed to be toughened up as a leader. His administrative practices, however, attracted SS investigators.[40]

Like several other equestrian leaders, Struve was not especially skilled in handling the financial operations of his unit. An SS investigation concluded that he improperly handled funds, falsified records, and probably enriched himself with SS money. He also displayed behavior unbecoming an SS officer in the presence of women. Struve was stripped of his rank and banished from the SS. Worried about his ability to find a job and support his family, Struve pleaded with the SS court to reduce his punishment because, he stated, he was only using funds to cover his actual expenses. The SS, reassessing its decision, found that he probably did not steal SS funds and simply discharged him.[41]

Shortly after his release, Struve applied to be reinstated. He had, in the meantime, been working at the University of Munich's riding school and another school rumored to be owned by Jews. The SS nevertheless readmitted him and attempted to use him as a cavalry instructor for Death's Head units. But Theodore Eicke, their leader, said he could use Struve only as a postal clerk. Several SS officials unsuccessfully attempted to transfer him to various units, but none wanted him. Finally, in June 1939, Struve became leader of Equestrian Regiment 20, recently organized in Tilsit in SS Main Sector *Nordost*. After the outbreak of war, he led a mounted auxiliary police detachment that evacuated Jews and Poles and engaged in cleansing operations, a euphemism for carrying out executions, in occupied Poland. His participation in the mass shooting of Jews in Lithuania in June and July 1941 – again with SS horsemen and members of the police – earned him a sentence of life in prison by a 1964 German court.[42]

To replace Struve as commander of Equestrian Regiment 12, the SS selected Austrian-born Herbert Gilhofer, an SS "old fighter," who joined in 1931. His activity in the SA, SS, and Nazi movement in his homeland earned him several arrests and fines. He left Austria for Germany in 1933 to report to Dachau to take a leadership training course and to train with the Militarized SS (Battalion 2 of Regiment I). At Dachau, Gilhofer received mostly favorable evaluations – a good leader, a good Nazi.[43]

But the commander of Company 8 of SS Regiment *Deutschland*, an SS lieutenant colonel, described Gilhofer as a man of peaceful character whose weak will needed toughening. Although Gilhofer was a good National Socialist, he was too timid and sensitive and he needed to show more enthusiasm for training, the infantry commander wrote. A poor evaluation by an infantry commander, however, seemed inconsequential when compared to another allegation. The wife of an SS member declared Gilhofer to be a communist sympathizer. After a brief investigation, Himmler reprimanded Gilhofer for "violating principles of decency and camaraderie" by expressing communist views. Gilhofer avoided serious punishment and continued his activity in the Militarized SS Troops as an officer in Company 6 and a platoon leader.[44]

Gilhofer took additional officer training courses in the armed SS units before being transferred to SS Main Sector *Nord* in July 1936 to become an adjutant and personnel director in SS District 33. On April 1, 1938, he became leader of Equestrian Regiment 12 in Schwerin in northern Germany. Gilhofer received several favorable evaluations as an equestrian leader, and he helped the SS gain access to an equestrian club in Rostok by becoming an adviser to the *Rostocker Pferdesport und Rennverein*. But Gilhofer also expressed his indifference to commanding an equestrian regiment and a desire to be transferred. The leader of SS Main Sector *Donau* asked that Gilhofer be transferred to Vienna to become personnel and training director for Sector 31 since he knew the region and had worked there previously. However, the SS personnel office rejected the transfer request because of Gilhofer's skills as an equestrian leader, especially since, as it stated, there was a general shortage of suitable equestrian officers.[45]

When SS Main Sector *Nord* requested Gilhofer's services to become a director in the Main Sector effective May 1, 1939, a position he previously held, Equestrian SS inspector Friedrich-Wilhelm Krüger intervened. Krüger wanted the transfer rejected because of potential detrimental consequences to Equestrian Regiment 12. He said the transfer would be a "significant loss" because Gilhofer had attended the recent training course for all equestrian regimental leaders designed to standardize training throughout the Equestrian SS. "A removal of equestrian unit leaders at this point in time would harm the entire training program," Krüger wrote. Despite his plea, the SS Main Office approved the transfer request effective June 1, 1939, a move that hardly adversely affected the Equestrian SS since Germany was at war two months later.[46]

Philip Hahn was another World War I veteran who served as an equestrian unit commander and, like Gilhofer, was an early supporter of the Nazi movement. He was a devout Nazi who had joined the party in 1926 and, like many devoted Nazis, had requested an Aryan (non-Christian) burial in his last will and testament. After serving in the SA from 1927-1930, he transferred to the SS in 1930 as leader of a cavalry unit of Regiment 10 (infantry) in Düsseldorf. In 1934 he became leader of Company 6 of Equestrian Regiment 14 in Karlsruhe. He became the regiment's leader in 1936 while working as a full-time civil servant in Pirmason, a city in the Rhineland-Palatinate. A vacancy in East Prussia prompted Hahn to request and receive a leave of absence to take command of Equestrian Regiment 1 in Insterburg, a major breeding area for the Trakehner breed of thoroughbreds.[47]

Hahn's leadership tenure in East Prussia evidences the difficulty the SS had in securing talented commanders. The Minister of Interior granted only a one-year leave, but the SS had not found a suitable replacement when Hahn had to return to his prior job. He unsuccessfully requested another furlough, and the SS sought an extension of his leave of absence because of his importance to the unit. With the requests denied, the SS discharged Hahn. But petitions to the minister of interior continued and eventually the Lord Mayor of Pirmasen granted the appeal.[48]

Another early Nazi to join the Equestrian SS was Dr. Hans Jacobson. His experience in the organization reveals the extent to which SS officers often compromised their positions. Born in Holland in 1905, Jacobson gained German citizenship through his father, a citizen of Bremen. Excited by the Nazi ideology, he joined the party in 1922. In the spring of 1923, during uprisings in the Saar, the French arrested him, and a military court sentenced him to five years of imprisonment, a punishment he avoided by fleeing to Germany. He enlisted in the army for three months and continued his activities in right wing politics as a member of the *Völkisch-Sozialen Block Kreis Konstanz*. He also went to college to study banking and later earned a law degree.[49]

Although Jacobson's SS officer file does not clearly mention the date he joined the SS, the evidence suggests that shortly after his enlistment he became a second lieutenant and legal adviser to the SS Main Riding School in July 1937. Clearly, Jacobson had skills valued by Himmler and the SS leadership, but he had a more important trump card for advancing in the SS: connections. Equestrian leaders Eberhard von Künsberg and Hermann Fegelein helped Jacobson receive rapid promotions, although they could not protect him from Gestapo snooping.[50]

As early as October 1936, the Gestapo warned SS Main Sector *Süd* of Jacobson's possible ideological shortcomings and especially of his activities as a lawyer for the *Bayerischen Vereinsbank*, a bank in Munich. Investigations discovered that Jacobson had been concealing the role of the bank's Jewish board members and therefore protecting Jews. Jacobson wanted to prevent the *Vereinsbank* from being classified as a "Jewish bank," a designation which would have led to numerous accounts being transferred to the *Deutsche Arbeitsfront* bank, the bank of the Nazi labor organization that replaced traditional unions. He simply did not want the bank to lose money, so he covered up the influence of Jews. An SS court judged Jacobson's behavior as unacceptable for a National Socialist, and Himmler dismissed him from the SS in 1939. In 1943, after being severely wounded while fighting on the eastern front, Jacobson petitioned for readmission. Himmler approved his request because, as one SS official remarked, Jacobson had been rehabilitated and his behavior had not been sufficiently damaging to prevent him from rejoining.[51]

Although most SS equestrian officers remained with the SS unless discharged, two regimental commanders were able to advance into the upper Nazi echelons outside of the SS. Dr. August Schwedler, leader of Equestrian Regiment 7 in Berlin in 1936, rubbed shoulders with diplomats and elites in Berlin and in 1938 became the adjutant and daily personal companion to Hitler's minister of economics and president of the *Reichsbank*, Walther Funk. Eberhard von Künsberg, leader of Equestrian Regiment 15 in Regensburg in Bavaria from September 1934 to April 1936, likewise associated with prominent nobles and Nazi officials. In 1936 he joined Joachim von Ribbentrop's diplomatic ministry.

The equestrian career of the well-educated Schwedler – he held a Ph.D. in agriculture – began in July 1933 when he became a director of training and personnel for equestrian units in SS Main Sector *Südost*. Later, as a member of the Berlin equestrian unit, he escorted foreign guests at Nazi functions. In late 1936, the SS transferred him to its main office (SS *Hauptamt*). His position as Funk's adjutant led several SS organizations to request the former cavalry leader's services, so Schwedler was posted to various SS departments – the SS Main Office, Himmler's personal staff, and the Race and Settlement Main Office. However, his credentials did not always impress all Nazi organizations. When the National Socialist People's Welfare Organization accused Schwedler of neglecting his Winter Relief Organization annual charity obligations (*Winterhilfswerk*) and failing to pay his welfare dues, he threatened to use his contacts in the Nazi Party to discover the source of the "unfounded attacks on his character." An unimpressed welfare officer contacted the SS Main Office, which resolved the issue.[52]

Schwedler remained a valuable member of the SS as he climbed the Nazi hierarchy. He accompanied Funk on many trips, both in Germany and abroad, the economic minister protecting his adjutant all the while. During World War II, Funk consistently demanded Schwedler's services, thereby keeping him from fighting in the Waffen SS. During the war, Schwedler became a director of the *Reichsbank*, and after the war, he defended Funk in affidavits at the Nuremberg Trials.[53]

Eberhard von Künsberg's name also appeared during the Nuremberg Trials, for he played a major role in plundering art in Nazi occupied territories. After the fall of France, Hitler agreed to the expropriation of Jewish-owned artworks. Because the Foreign Office had jurisdiction over the operations, von Ribbentrop instructed Otto Abetz, the German ambassador of occupied France, to coordinate the looting campaign. Abetz entrusted three employees, one being von Künsberg, to collect and transport to the Louvre Jewish-owned artworks hidden by the French in chateaus along the Loire River. Once catalogued, certain pieces would be sent to Germany. In just over a month, von Künsberg's commandos had ferried about 1,500 paintings to the embassy depot.[54]

After Alfred Rosenberg received a virtual monopoly on plunder in France, the foreign minister transferred von Künsberg east to lead Special Forces Ribbentrop (*Sonderkommando* Ribbentrop), a new unit composed primarily of SS members attached to the Foreign Ministry. Like von Künsberg, many were experienced at gathering French art. The brigade included three battalions (initially consisting of about 100 men, later almost 400), which moved eastward into Russia behind the invading army groups and with their support. The unit, sometimes referred to as *Sonderkommando* Künsberg because its leader was frequently found at the front with his troops, began operations on August 5, 1941.[55]

The unit caused tremendous destruction while pilfering numerous valuables from the East. It was estimated at the Nuremberg Trials that von Künsberg's brigade filled between forty and fifty freight cars per month with booty taken in their raids. It ransacked palaces formerly belonging to the czars and their relatives, including Peter the Great's estate, Montplasir, at Peterhof, the Pavlosky palace at Pavlovsk, and a residence called Marly Castle by the Germans. At Nuremberg, the Soviet prosecutor declared that 34,000 objects had been looted from these three palaces alone, along with the entire Amber Room, the gift given to Peter the Great by Friedrich Wilhelm I. The unit combined thievery with destruction, leaving all three castles and the homes of Pushkin and Tolstoy in ashes. Von Künsberg, who left the *Sonderkommando* in 1943, served in the Waffen-SS for the duration of the war.[56]

While von Künsberg plundered art in the East, one-time equestrian regimental commander Hermann Florstedt worked in the SS concentration camp system. Florstedt was officer-in-charge at Buchenwald and Sachsenhausen and commandant of the camps in Lublin and Majdanek in Poland. Florstedt, who received impressive evaluations as a guard at Buchenwald and Sachsenhausen, was recognized as an excellent commandant of the Lublin camp. He developed a reputation for brutality and for treating children with great cruelty. He was remembered by historian and Buchenwald survivor Eugen Kogon as a particularly vicious anti-semite.[57]

Like many older equestrian leaders, Florstedt, born in 1895, had World War I experience and had spent time in the Steel Helmet (five years) and in the SA. He joined the Nazi Party and the SS in 1931 and became active in various SS infantry units. He took command of SS Infantry Regiment

73 in 1934, the year he received an evaluation calling him an experienced horseman who would be useful as an equestrian unit leader. A scarcity of experienced cavalrymen led to his transfer to become leader of Equestrian Sector VI in Main Sector *Südwest* and commander of Equestrian Regiment 14.[58]

A street fighter and beer-hall brawler, he had had a seedy life, including several run-ins with the police, before joining the SS. His unlawful behavior continued after he donned the black uniform. An altercation in 1934 ended in the death of one participant. Intervention by his SS commanders saved him from manslaughter charges. In 1935, he quarreled with a train conductor after being assigned a sleeping compartment with a Jew. Florstedt, in uniform, insulted the conductor and demanded another compartment. The conductor sarcastically asked if Florstedt was certain – had he seen the occupant's birth certificate – and reminded the SS officer that Jews were permitted to travel by train. Another conductor allowed the unamused Florstedt then to buy a first class ticket to change cars. But because he threatened to slander the conductors in the notoriously antisemitic tabloid, *Der Stürmer*, the SS formally reprimanded him.[59]

On another occasion, drunk and disorderly, he fought with a policeman after the officer attempted to arrest his drinking companion for allegedly running over three people with his car. An attempt to intimidate the police with his SS credentials failed, and so Florstedt was arrested and ordered to pay 300 RM or spend thirty days in jail. SS officials sided with Florstedt since, as they reasoned, the police in Bruchsal were known for roughing up suspects. But Florstedt's abbreviated service as a cavalry commander ended in March 1936. Although he had acquired appropriate skills – he completed two training courses at the Forst Riding School – the SS thought it wise to transfer Florstedt out of the region to command SS Infantry Regiment 31 in Kassel.[60]

Because chronic illnesses had physically weakened Florstedt, shortly after the outbreak of World War II, the SS shipped him to Buchenwald where he led a guard battalion and supervised the transfer and training of SS guard reinforcements. He moved to Sachsenhausen before becoming commandant of the camp in Lublin. He returned to Buchenwald to work with his friend, Karl Koch, camp commandant. Florstedt was closer, however, to Koch's wife, the notorious Else, "the monster of Buchenwald"; in fact, the two were lovers. Florstedt then went to Majdanek as camp commandant to supervise the extermination of Jews. Meanwhile, Commandant Koch became the center of an SS investigation into a scandal involving widespread corruption and fraud at Buchenwald. Investigators accused Florstedt of being an accomplice in Koch's embezzlement schemes. The two associates were tried and executed.[61]

Conclusions

SS equestrian units represented a unique group within the SS. Because they served as an instrument for the recruitment of traditional elites and entree into the establishment, in no other SS organization was there as high a percentage of the nobility, most of whom were dedicated National Socialists. An analysis of the Equestrian SS leadership also reaffirms earlier findings that the base of Nazi support was the lower middle class, even though recruits came from all strata of society. Indeed, many of these men had committed themselves to the Nazi cause and SS creed prior to the seizure of power.

The SS equestrian leaders, however, were not always exceptionally gifted commanders. Many had prior cavalry and leadership experience and were quite successful in equestrian competitions. But according to their personnel files, some of them commanded like unseasoned amateurs and opportunists willing to violate SS procedures. In part this reflected the dual nature of the Equestrian SS. Alongside a core of talented jockeys existed the mass of SS horsemen, many of whom were farmers and urbanites with limited equestrian skills. And the Equestrian SS was hardly unique in attracting qualified personnel. Essentially the General

SS was composed of amateurs and part-time SS "political soldiers," and other studies also have revealed how the General SS lacked truly professional commanders.

Most significantly, an examination of the personnel files of equestrian officers exposes the great extent to which the Equestrian SS was affiliated with the entire SS organizational structure. Many equestrian leaders held various posts in the SS both before and after their association with the Equestrian SS. Being an Equestrian SS officer certainly did not preclude one from having a career in another SS formation nor from advancing in the SS.

CHAPTER NINE

The SS Cavalry
in World War II

Before the outbreak of World War II on September 1, 1939, Himmler ordered Hermann Fegelein to create and command a cavalry unit for action in Poland. The mounted unit would serve as an occupation force in conjunction with SS Death's Head formations that followed on the heels of the successful German invasion. The Equestrian SS, the police, and various SS units, especially the Death's Head formations, composed the core of the unit. For the Equestrian SS, the creation of an SS cavalry regiment allowed many SS horsemen to fulfill their duty as ready-for-action political soldiers prepared to serve their country.[1]

During the first week of World War II, Equestrian SS inspector Friedrich-Wilhelm Krüger informed all equestrian regiments of a special mounted unit being formed in Berlin within the framework of the SS police reinforcement program. All equestrian regiments had to report the names of personnel and the number of horses to be assigned to the unit. To prevent the army from drafting its men, all SS horsemen had to have been reserved by the SS through its police reinforcement program or through a draft exemption. Otherwise the army could draft the men and disrupt the unit.[2]

Each SS main sector had to send a designated number of Equestrian SS members and horses to Berlin for training by Fegelein and his officers. SS Main Sector *Ost* was required to send the most men and horses, sixty-eight and fifty-four, respectively, but most main sectors had to send fewer than twenty-five men and supply fifteen horses. The SS designated all other qualifying men (and horses) as replacements. All men had to appear in uniform and horses had to be completely outfitted and certified as healthy by a veterinarian. Horses unfit for duty were immediately sent home.[3]

Fegelein's riding academy, the SS Main Riding School in Munich, had already been reserved by the SS in the event of war. Its men and horses were assigned to the new mounted unit, and the school itself became a training center for replacements for Fegelein's unit.[4]

The first SS mounted regiment formed during the second week of September. Officially called the SS Death's Head Cavalry Regiment (*Totenkopf-Reiterstandarte*), it initially consisted of a staff and four squadrons, two in Lodsch and two in Posen. Most of the regiment's members were SS men who had transferred to the unit, many from the Equestrian SS. But because the army controlled the draft destiny of most SS horsemen, Fegelein supplemented his troops with police forces (whose barracks housed men of Squadrons 2 and 3 during their formation). The regiment's initial strength totaled twenty-seven officers, four hundred and twenty-four men, and three hundred and ninety-nine horses.[5]

The Equestrian SS dominated leadership positions in the cavalry unit. Fegelein was regimental commander, and two squadron leaders transferred directly from Equestrian SS leadership positions. Several mounted platoons were led by Equestrian SS officers. Herbert Schönfeld, an officer at the SS Main Riding School, commanded Squadron 2, and Rolf Becher, leader of Equestrian Regiment 10 in Arolsen, led Squadron 4. Another squadron leader, Franz Magill, had once served with Equestrian Regiment 7 in Berlin. Most of the SS's best jockeys, along with their prized steeds, found a home in the SS cavalry in Poland.[6]

The regiment received explicit instructions concerning their behavior in Poland. It had to carry out completely all orders and work in conjunction with Death's Head units in Poland. Cavalry leaders ensured that their men fully understood the nature of operating in an enemy's country; military matters could be discussed only in the barracks. SS horsemen had to remember the importance of racial purity. Fraternization with Poles, especially with Polish women, was strictly forbidden. A man who strolled arm in arm with a Polish woman or who had sex with one faced serious consequences.[7]

The Death's Head Cavalry Regiment was assigned as an occupation force in Poland ostensibly to restore order and maintain safety; frequently it carried out its assigned tasks with great brutality. The regiment sometimes worked in conjunction with other German units and, on occasion, with the Polish police. Although the regiment officially began operating in late September, under the control of Kurt Daluege, commander of Germany's regular, uniformed police forces, the Order Police (*Ordnungspolizei*), most units were still setting up barracks at the time.[8]

Generally, the regiment engaged in mopping-up operations against by-passed Polish soldiers and battled the Polish resistance. It carefully combed through villages searching for and confiscating weapons. It captured escaped convicts, guarded and transported Poles and Jews, rounded them up for deportation to work camps. The regiment often used Jews for work details, especially to clean up debris and to construct roads. Regimental personnel also confiscated property, set up ethnic German (*Volksdeutsche*) villages, and enforced policies of resettlement and immigration.[9]

SS horsemen also assisted in harvesting crops, a familiar task since many in the regiment were farmers themselves. They protected local farmers from field thieves and, when produce was brought to market, armed robbers. As part of Himmler's plans for the East, SS horsemen carried out executions. On October 4, Squadron 4, led by Rolf Becher, was dispatched to Kutno for a "special assignment," a euphemism for conducting executions. This marked the beginning of many similar assignments for the SS cavalry.[10]

The regiment's success in carrying out its assigned tasks and the need for a larger occupation force in Poland prompted Himmler to expand his cavalry force. On November 15, the SS Death's Head Cavalry Regiment was organized into twelve squadrons scattered throughout Poland. This was the first of several peculiar reorganizations. With the army having first priority over most General SS personnel, Fegelein continued to search beyond the Equestrian SS to supplement his units. About eighty percent of recruits for the reorganized regiment were non-cavalrymen, many with poor riding skills. In January 1940, the SS Cavalry became subordinate to former inspector of the Equestrian SS Krüger, who, since late 1939, was Higher SS and Police Leader *Ost*.[11]

The expanded SS cavalry faced several immediate problems. In addition to the influx of poorly trained recruits, distances of as much as 500 kilometers existed between the headquarters of some squadrons and Fegelein's staff headquarters in Warsaw. With the arrival of winter, heavy snowfalls and cold weather wreaked havoc on the few telephone lines. Furthermore, most formations had insufficient cold weather gear and clothing, which forced them to scour Poland for supplies. Winter also could be distressful on horses. Although former tournament steeds could be found in the units, most horses had previously been used in agricultural work. The SS cavalry required a significant number of veterinarians and shoesmiths to maintain its fighting strength.[12]

Krüger deployed SS mounted squadrons almost daily against partisans, although he reserved some squadrons especially for Himmler's extermination campaigns. Squadron 1 in Warsaw, led by Hermann Fegelein's younger brother, Waldemar, regularly carried out executions. Regimental commander Hermann Fegelein expressed great pride in the manner in which his brother's squadron conducted "special assignments." He reported that all men performed as ordered and without hesitation, that the rigorous training they had received had strengthened their resolve, and that none questioned orders or excused themselves from an assignment.[13]

The SS cavalry participated significantly in Himmler's schemes to concentrate Polish Jews in designated areas in occupied Poland. On December 1, 1939, Squadron 5 in Chelm, commanded by Wilhelm Reichenwallner, received orders to transport 1,018 Jews from Chelm to Sokal.[14] During the march, many tried to flee, but Reichenwallner's troops opened fire, reportedly killing 440 Jews. Those remaining were handed over to the German police in Prupiessow.[15]

Just over one month later, a few of Reichenwallner's men helped to execute 600 Jews transported to Chelm from Lublin. Some forty Jews had died in the over-crowded cars during the journey. With the cars full of excrement, Reichenwallner gathered that dysentery had broken out and so decided to shoot everyone rather than risk infecting others. But the squadron, which had expected only to guard the transport, had insufficient ammunition to carry out the executions. When the army refused to provide ammunition, Reichenwallner let the Gendarmerie do the shooting, although eleven of his men participated.[16]

Harsh German occupation policies naturally increased resistance, and so skirmishes with strong partisan forces occurred with increasing frequency. Squadron 3 in Seroczyn fought uninterrupted for weeks against Polish resistance forces. Polish partisans, often led by officers, became adept at hit-and-run tactics, gaining the respect of SS cavalry leaders as worthy opponents.[17]

The regiment's largest engagement to date occurred in late March and early April 1940. On March 30, Krüger ordered all available units in Warsaw, Krakau, and Kielce to march to Skarzysko-Kamienna, the headquarters of Squadron 10. Reportedly, a large band of Polish partisans, perhaps as many as 300, roamed the forests around Kamienna. The SS cavalry at that time was short-handed because its units contained a large number of farmers on leave to harvest crops in the homeland. Fegelein could therefore assemble only half of the regiment's squadrons, but Police Battalion 51 supplemented SS forces.[18]

After SS reconnaissance patrols identified the location of the Polish irregulars, the mounted units moved to surround the enemy. An initial breakout attempt against Police Battalion 51 resulted in several hours of heavy fighting before Squadron 10's infantry cannons forced the Poles to retreat to hilly, swampy areas in the forest. Although Polish snipers and partisan bands using hit-and-run tactics slowed the encirclement, the Germans methodically tracked the enemy, employing "atonement actions" in the process: burning down towns and villages, rounding up and executing males, and evacuating women and children. On April 8, with the resistance completely surrounded, the Germans opened fire, killing all partisans.[19]

Fegelein commended his horsemen for performing marvelously in the engagement, an action, he declared, which revealed the necessity of relying on cavalry forces to control the Polish countryside. He regarded the engagement as an opportunity to strengthen his unit. Poland, with its wide, flat lands, its thick forests, and large areas of swampland, required the presence of the SS cavalry, which Fegelein believed would benefit from the addition of a convoy of motor vehicles. He also thought the regiment should be strengthened with fresh personnel, since the unit's many farmers required long absences to finish their agricultural work.[20]

Fegelein's aspirations for an expanded SS cavalry achieved fruition. In mid-May 1940, Himmler reorganized his cavalry unit, which at that time totalled 1,908 officers and men. On May 15, Fegelein's regiment became two formations: SS Death's Head Regiment 1, headquartered in Warsaw and commanded by Fegelein, and SS Death's Head Regiment 2, headquartered in Lublin and commanded by Franz Magill. Each regiment consisted of six squadrons, including a heavy squadron and a horsed battery squadron. Each regiment's staff had a signals platoon, a motor-cycle dispatch platoon, an engineer platoon, and a trumpet corps.[21]

After the reorganization, most of it done by Fegelein personally, the SS cavalry continued its normal operations. Search and seizure (or destroy) actions, resettlement operations, and skirmishes with Polish partisans occupied the time of some squadrons, while others rounded up Jews and Poles for work details or to be transported to concentration camps in Poland and Germany. The procedure for conducting searches was generally consistent by this time. Small patrols performed the first searches at night, shortly after the occupation of the village. They searched every residence and farm looking for Poles hiding practically anywhere – in chicken coups, barns, sheds. Occasionally, Poles defended themselves with whatever they could find, including pitchforks.[22]

The complex arrangement of German resettlement policies confused some SS horsemen and, at times, they appeared unsure of whom to evacuate and whom to allow to remain in occupied villages. SS cavalrymen often simply turned Poles over to the SD to avoid making a decision. Those evacuated were turned over to immigration and had their farms seized. Usually, ethnic Germans could be settled on the farm on the very same day, although the unexpected consequences of resettlement policies exasperated some SS horsemen. Some ethnic Germans apparently considered themselves privileged. According to the war diary of SS Death's Head Equestrian Regiment I, too many of them, having lost their spirit of enterprise and willingness to work, egotistically took in Poles to work as servants.[23]

By July 1940 the SS cavalry consisted of nearly 3,000 men. Regiment I in Warsaw consisted of 1,585 men, including 190 non-commissioned officers (NCOs) and 54 officers; Regiment II in Lublin totaled 1,360 men, including 140 NCOs and 31 officers. The arrival of new recruits relieved men over thirty-five to return to Germany, although new troops frequently required extensive training to improve their cavalry skills.

By fall, the SS had decided to expand the two regiments into a cavalry brigade. In the process, the regiments were initially grouped into two half-regiments, each with two detachments. One detachment consisted of four mounted squadrons and one heavy machine gun squadron, while the second detachment contained motorized and heavy-weapons squadrons.[24]

Early 1941, SS cavalry squadrons engaged in routine, largely uneventful activities while the regiment underwent reorganization yet again. The monotony of assigned tasks frustrated some horsemen. On January 1, 1941, the two half-regiments officially became SS Cavalry Regiment 1 (SS-*Kavallerie-Regiment* 1), thereby severing the SS cavalry from the pre-war paramilitary terminology (*Reiterstandarten*) used to designate Equestrian SS regiments. In March, in anticipation of the creation of the SS Cavalry Brigade, the SS eliminated the two half-regiments with the formation of SS Cavalry Regiment 2. Some previous Equestrian SS personnel remained in key positions, but young graduates of SS officer schools in Bad Tölz and Braunschweig increasingly replaced earlier commanders.[25]

Legt an, Gebt Feuer[26]

On June 21, 1941, the two regiments were assigned to the Headquarters Staff (*Kommandostab*) *Reichsführer-SS*, which was created to pacify rear areas during Operation Barbarossa, the massive June 22 invasion of the Soviet Union. Initially, the Headquarters Staff was assigned to safeguard rear areas of the 42nd Army Corps to confront by-passed Soviet forces. Himmler, though, had other plans in mind. Shortly after the invasion began, he ordered their removal from army command; he needed them for "other tasks." These concerned pacification of areas not covered, or only covered superficially, by the *Einsatzgruppen*, the SS murder squadrons operating behind invading German armies. More specifically, Himmler himself directed elements of the Headquarters Staff as his private army to exterminate Jews.[27]

The two cavalry regiments, formally announced as the SS Cavalry Brigade on August 2, were assigned to Higher SS and Police Leader Erich von dem Bach-Zelewski to cleanse the area of the Pripet Marshes in Belorussia. The SS used the euphemisms "cleansing operations," "partisan warfare," "purification," or "pacification" to camouflage the murder of Jews. SS forces were told that Jews were either partisans or supporters of partisans and therefore had to be shot. By this twisted reasoning, in occupied territories, soldiers who "imposed peace" by murdering Jews could imagine their actions as legitimate operations against partisans.[28]

Himmler assigned the SS cavalry to cleanse the Pripet Marshes, an oval pocket of 300 kilometers by 200 kilometers near the Pripet River, to complete extermination actions begun by the undermanned *Einsatzgruppen*. Cavalry, rather than mechanized forces, seemed better suited to the terrain of the region. It consisted of deep forests and marshes, extensive swamps, numerous rivers, streams, ponds, and of lakes with sedge islands; there were also populated areas with canals and paved thoroughfares. But summer storms and flood waters could turn hard, dry land into mud and morass, making short distance travel an hours-long task even for the cavalry. Furthermore, SS maps often erroneously listed pathways as main thoroughfares, thus hampering the movement of cavalry forces.[29]

Strict guidelines informed the men of their assignments. The villages and towns were awash in "partisans" and "plunderers" (Jews). While all partisans and their supporters had to be shot, Himmler, obviously recognizing the added emotional burden involved, preferred evacuating Jewish women and children. And, whether the towns and villages were burned depended on the support of locals. Residents who supported the SS got a share of the booty.[30]

Himmler's orders to Fegelein and von dem Bach-Zelewski on June 28 eliminated the euphemisms. They were direct and explicit: All Jews must be shot; drive Jewish women into the swamp. Commanders had to report daily on their activities and to refer to Jews as plunderers or partisans. Fegelein dutifully relayed Himmler's orders. According to him, "Only villages that are free of Jews do not become partisan bases."[31] During their operations, SS horsemen killed almost every Jew they could find. Two mounted detachments commanded by Gustav Lombard and Franz Magill carried out most executions.[32] SS horsemen operated independently and also in conjunction with other units, such as the Order Police and the SD. Fegelein's summation report on the "cleansing" of the Pripet Marshes from July 29 to August 12 listed the execution of 14,178 "plunderers," 1,001 partisans, and 699 Red Army soldiers; 800 others were taken prisoner. In about two weeks the SS Cavalry Brigade slaughtered 15,878 men, women, and children while suffering only minimal losses (two dead).[33]

The killing began by July 31. Executions proceeded largely without incident and with only limited objections from participating troops. Magill and Heino Hierthes, commander of Cavalry Regiment 2, apparently considered the orders unjust and complained to Fegelein. Both, nevertheless, dutifully relayed the orders to their units.[34]

In some areas, Ukrainians enthusiastically greeted their German conquerors. A band and villagers bringing food greeted members of Magill's unit. Lombard recalled the delight of others over the departure of communists (some wanted their livestock returned from the collective farms). The degree of anti-semitism varied. Some were quite outspoken in their hatred of Jews, while others held more favorable views. Although no anti-Jewish measures had been enacted, nevertheless Ukrainians, White Russians, Poles, and other locals, especially militia members, energetically assisted the SS. They rounded up Jews, helped comb through villages, and assisted in house searches. "The Ukrainian clergy was very cooperative and made themselves available for every action," Magill wrote.[35]

Generally, SS troops entered a town and, sometimes using placards, ordered Jewish males aged 16 to 60 to assemble for work the next morning. For instance, on August 8, Squadron 1 of Magill's Mounted Detachment of SS Cavalry Regiment 2 was dispatched to Pinsk, a city whose Jewish population exceeded 30,000; they were to kill all Jews. The squadron found about 2,000 Jewish people assembled for work. A few succeeded in fleeing during the march to the designated shooting area, but SS horsemen rounded up and shot most of them.[36]

Jews were led in groups to mass graves, dug by locals, with each SS horsemen assigned to murder one person. There, lying face down in their underwear, they awaited death. Small groups at a time approached the edge of the graves, all looking down. About five paces behind, shooters raised their rifles. The victims went to their graves peacefully and with dignity, occasionally praying and singing. The killing lasted until evening. As darkness fell, a machine-gunner arrived to ensure that all would be killed that day. But, of the 2,000 Jews assembled in the morning, about fifty survived.[37]

The killings continued in Pinsk until August 8. Squadron 4 had arrived to assist in the murders, and the SS cavalry was able to count on the support of locals. At first, the SS slaughtered all Jewish males between the ages of 16 and 60. But when some took along their children, machine gun fire eliminated them some distance away from the grave site.[38]

Later the SS lowered the age limit – they shot those above age six. On one occasion, as Himmler ordered, Jewish women and children were driven into the swamp, but, according to a Magill report, "...this did not have the desired effect as the swamp was not deep enough for them to drown. At a depth of one meter it was possible in most cases for them to reach firm ground (possibly sand)." Mothers raised their children up high. SS troops therefore resorted to the preferred method of execution. Thus, the SS cavalry was perhaps the first of Himmler's murder brigades to receive and follow orders to shoot women and children.[39]

After reading various reports of the operations, an unimpressed Himmler regarded the number of people shot as "too insignificant"; commanders had been "too lenient in their conduct of operations." He ordered the brigade to toughen up, to "act radically," and to report daily the number of Jews shot.[40] But on the evening of August 8, Magill received orders to leave Pinsk to continue combing the area. Thus, the SS cavalry was unable to annihilate completely the Jews of Pinsk. Nevertheless, when the killing had ended, Magill declared the operation a success: 6,526 Jewish "plunderers" had been murdered.[41]

The SS cavalry had achieved similar successes elsewhere during the operations. The entire Jewish population of Bobruisk, some 7,000, was murdered, and on August 7, an SS Cavalry Brigade radio report intercepted by British intelligence claimed the execution of 7,819 Jews in the Minsk area. Gustav Lombard's mounted detachment, operating in the Starobinsk district, killed 6,504 Jews.[42] In his final report, Fegelein commended his troops for their success under difficult conditions and wondered why no member of the Cavalry Brigade had been decorated with the Iron Cross. Fegelein intended the honor to sanction the mass murder of Jews in order to spare his men from unpleasant crises of conscience. Lombard and Waldemar Fegelein received the Iron Cross First Class. Magill and others earned the Iron Cross Second Class.[43]

Because the killing of Jews was incomplete, Himmler ordered a second "combing through" of the Pripet Marshes to annihilate all those remaining. The SS Cavalry Brigade continued its murderous pursuit of Jews in the region. By the end of September, Fegelein reported apprehending 31,403 more prisoners. It seems reasonable to assume that most were Jews and that most were executed.[44]

In December 1941, the precarious situation on the Eastern Front necessitated the removal of the SS Cavalry Brigade from its liquidation operations to confront the advancing Red Army. The brigade guarded the supply lines of the 9th Army, the rail line from Weliki-Luki to Toropez to Dubno, against partisans operating in the area. Like most German units, brigade personnel became victims of the bitter Russian winter. Frostbite plagued many horsemen, individuals froze to death, horses became incapacitated, and both light and heavy weapons broke down in well-below-freezing temperatures.[45]

Pressed into action as a front-line force, the brigade fought valiantly but suffered devastating losses. Soviet forces virtually destroyed the 500-man Bicycle Reconnaissance Detachment commanded by Günter Temme. Of 109 survivors on January 19, 91 suffered mild to severe frostbite. During the Battle for Rshev in December 1941 and January 1942, Cavalry Regiments 1 and 2 faced heavy losses. The SS began withdrawing parts of the devastated brigade, and in March commander Fegelein went to Debica, Poland, to begin rebuilding the SS cavalry. By then the 3,100-strong brigade had suffered nearly 2,100 casualties.[46]

Fegelein's report in early April detailed the precarious existence of the SS Cavalry Brigade. Its remaining fighting element, completely exhausted, had operated since early March without reserves and without sufficient officers and NCO's. After surviving the harsh winter, troops still faced difficult conditions as the snow thawed. With shoes and clothes constantly drenched, many suffered from coughs and colds. Morale, already declining, worsened. Squadron leaders continually dispensed medication, which often made the men lethargic. Brigade horses suffered severely; none was healthy enough to be taken back to Poland. Fegelein suggested withdrawing the remaining troops from the front to recuperate and to serve as a cadre for a rebuilt SS Cavalry Brigade. For operations at the front, a battle group could be organized under the leadership of August Zehender, a Waffen SS commander recently assigned to the Cavalry Brigade. Otherwise, Fegelein wrote, the brigade would fight to the last man without any regard to the future importance of an SS cavalry.[47]

Fegelein's request met with favor. Battle Group Zehender formed and remained in Russia until the 500-strong force returned to Poland to form the cadre of a new cavalry unit. Although the SS had intended originally to replenish the Cavalry Brigade bled white during the Russian winter offensive, Hitler, his gaze on Stalingrad, decided to expand the Waffen SS. He authorized the creation of an SS cavalry division, which became operational on June 21, 1942. It included two cavalry regiments, a horse-drawn artillery regiment, a motorcycle reconnaissance battalion, and a veterinarian company. The division, which required about 6,000 horses, consisted of 4,400 men with 819 NCOs and 159 officers.[48]

The establishment of the SS Cavalry Division severed the bonds with the pre-war Equestrian SS; only a small percentage of its men had served in the Equestrian SS, for most of its personnel had been drafted into the army by that time. With the pre-war Equestrian SS depleted, Himmler was forced to look elsewhere for recruits. He turned to Hungary, relying on ethnic Germans to fill the ranks of the unit. The Waffen SS cavalry was primarily an ethnic German force under German leadership. Most recruits had no prior military training, a large number of Hungarian Germans knew only a few German words, and many spoke no German at all. Himmler's cavalry had undergone a radical transformation, although, in general, the Waffen SS increasingly relied on ethnic Germans as replacements.[49]

By this time, the prewar Equestrian SS in Germany existed primarily on paper. During the first two years of the war, SS equestrian units attempted to conduct normal pre-war activities, such as organizing and riding in tournaments; however, with the critical situation in the East, the German armed forces drained the Equestrian SS of its men and horses, especially its leaders and trainers. The SS attempted to fill administrative posts with those unfit for warfare and the war wounded, but conducting normal operations proved futile. As the commander of Equestrian Regiment 10 stated, only after the war could his unit expect to participate in equestrian sports. It had to be content with helping the General SS in its "paper war."[50]

Himmler had little time to concentrate on his dwindling Equestrian SS. His main concern was with winning the war and eliminating the Jews of Europe. Not surprisingly, he used the SS Cavalry Division as he had the Cavalry Brigade: for anti-partisan operations. These "SS horsemen" again committed atrocities. From 1942 to 1943, the division fought mainly in Belorussia – another stint near the Pripet Marshes – and along the southern and central sectors of the eastern front. In late 1943 it fought in Yugoslavia. Designated the 8th SS Cavalry Division on October 22, 1943, it added the title Florian Geyer on March 12, 1945, in honor of the great peasant leader in the German Peasants' War (1524-1526). With numerous SS cavalrymen receiving the Knight's Cross, Florian Geyer became the sixth most decorated Waffen SS division.[51]

As the Russians methodically advanced, the division battled large mechanized forces. In the fall of 1944 it fought rapidly advancing Soviet troops in Hungary. In early 1945 the Russians annihilated the division in Budapest; its commander, Joachim Rumohr, committed suicide after being wounded.[52]

The SS established other cavalry divisions toward the end of the war. The 22nd Cavalry Division, organized in 1944, was created from Regiment 17 of Florian Geyer. The division, consisting primarily of Hungarian ethnic Germans, was trapped and destroyed along with Florian Geyer in Budapest. Near the end of the war, Himmler formed the 37th SS Cavalry Division using the few survivors of the two destroyed cavalry divisions along with additional ethnic Germans, Hungarians, and elements of both the German and Hungarian armies. The Red Army annihilated the division in Hungary in May 1945.[53]

Himmler's Knight in Shining Armor: Hermann Fegelein

Although the various cavalry units were never considered elite Waffen SS formations, they produced one of the SS's most decorated military officers: Hermann Fegelein. No other Equestrian SS officer had a greater role in creating the SS cavalry. Fegelein, who had earlier requested command of a mounted unit in the event of an invasion of Czechoslovakia, created the first SS cavalry regiment. For his command in Poland, he received the Iron Cross, the first of many honors that made him the most decorated of SS horsemen. The Waffen SS chief of staff called Fegelein "a born cavalry leader. . . [who]. . . in spite of his relative youth. . . possesses sufficient military knowledge." He "enjoys the trust of his men and officers. . . [and is]. . . willing to accept responsibility." The chief of staff added that Fegelein "is a good organizer who has successfully mastered all difficulties with regard to accommodations, rationing, and equipment for man and horse. The continued existence and condition of the horses are exemplary and outdo the army's squadrons."[54]

Fegelein always considered his command of the SS cavalry in Poland an extension of his prominence in the Equestrian SS. For Fegelein, the war simply signified a transformation of the pre-war Equestrian SS into a full-fledged SS cavalry officially recognized as part of the German armed forces. Fegelein pondered the role and future of the SS cavalry while stationed in the East. For him, the establishment of the SS Death's Head cavalry regiments meant that SS horsemen had a permanent home and career as officers. Like the pre-war armed SS units, the SS cavalry had proven and established itself through its actions, stressed Fegelein.[55]

His grandiose plans for the SS Main Riding School in Munich called for it to be the headquarters of the Equestrian SS and the pre-eminent equestrian academy in Europe. It would, he believed, be affiliated with SS officer-training schools in Bad Tölz and Braunschweig so that all future SS cavalry officers would train in Munich. Fegelein gathered the best horses he could find in Poland to ensure the school's future success. He, however, still regarded the army as the main deterrent to his ambitions, and he regularly begged Himmler to seek Hitler's approval for Equestrian SS commanders to be considered as full-fledged military officers.[56]

Fegelein assumed all of the discharged SS cavalrymen would join the Equestrian SS once the war ended. In effect, he expected to combine war veterans with peacetime SS horsemen in a new Equestrian SS. Unlike the situation in the prewar years, commanders of all equestrian regiments would be expert cavalrymen. Thus recruiting would be much easier since the Mounted SA would no longer offer similar opportunities. SS horsemen would be afforded a career as legitimate cavalry officers, and the SS could be much more selective in recruiting. Furthermore, with the expanded German empire, the Equestrian SS would have installations throughout Europe and stud farms in Holland and the Ukraine.[57]

Fegelein wanted no interference in his ambitions to have complete control over the postwar Equestrian SS. When a proposal to name a replacement for Friedrich-Wilhelm Krüger as inspector of the Equestrian SS reached his desk, Fegelein exploded. The replacement, Rudolf Bösel, was an equestrian regiment leader and an SS main sector equestrian inspector before the war, positions Fegelein regarded as insignificant, for the Equestrian SS needed someone with experience in battle. For Fegelein, the actual Equestrian SS served in the East, not on the homefront. SS horsemen were both soldiers and jockeys. But events in the East prevented Fegelein from excessively intervening in General SS affairs; the war had meanwhile turned the inspector of the Equestrian SS into a meaningless position.[58]

While in Poland, between commanding his unit and organizing a few equestrian shows to display the riding abilities of his cavalrymen, Fegelein found time to indulge in his many questionable passions. The Iron Cross holder became the subject of a lengthy SS investigation into sexual relations with Polish women, looting in Poland, shipping goods to the SS Main Riding School in Munich (his personal residence), and allowing troops of his mounted regiment to sell confiscated delicacies, such as dried grapes and hazelnuts, for a handsome profit. Any of these charges would have doomed a man of lesser talents and connections. But Fegelein was a flatterer who had close contacts among a few important SS leaders and, most importantly, he maintained a personal friendship with Himmler.

Throughout the lengthy investigation of Fegelein's illegal activities, he routinely corresponded with Himmler. The impression given by his letters is that of a cavalry leader who hardly took the accusations against him seriously. He seemed certain that Himmler would protect him from zealous SS prosecutors.

The SS investigation began in 1940 over rumors of illegal shipments of merchandise from Poland to Fegelein's riding school in Munich. The Munich school had become the depository for an impressive quantity of stolen goods, for men of the SS cavalry had conducted an impressive looting campaign. A Gestapo search of the school discovered numerous items, including two Mercedes Benz cars, a two-seat Stoda convertible, a large flatbed truck, fifty pounds of coffee, ninety pounds of tea, liquor (including Schnapps and Brandy), a variety of clothing (including silks and furs), and several hunting and military rifles. More war booty ended up in the homes of SS cavalry members, although when their wives learned of the Gestapo's investigation, they managed to make the loot disappear.[59]

Martin von Barnekow, in charge of the school in Fegelein's absence, contacted Fegelein in Poland to report on the Gestapo's actions. An angry Fegelein told von Barnekow that the police action at the riding school was not only improper but illegal since the academy had become a military installation affiliated with the Death's Head units. He brazenly reprimanded the officers at the school for not brandishing their weapons and using their firearms against the Gestapo.[60]

In a letter to Himmler, Fegelein naturally refused to accept blame for any impropriety. Everything was legitimate and legal, he believed, for the chief of administration had distributed all of the items to the SS cavalry. Furthermore, Fegelein charged, Karl Friedrich Freiherr von Eberstein, SS police leader in Munich, had overzealously attempted to destroy him by systematically gathering inaccurate information. Von Eberstein intimidated von Barnekow – who apparently felt compelled to relieve his burdened conscience, Fegelein added – but he could not be trusted. Fegelein wondered how he and von Eberstein, once friends, could end up having problems. He surmised that the police leader's recent health problems had probably made him irritable and oversensitive, causing him to believe in such illogical and corrupt incidents at the SS Main Riding School. Fegelein declared his youth to be his significant burden; he blamed older SS comrades like von Eberstein for envying his rapid rise in the SS. Himmler accepted Fegelein's assessment. In a letter to SS security chief Reinhard Heydrich, he charged the entire affair to a sudden change of heart by von Eberstein. This was not the last time Himmler protected his young cavalryman.[61]

Fegelein knew his direct appeals to Himmler would prove fruitful; the *Reichsführer* defended his young cavalry commander whenever new allegations arose, for, despite Himmler's support, the investigation of Fegelein broadened and revealed additional questionable activities. It was generally known that Fegelein, a bachelor, was a womanizer. Friends admired his ability to attract members of the opposite sex. Shortly after the SS cavalry was stationed in Poland, he romanced a Polish woman, a violation of SS regulations. In December 1939, he had arranged an abortion for his Polish mistress to conceal his illicit activities. The woman, however, gave a detailed statement to the Gestapo about their affair as well as other liaisons between Polish women and SS officers. Fortunately for Fegelein, Himmler looked the other way, although he expected the other SS officers involved with Polish women to be duly punished.[62]

Himmler seemed more concerned with Fegelein's marital status than with the allegations surfacing in Poland. A personal letter to Fegelein, dated February 31, 1940, called upon the cavalryman to put aside his youthful behavior and find a bride. After opening the letter with pronouncements about how he understood the difficulty in the East because of the weather and the harsh fighting conditions, Himmler admonished his young officer to consider the importance of having children and to ponder what was expected of SS officers. SS men, as part of Germany's

new racial elite, were required to marry racially pure women and to produce offspring in order to perpetuate Germany's new nobility.

Himmler admonished Fegelein to get married and to announce his
betrothal quickly. Fegelein had had sufficient time to find a wife; the war
was no excuse, Himmler proclaimed, but made the issue especially ur-
gent. He advised Fegelein to use spring to find a bride and to announce
his engagement by the end of May. Although Fegelein professed deep
loyalty to Himmler and the SS, he remained a bachelor. In the meantime,
the spoils of war attracted his attention.[63]

Fegelein seemed incapable of provoking Himmler's wrath. In another incident, Fegelein and a member of his staff, Albert Fassbender,
confiscated and ran a furriery in Warsaw. The store was simply looted; its
contents curried favors with important SS officers whose wives received
expensive furs. A woman, a half-Russian who had previously worked
there, maintained the store's books. She had earned a reputation for her
many love affairs, her most recent being with Fassbender, whose child
she bore and whom she intended to marry. A Gestapo investigation charged
Fegelein with illicitly acquiring a fortune – sufficient to build a new riding
school – while approving Fassbender's relationship with a woman of
questionable racial stock.[64]

Himmler intervened to protect Fegelein and, by default, Fassbender.
The Reichsführer informed SS investigators that he would personally investigate the matter and decide on the proper punishment. He found little
incriminating evidence against Fegelein, inasmuch as he did not enrich
himself but accepted money only for the Munich riding school. In fact,
Himmler expressed approval of Fegelein and Fassbender's confiscation
of furs. Their diligence, Himmler declared, saved the furs. He also ordered that no future house searches related to the investigation be conducted without his consent; in addition, he expected to be immediately
apprised of any new allegations concerning Fegelein.[65]

Fassbender's affair with the so-called "half-Russian" troubled
Himmler more than the other incidents. It concerned a matter of racial

purity and, therefore, was possibly a serious transgression by an SS officer. But, after meeting with the woman and observing her Aryan features, Himmler settled the matter. Declaring she had German ancestors, Himmler announced her as an ethnic German and praised her for being an especially cooperative informant.[66]

Despite his disreputable behavior, Fegelein managed to remain in Himmler's good graces and continued as commander of the SS cavalry. By the time the invasion of Russia began, he had enlarged his regiment to brigade strength. He commanded the SS Cavalry Brigade in the East.

While the brigade slaughtered Jews in the Pripet Marshes, Fegelein conveniently absented himself from most of the killings – actions not too pleasing to his immediate superior von dem Bach-Zelewski. "While the SS men of the Cavalry Brigade were fighting like heroes, Mr. Fegelein was in Warsaw," von dem Bach-Zelewski recorded in his diary. Although he admired Fegelein's organizational skills – "he created a cavalry brigade from nothing" – he generally referred to Fegelein as a loafer, a buffoon, and a braggart. Concerning Fegelein's bravery: "This clown fulfills his duty only when the war adorns him with nice weather and good quarters.... When you hear his reports, it sounds like he's fighting the campaign in Russia all on his own."[67]

With the brigade thrown into bitter fighting beginning in December 1941, Fegelein's bravery emerged and he received the Knight's Cross to the Iron Cross in 1942. The Soviets, however, essentially destroyed his brigade; Fegelein then concentrated on creating a cavalry division. Once this was accomplished, Himmler called Fegelein from the East to oversee the creation of the Waffen SS remount offices, stud farms, and cavalry schools. He returned to the front in December 1942 as commander of his own unit: Battle Group Fegelein. It was dispatched to the Don Basin in southeastern Russia during the rapidly deteriorating situation at Stalingrad. Hitler awarded a wounded Fegelein the Oak Leaves to the Knight's Cross.[68]

After a short convalescent leave in Munich, Fegelein became commander of Florian Geyer in May 1943. Hitler then promoted the horseman, who began the war as a colonel, to brigadier general. Fegelein again proved to be a successful commander, although most commendations by his superiors praised the cavalryman's exemplary bravery and personal courage rather than his skills as a tactician. During his command, the SS cavalry captured a Russian general. The general gave his Order of Lenin to Fegelein, who, ever the sycophant, presented it to Hitler. The Führer later returned the medal after mounting it in a silver case. Near the end of the year, after being wounded, Fegelein returned to Germany as a rapidly advancing member of the SS.[69]

On January 1, 1944, he became Himmler's liaison officer with Hitler. Present during military discussions at Hitler's headquarters, Fegelein reported on all matters concerning the Waffen SS. He became an influential member of Hitler's inner circle: He advised the Führer to intensify the war effort and to withdraw from the Geneva convention. And, after the disgrace of the *Abwehr*, the counterintelligence service of the army high command, it was Fegelein who prompted Hitler to entrust the SS with a unified intelligence service.[70]

Fegelein gloried in his newfound status. Always dressed in full regalia, he charmed ladies and guests at the court of the Führer. A penchant for alcohol made him a drinking buddy of Martin Bormann, Hitler's personal secretary. The two became close friends and often took morning walks and meals together. Reportedly, they struck up an alliance which made Fegelein less dependent on Himmler's good graces. Along with Wilhelm Burgdorff, Hitler's military adjutant, they ultimately formed an intimate circle around Hitler, which, according to Albert Speer, kept outsiders away.[71]

In June 1944, to solidify his position in the Nazi hierarchy, Fegelein married Gretl Braun, sister of Hitler's mistress, Eva. The elaborate ceremony took place at Bormann's house at Obersalzberg with several dignitaries in attendance. Supposedly Eva insisted on a lavish ceremony, knowing that she would never have one of her own. The wedding celebration lasted several days, and rumors spread about the enormous consumption of delicacies and French champagnes and liquor.[72]

The marriage made Fegelein one of Hitler's closest advisors.[73] Shortly thereafter, Hitler promoted him to lieutenant general and again bestowed military honors on him. Fegelein was present during the attempted assassination of Hitler at his East Prussian headquarters at Rastenburg on July 20, 1944. According to *Das Schwarze Korps*, he was only two steps from the Führer. Hitler awarded a slightly wounded Fegelein the Oak Leaves with Swords to the Knights Cross of the Iron Cross for previous service on the Eastern Front.[74]

Fegelein's close relationship with the Führer ended abruptly in late April 1945. Although the details of his final days remain uncertain, he apparently realized the implications of remaining in Hitler's bunker to await capture by the Russians and so fled to his nearby apartment in Charlottenburg on about April 26. Shortly after detecting his absence, Hitler dispatched SS guards to locate and return the deserter. They found a drunken Fegelein in civilian clothes, who, after some difficulty, was brought back to the bunker. Confusion and suspicion reigned in the bunker, and by this time Hitler had learned of Himmler's peace negotiations with the West, a plot, he suspected, that also involved Fegelein. During questioning, Fegelein apparently admitted knowledge of Himmler's actions. After being stripped of rank for desertion, Fegelein was shot in the Chancellery garden for treason on April 29. On the following day, Hitler committed suicide; the Third Reich surrendered a week later.[75]

The events surrounding the execution of Fegelein have prompted considerable speculation. Sources inside the bunker claimed that Fegelein intended to flee Berlin and had gathered diamonds and other precious stones and jewelry, fake passports, and Reichsmarks and Swiss Francs for his escape. James P. O'Donnell, who interviewed several survivors, believed that Fegelein left to be with his mistress, who immediately fled, when SS troops arrived. Hitler and Bormann, O'Donnell wrote, believed her to have been the source, through Fegelein, of secret information broadcast by the British during the final months of the war. O'Donnell relied on postwar recollections of individuals who generally despised the SS horsemen. Although he rose to the upper echelons of the SS and Nazi system, Fegelein died as one of the characters around Hitler most despised by bunker survivors.[76]

Immediately after the war, the Allies were unsure of Fegelein's fate. Working for U.S. military intelligence was Walter Hirschfeld. Impersonating an SS officer, he visited Fegelein's parents on several occasions with tales of money, gold, and diamonds stashed in Austria – and 15,000 RM for the father, Hans —hoping to find Fegelein's whereabouts. Hans expressed his belief that his son was alive with Hitler and preparing for another war against the Russians, for he had been contacted by young Fegelein shortly after the capitulation. Hirschfeld bought the story and briefly continued to meet with the Fegeleins. The truth, however, was soon discovered.[77]

Fegelein's SS career reveals how closely integrated the Equestrian SS was into the SS system. Fegelein gained a reputation in equestrian circles in Germany through his service in the Equestrian SS; he served his entire SS career in Himmler's mounted units. This rising star in the prewar SS as commander of the SS Main Riding School and captain of the school's equestrian team became a leader of mass murderers in World War II. Among his troops were members of the Equestrian SS, the organization which formed the basis on which SS cavalry regiments developed. Himmler's original intentions for establishing the Equestrian SS included a desire to control a mounted force prepared to carry out orders with unflinching loyalty. He found the appropriate commander in Fegelein, a leader who directed SS horsemen to fulfill their duty in the SS cavalry in World War II.

CHAPTER TEN

The Equestrian SS and the Nuremburg Trials

One of the great trials in world history opened on November 30, 1945, in Nuremberg, a city which had annually played host to spectacular Nazi Party rallies. A tribunal composed of one judge and one alternate from the United States, the Soviet Union, France, and Great Britain indicted twenty-two leading German officials on counts of waging an aggressive war, crimes against peace, war crimes, and crimes against humanity. Twelve defendants were sentenced to death by hanging, three to life in prison, and four to prison terms of varying lengths. Three were exonerated.

The tribunal also indicted six organizations on criminal charges. It judged the SS and two other Nazi organizations to be criminal in nature. Members could be given any sentence, which could not be appealed. However, members could be exonerated if they had no knowledge of their organization's criminal purposes or had been drafted into the enterprise and had not participated directly in SS crimes. The tribunal excluded those "who had ceased to belong to the organizations ... prior to September 1, 1939."[1]

The SS, beyond any doubt, committed widespread crimes against humanity. Not all SS members took part in these acts, but all knew the nature of the organization. The tribunal ruled that the General SS, the branch to which the equestrian units belonged, "was an active participant in the persecution of the Jews and was used as a source of concentration camp guards."[2] But the tribunal's verdict removed the Equestrian SS from the SS, declared it a special organization, and acquitted SS horsemen.

It based its judgment on a variety of factors, one being the spirited defense of the SA Equestrian Corps. The tribunal exonerated the SA and regarded the Mounted SA as a typical equestrian club found in many countries. SA horsemen were simply involved in sporting and breeding activities and in instructing farmers in the proper care of horses. According to the tribunal, the Equestrian SA leadership was tied to the SA only at the top level. Furthermore, neither it nor the National Socialist Equestrian Corps was affiliated with the army. It was purely an athletic organization, the judges determined.[3]

Some SA defense affidavits were quite remarkable. Former SA riders claimed that they received only athletic training, military training being expressly forbidden. Oddly enough, some even called the Mounted SA a haven for the politically persecuted. Members and supporters were leading anti-fascists, and even communists and Jews joined the ranks, they declared. Farmers in particular were pacifists and therefore would have nothing to do with a cavalry formation.[4]

SS horsemen, in testimony and affidavits, provided similar defenses of their organization. Wilhelm von Woikowski-Biedau, a former equestrian regimental commander and inspector of the Equestrian SS, testified that Equestrian SS activities were athletic and non-military – "pre-military training...was expressly prohibited" – that SS horsemen were not involved in disseminating propaganda, and only limited ideological training occurred, and then only with public party pamphlets. He stated that German riding associations joined the SS or SA simply to continue to participate in tournaments – for an amateur, it was impossible to do so otherwise. The choice to join either group was based on convenience corresponding to horse-breeding areas.[5]

Dr. Guenther Reinecke, chief judge of the Supreme SS and Police Court, protected SS horsemen on the stand at Nuremberg. He falsely testified that the Equestrian SS "had nothing whatever to do with the later cavalry units of the Waffen SS nor were these later units built up from the mounted units."[6] On the basis of this testimony and the affidavits of a few other SS horsemen who testified similarly, the tribunal excluded equestrian units from condemnation and concluded that they had the same characteristics and history as the Mounted SA.[7]

Clearly, von Woikowski-Bidau had a selective memory. He did not mention the paramilitary function of the Equestrian SS nor did he report on the ideological programs regularly attended by SS horsemen. His own role in purchasing horses for both the Equestrian SS and the Militarized SS Troops was never discussed. The commission investigating the Equestrian SS gave SS horsemen little attention. Only von Woikowski-Biedau was questioned, and then only briefly. The commission spent considerably more time on the Mounted SA as it attempted, unsuccessfully, to implicate it with preparing troops for the German army.

The Equestrian SS certainly participated in sporting events and assisted in various agricultural activities. SS horsemen with agricultural obligations at home or who cared for their regiment's horses occasionally were exempted from some SS duties. However, SS riders after the war greatly exaggerated the degree of Equestrian SS autonomy. SS horsemen, like their General SS brothers, understood the nature and objectives of Himmler's organization.

The Equestrian SS was intended to be an SS cavalry. As part of the General SS, SS riders were to be used for security in emergency situations. They fulfilled this duty by serving as a mounted police force in occupied Poland. They also fulfilled their role as an SS cavalry. Although most members were drafted into the army, the Equestrian SS formed the basis from which the initial Waffen SS cavalry units emerged. Even various SS publications disclosed this fact.[8]

As members of these mounted units, SS horsemen committed numerous atrocities in the East, especially the slaughter of thousands of Jews. The SS cavalry became an integral component of the SS murder machinery under Himmler's direct command. It executed thousands of Jewish men, women, and children in the Pripet Marshes. Not only did the SS Cavalry Brigade commit atrocities, an east Prussian SS equestrian regiment shot Jews on the Lithuanian border without being ordered to do so. From June to July 1941, members of Equestrian Regiment 20, together with the border police and an SS infantry regiment, exterminated at least 220 Jews.[9]

Waffen SS General Paul Hausser, a staunch defender of the Waffen SS, claimed that he had heard rumors that the Equestrian SS was acquitted because it contained an internationally known (but unnamed) person whose conviction could have led to embarrassing political problems. He was undoubtedly referring to Prince Bernhard zu Lippe-Biesterfeld, the Dutch prince regent, once an active member of the Equestrian Regiment 7 in Berlin. Another SS member gathered that the acquittal was quite fortunate, otherwise the Dutch prince would have been declared a criminal. Hausser added that SS horsemen appeared astonished by the tribunal's decision to exclude them from the judgment against the SS.[10]

Hausser's views should be treated with suspicion, but SS horsemen did compete in international tournaments, and members of Equestrian Regiment 7 in Berlin, a unit steeped in social graces, escorted foreign guests at Nazi functions. The Berlin regiment was significantly blue-blooded; many of its members worked in the foreign and intelligence ministries and in the justice department. Some established cordial relations with foreign diplomats. Wolfgang Jaspar, a member of the regiment, testified that the Belgian ambassador twice invited him to his home.[11]

The inherent prestige of the Berlin regiment certainly benefitted the Mounted SS at Nuremberg, and the testimony of von Woikowski-Biedau, chief spokesman for the Equestrian SS at Nuremberg, added more advantages. An elderly aristocrat known in equestrian circles, he served as an excellent mouthpiece for those SS horsemen hoping to dissociate themselves from Himmler. Perhaps the Equestrian SS profited significantly from having famous jockeys and the Dutch prince regent in its ranks.

Above all, Hermann Fegelein's execution saved the Equestrian SS from serious scrutiny. Had Fegelein survived the war, undoubtedly he would have been indicted as a major war criminal (the Russians wanted him dead). He certainly would have been an important figure at the trials. The Nuremberg Tribunal would then have been hard-pressed to consider the Equestrian SS as anything but a genuine SS organization. Hardly an outsider, Fegelein rose to the upper echelons of the SS exclusively through his career as an SS horseman, and he maintained a close relationship with Himmler until the end of the Third Reich.

Although the Nuremberg tribunal refused to convict the mounted SS as a criminal organization, postwar trials in West Germany provided a small measure of justice. The veteran SS horseman Karl Struve, commander of Equestrian Regiment 20, received a life sentence for his role in exterminating Jews in Lithuania. A German court sentenced four members of the SS Cavalry Brigade from four to five years for their roles in the murder of at least 5,254 Jews in 1941. Two of them, Walter Dunsch and Franz Magill, were former members of the Equestrian SS recruited by Fegelein for the SS cavalry in Poland. However, only a few commanders were prosecuted at the trials; common soldiers who carried out orders were spared indictment.[12]

In trial affidavits by members of the SS Cavalry Brigade, most men refused to conceal their actions as legitimate operations against partisans. They realized that the slaughter of Jews had no military justification; killing men, women, and children were crimes. Some recalled the horror, the disgust, and the revulsion of having to murder civilians. Others enthusiastically participated in the savagery.[13]

Despite the routine indoctrination sessions, for some ideology played a minimal role. Most who participated stressed an overriding fear of reprisals – arrest, imprisonment in a concentration camp, execution. One said he shot Jews as a matter of fulfilling his duty, not for antisemitic reasons.[14]

Clearly, though, SS ideology contributed to the inhumanity. SS discipline prepared men to become political soldiers. Some members of the squadrons were quite brutal during roundups and forced marches. A member of the Cavalry Brigade's Bicycle Reconnaissance Detachment explained, "It was naturally clear they would be shot because they were Jews." He added that since the men had been hardened by warfare and SS training, no justification was offered, or required; the men followed orders and no one wondered why Jews had to be killed.[15]

Yet not all members were willing to acknowledge their actions. Some were concerned that such an admission would further disgrace the image of Waffen SS. As one recalled, "I was never in a special commando unit in which Jews were shot. I was completely engaged in actions against partisans, during which no Jews were exterminated."[16]

As the postwar trials revealed, the Nuremberg Tribunal erroneously considered SS horsemen as something other than genuine SS members. The fact remains, however, that the Equestrian SS was intimately tied to Himmler's organization. Most SS horsemen were probably not criminals because most individual SS horsemen, particularly farmers uninvolved in competitions, were drafted into the army. Even some who rode for the SS in tournaments, like Hans von Salviati, rejected the SS system after 1939.

But a core of Equestrian SS officers, Hermann and Waldemar Fegelein, Gustav Lombard, and Walter Dunsch among them, commanded murder brigades in the SS cavalry in World War II. Among their troops were many former members of the Equestrian SS. When called upon by Himmler in World War II, SS horsemen fulfilled their roles as political soldiers by willingly executing the innocent.

Essentially the tribunal did not understand the complexity of the multi-faceted SS. The judgment itself was intrinsically flawed. It found guilty "all persons who have been officially accepted as members of the SS including the members of the *Allgemeine* (General) SS." The tribunal added that the judgment "does not include the so-called riding units."[17] By including all members of the General SS in its verdict the tribunal effectively condemned all members of the Equestrian SS who remained in the organization after September 1939. Obviously, the tribunal, primarily concerned with major war criminals and the SS police and concentration camp system, did not comprehend the intricate organizational structure of the SS. It instead relied excessively on the testimony of a few self-serving former SS horsemen in exonerating the Equestrian SS.

The uniqueness of the Equestrian SS, then, was its exoneration by the Nuremberg tribunal. The tribunal condemned the General SS for its criminal nature, even though the army drafted two-thirds of its members, an action which made it generally insignificant during the war. Although all Equestrian SS personnel were also members of the General SS, in its judgment the tribunal mistakenly regarded SS equestrian units as essentially non-SS formations; it simply did not understand the strong connections between the Equestrian SS and the General SS. To the tribunal, the Equestrian SS was no different from riding clubs throughout Europe.

The Equestrian SS leadership, unlike that of the Mounted SA, was closely connected to its parent organization, and the SS riding schools were intimately tied to prewar armed SS units. Furthermore, many equestrian officers had served in other SS agencies, especially the General SS, and some were transferred to other SS branches after serving as equestrian leaders. Any independent tendencies were curtailed, and members, with exceptions, who violated SS regulations were punished and expelled.

Even though many members of equestrian units joined simply to continue to participate in tournaments, little evidence exists that SS horsemen, especially officers, resented being part of the SS. The SS offered benefits, advancement, prestige, and a sense of community.

Many of the difficulties experienced by the Equestrian SS, especially its leadership and administrative problems, reflected patterns existing throughout the General SS system. Suspect training methods generally resulted from a lack of available funds to hire skilled instructors. The General SS itself suffered from persistent financial problems which forced regiments to rely excessively on part-time volunteers to staff important positions. The SS did not provide sufficient financial resources to enable General SS units to hire enough competent personnel.

As part of the General SS, equestrian units trained regularly to be prepared to mobilize for security operations to quell domestic unrest. So that they could become Hitler's faithful warriors, Himmler's horsemen received both paramilitary training and ideological instruction, generally within each unit and occasionally at SS riding schools and leadership conferences. Periodic ideological instruction reminded them to embody what their black uniforms represented: political soldiers with unflinching loyalty to the state. Although instruction and training sometimes was conducted haphazardly, the Equestrian SS provided a pool of trained individuals ready when called upon.

World War II allowed the Equestrian SS to fulfil its role as a mounted police force in occupied Poland. Equestrian SS personnel dutifully served in the SS cavalry in the East and formed the basis from which the initial Waffen SS cavalry units emerged. As members of these mounted units, SS horsemen committed numerous atrocities in the Pripet Marshes. The SS cavalry, under Hermann Fegelein's leadership, became an integral component of the SS murder brigades directed by Himmler. As perhaps the first unit to receive and carry out Himmler's order to shoot women and children, the SS Cavalry Brigade executed thousands of Jews. Prewar indoctrination and training programs and Fegelein's leadership prepared SS horsemen to carry out Himmler's orders in the East. And, Fegelein conceived that this battle-tested, hardened SS cavalry force would form the core of a new, postwar Equestrian SS under his command.

Although Fegelein emerged as the most recognized member of the Equestrian SS and SS cavalry, other SS horsemen gained notoriety for their activities. Some, notably Hermann Florstedt, staffed Himmler's concentration camps during World War II. Eberhard von Künsberg plundered art on both fronts. Friedrich-Wilhelm Krüger practically ran the Holocaust in Poland. Kurt Becher became Himmler's special representative in Hungary in 1944 and special commissioner for all concentration camps in 1945. Dr. August Schwedler rose in the Nazi hierarchy to become a director of the *Reichsbank* and a close companion of Walter Funk, Hitler's minister of economics.

Behind the scenes, SS horsemen contributed to Himmler's expanding SS empire by serving in equestrian units and in other SS agencies. Equestrian SS members, like their fellow SS comrades, moved throughout the SS system before and during the war. They trained as SS men, followed SS procedures, recruited SS members, represented the SS at public functions, and regarded themselves as SS political soldiers just like all others.

Despite the judgment at Nuremberg, Himmler's mounted units served an essential role in his attempt to control Germany. Himmler gained access to rural Germany, influence among segments of the establishment, and prestige through his equestrian units. Driven by SS training, Himmler's horsemen became true political soldiers in World War II when they murdered thousands. Although the Nuremberg Tribunal ruled otherwise, the Equestrian SS bore the indelible stamp of a criminal organization.

Endnotes

Introduction

1. Charles W. Sydnor Jr., *Soldiers of Destruction: The SS Death's Head Division, 1933-1945* (Princeton: Princeton University Press, 1977), xiv.

2. The tribunal also indicted the SA, the Gestapo and the SD (indicted together), the Reich Cabinet, the leadership of the Nazi Party, and the General Staff and High Command. The SA, the original Nazi paramilitary formation, the Reich Cabinet, and the General Staff and High Command received acquittals. The tribunal convicted as criminals organizations the Nazi Party leadership, the Gestapo, and the SD (*Sicherheitsdienst*), the SS intelligence and security service.

3. Office of the United States Chief of Counsel for Prosecution of Axis Criminality, *Nazi Conspiracy and Aggression: Opinion and Judgment* (Washington: United States Government Printing Office, 1947), 101-02.

4. Robert L. Koehl, *The Black Corps: The Structure and Power Struggles of the Nazi SS* (Madison: University of Wisconsin Press, 1983), 23-24; Heinz Höhne, *The Order of the Death's Head: The Story of Hitler's SS*, trans. Richard Barry (New York: Ballantine Books, 1971), 27-28.

5. Ibid., 65; Koehl, *The Black Corps*, 79.

6. Helmut Krausnick et al., *Anatomy of the SS State*, trans. Richard Barry (New York: Walker and Company, 1968), 142; Koehl, *The Black Corps*, 46; Höhne, *The Order of the Death's Head*, 65, 73-77, 146-49.

7. Manfred Wolfson, "The SS Leadership" (Ph.D. diss., University

of California, Berkeley, 1965), 249; Robert John Shalka, "The General-SS in Central Germany, 1937-1939: A Social and Institutional Study of SS Main Sector Fulda-Werra," (Ph.D. diss., University of Wisconsin, 1972), iii-iv; George H. Stein, *The Waffen SS: Hitler's Elite Guard at War, 1939-1945* (Ithaca and London: Cornell University Press, 1966), xxvii.

8. Ibid.

9. A good research source is Mark C. Yerger, *Allgemeine-SS: The Commands, Units and Leaders of the General SS* (Atglen, PA: Schiffer Publishing Ltd., 1997).

10. Höhne, *The Order of the Death's Head*, 156.

Chapter 1

1. Felix Gilbert with David Clay Large, *The End of the European Era, 1890-Present* (New York: W.W. Norton and Company, Inc., 1991) 23-24.

2. The German army, however, relied extensively on horses. Office of the United States Chief of Counsel for Prosecution of Axis Criminality, *Nazi Conspiracy and Aggression* (Washington: United States Government Printing Office, 1946), 4:793; *Völkischer Beobachter* (hereafter cited as *VB*), 17 July 1935.

3. *SS-Kavallerie im Osten*. Herausgegeben von der SS-Kavallerie Brigade für Ihre Führer und Männer (Braunschweig: G. Westermann, 1942), 1; Chef-Abteilung II to Oberste SA-Führer, National Archives Microfilm (hereafter cited as NA) *T-354*/Roll 194/Frame 3852248.

4. *Statistisches Jahrbuch der Schutzstaffel der NSDAP 1938* (Berlin: Reichsführer-SS, 1939), NA *T-175*/205/4042319, 4042306); Aufstellung von SS-Reiterverbänden, 26 January 1934, NA *T-354*/400/4112542-44; Reichsführer-SS (hereafter cited as RFSS) to Chef-SS-Amt, 21 February 1934, NA *T-354*/400/4112536-39.

5. Chef-Hauptamt (hereafter cited as HA) to SS Oberabschnitt (hereafter cited as OA) Rhein, 8 April 1935, NA *T-354*/400/41122028.

6. *"SS-Reiterei," Das Schwarze Korps* (hereafter cited as *DSK*), 6 March 1935, 6; Foundation dates of the equestrian regiments, Bundesarchiv (hereafter cited as BA) Koblenz/NS33/21; Reitereinheiten des SS-Oberabschnittes, NA *T-175*/574/19, 29, 49, 59; Koehl, *The Black Corps*, 109; Statistische Jahrbuch der Schutzstaffel der NSDAP 1938, NA *T-175*/205/4042319, 4042354.

7. RFSS, SS-Gericht (Tondock) to Chef-Persönlichen Stab RFSS, 24 January 1938, and Führer-SS-Reiterabschnitt VI to Führer-SS-OA Südwest, 21 November 1935, Berlin Document Center (hereafter cited as BDC), SS Officer File, Georg Skowronski. The Berlin Document Center

is now the Bundesarchiv Berlin. SS personnel files are also located in the National Archives II in College Park, Maryland.

8. He suggested that Josius Erbprinz zu Waldeck-Pyrmont, leader of SS Main Sector *Fulda-Werra,* would make a better cavalry inspector. Krüger assumed a more prestigious position when he became Higher SS and Police Leader *Ost,* the supreme SS police commander in Poland, in 1939. Among other units, the SS cavalry in Poland reported to him. Known for his frequent disagreements with Hans Frank, the Nazi governor of Poland (the General Government), Krüger later became a general in the Waffen SS. He committed suicide on May 10, 1945. Lebenslauf, BDC, SS Officer File, Friedrich-Wilhelm Krüger; Mark C. Yerger, *Riding East,* 32.

9. RFSS to Chef-SS-Amt, 21 February 1934, NA *T-354*/400/4112536-39.

10. Stellenbesetzungsliste, 1 November 1934, NA *T-175*/203/2744724-25.

11. Aufstellung von SS-Reiterverbänden, 26 January 1934, NA *T-354*/400/4112542-44.

12. RFSS to Chef-SS-Amt, 21 February 1934, NA *T-354*/400/4112536-39; SS-Oberabschnittsreiterführer Süd (Fegelein) to Sondereinheiten, 28 March 1935, NA *T-354*/357/4063166.

13. Höhne, *The Order of the Death's Head,* 138, 156.

14. Von Hohberg und Buchwald was the only SS horsemen executed during the Night of the Long Knives (Röhm purge). "Affären von dem Bach-Zelewski. Die Toten stehen auf," *Der Spiegel,* (7 January 1959), 22-23; Koehl, *The Black Corps,* 92; Gestapo Report, Karlsruhe, 3, February 1934 in *Die Lageberichte der Gestapo und des Generalstaatsanwalts Karlsruhe 1933-1940, Verfolgung und Widerstand unter dem Nationalsozialismus in Baden* ed. Jörg Schadt (Stuttgart: Verlag W. Kohlhammer), 62.

15. Inspekteur des Reitsports, NA *T-354*/148/3852365.

16. Chef-Stab to Obergruppen, Gruppen, 12 September 1933, NA *T-354*/194/3852360.

17. Leistungsbericht der Pferde-Unterstützungskasse, 1 October 1934, NA *T-354*/401/4113010; Inspekteur-Reitsports to Gruppenreiterführer, Oberabschnittsreiterführer, Sämtliche SA-und SS-Reiterstürmen, 20 January 1935, NA *T-354*/401/4112960; 25 January 1935, NA *T-354*/401/4112961-62.

18. Ibid.

19. Foundation Dates of the Equestrian Units, BA Koblenz/NS33/21; Koehl, *The Black Corps,* 311-12 n. 20; Aufstellung von Reiterverbänden, 26 January 1934, NA *T-354*/400/4112542-44.

20. RFSS to Chef-SS-Amt, 21 February 1934, NA *T-354*/400/ 4112536-39; Aufstellung von SS-Reitervervänden, 26 January 1934, NA *T-354*/4112542-44.

21. Equestrian Regiment 19 (Main Sector unknown), organized in 1935 and dissolved in October 1936. *Statistische Jahrbuch der Schutzstaffel der NSDAP 1936* (Berlin: Reichsführer-SS, 1937); NA *T-175*/574/19, 29, 49, 116; Chef-SS-Hauptamt to SS-OA Main, 10 November 1936, NA *T-354*/357/4062995; Reitereinheiten des SS-Oberabschnittes, NA *T-175*/574/19, 49, 106.

22. Führer-SS-OA Elbe to Chef-SS-Hauptamt, 2 April 1936, NA *T-175*/201/2742707-10.

23. Standartenbefehl 56, 8 July 1935, NA *T-175*/203/2744656.

24. In 1939 the SS established two additional units. Equestrian Regiment 23, originally organized in Freiburg in March 1935, dissolved in September 1936, and reformed in Pirmasens (Main Sector *Südwest*) in late 1939. In April 1939 the SS established Equestrian Regiment 20 in Main Sector *Nordost* with headquarters in Tilsit. Ibid.; Foundation Dates of the SS Equestrian Units, BA Koblenz/NS33/21; *Statistische Jahrbuch der Schutzstaffel der NSDAP 1938*, NA *T-175*/205/4042319.

25. RFSS to Chef-SS-Amt, 21 February 1934, NA *T-354*/400/ 4112537-39.

26. As a paramilitary organization, the SS had its own ranking system (from private to general). BA Berlin/NS31/108.

27. Equestrian victories were routinely published in the SS journal *Das Schwarze Korps*. See for instance SS-Reitersieg in der Tschechei, *DSK*, 31 October 1935, 4; "SS-Reiterei," *DSK*, 9 April 1936, 4; "Hauptreitschule," *DSK*, 9 June 1938, 4; Werner Menzendorf, *Reitsport: Ein Bildband 1900-1972*, Textliche Bearbeitung von Hans-Joachim von Killisch-Horn (Berlin and Hamburg: Paul Parey, 1972), 203.

28. Some clubs allowed SS members to rent horses and equipment, enabling the SS to recruit individuals who did not own horses. Chef-SS-Amt to SS-OA Rhein, 8 July 1934, NA *T-354*/400/4112437; Chef-SS-Amt to SS-OA Rhein, 12 July 1934, NA *T-354*/400/4112414.

29. Unlike the others, Nagel was a recent addition to the SS. He joined the staff of the SS Officer School Braunschweig as a riding instructor in 1937 after being discharged from the army's Cavalry School Hannover. BDC, SS Officer File August Nagel; Standartenbefehl 30, 22 February 1935, NA *T-175*/203/2744693; Gesamterfolge der SS-Reiterei, undated, NA *T-354*/445/4177091; Erfolge in den Championaten, 15 February 1939, NA *T-354*/445/4177090.

30. Equestrian SS training programs are discussed in Chapter 3. Karl Otmar von Aretin called these units "pure riding clubs." Karl Otmar von

Aretin, "Der bayerische Adel. Von der Monarchie zum Dritten Reich," in *Bayern in der NS-Zeit: Herrschaft und Gesellschaft im Konflikt*, eds. Martin Broszat, Elke Fröhlich, Anton Grossman (Munich, Vienna: R. Oldenbourg Verlag, 1981), 3:555; IMT, 42:523.

31. A circular from Oberabschnittsreiterführer-OA Süd, 4 April 1934, NA *T-354*/357/4063181.

32. Newspaper article from *Schwetzinger Zeitung*, 23 April 1935, Führer-SS-Reiterabschnitt VI to SS-OA Südwest, 14 May 1935, and Stabsführer-SS-OA Südwest to SS-Hauptamt, SS-Gerichtsamt, 16 May 1935, all in BDC, SS Officer File, Fritz Hausamen.

33. Ibid.; RFSS to SS-Standartenführer, Dr. Fritz Hausamen, 25 May 1935, and Vernehmungsprotokoll, 15 May 1935, BDC, Hausamen.

34. The prosecution at the Nuremberg Trial incorrectly believed that the Equestrian SS could not acquire this certificate, IMT, 21:575; "Die Reiterscheine für 1937," *DSK*, 28 January 1937, 3; BA Berlin/NS31/108.

35. "SS Reitersturm 4/21," *DSK*, 21 January 1934, 4; "Um den Reiterpreis des Reichsführers-SS," *DSK*, 17 October 1935, 3; IMT, 42:523.

36. Sturmbefehl für November 1936, 29 October 1936, NA *T-354*/418/4138469; Führer-SS-Reitersturm-SS-OA Rhein to SS-OA Rhein, 11 December 1934, NA *T-354*/402/4114733.

37. Hans-Jürgen Döscher, *Das Auswärtige Amt im Dritten Reich: Diplomatie im Schatten der > Endlösung<* (Berlin: Wolf Jobst Siedler Verlag, 1987), 116. Prince von Braunschweig und Lüneburg of Hannover and the future German rocket scientist Werner von Braun (though only briefly) were other members of the unit. Reichskanzlei, December 1937, BA Berlin *R43*/II/386a.

38. "SS Begleitkommando für Mussolini," *DSK*, 7 October 1937, 4; IMT, 42:523-24.

39. Letters dated 1 February 1936, 4 April 1936, 14 October 1937, 14 January 1937, 7 May 1938, in BDC, SS Officer File, Paul Brantenaar.

Chapter 2

1. It was not SS training sessions alone which horsemen had difficulty attending. After the reintroduction of the draft, some did not voluntary report to the army, particularly those studying for medical and law school examinations and those running a farm. Sturmbefehl für Juni/Juli 1936, 28 May 1936, NA *T-354*/418/4138464; Standartenbefehl 79, 22 January 1936, NA *T-175*/203/2744572; Sturmbefehl, 11 Juni 1934, NA *T-354*/402/4114493.

2. 4 Monatiges Ausbildungsprogramm, NA *T-354*/400/4112368-70; 4 Monatiges Ausbildungsprogramm, NA *T-354*/400/4112364-66; 21. SS-Reiterstandarte to SS-Reiterstürme 1, 2, 3, 4, NZ/R21, 29 May 1936, NA

T-354/418/4138309; Dienstplan für den Monat Februar 1939, 27 January 1939, NA *T-354*/418/4138384.

3. On rare occasions unexpected outbreaks of hoof and mouth disease altered, or cancelled entirely, training schedules (sometimes for months). Führer SS-Reitersturmes 3/R 17 to 17. Reiterstandarte, 16 February 1938, NA *T-354*/358/4064119; 6 January 1939, NA *T-354*/445/4177343; Standartenbefehl 45, 22 May 1935, NA *T-175*/203/2744671.

4. RFSS to Chef-SS-Amt, 21 February 1934, NA *T-354*/400/4112537-39; Stabsführer-SS-OA Rhein to SS-Reitersturms, SS-OA Rhein, 14 January 1935, NA *T-354*/402/4114289.

5. Ibid.

6. Standartenbefehl 14, 22 November 1934, NA *T-175*/203/2744714; Sturmbefehl für Januar 1937, 1 January 1937, NA *T-354*/418/4138474.

7. Koehl, *The Black Corps*, 83, Standartenbefehl 28, 9 February 1935, NA *T-175*/203/2744695.

8. Standartenbefehl 69, 24 October 1935, NA *T-175*/203/2744617; Standartenbefehl 71, 14 November 1935, NA *T-175*/203/2744610; SS-Reitersturm 1, 21. SS-Reiterstandarte to Zugführer I, II, and III, 10 November 1937, NA *T-354*/418/4138495; Standartenbefehl 73, 6 December 1935, NA *T-175*/203/2744602.

9. Sturmbefehl 84, 10 March 1936, NA *T-175*/203/2744560-61.

10. Patriotic German history was one popular theme for indoctrination sessions. In early 1936, leaders assigned men to scour caves for historically significant writing or artifacts. The SS took great pride in German ancestry, so much so that it forbade the wearing of "teutonic costumes" which mocked their forefathers at any parade, festival, or official function. Standartenbefehl 63, 27 August 1935, NA *T-175*/203/2744639; 21. SS-Reiterstandarte to 1,2,3,4/R21, 12 November 1936, NA *T-354*/418/4128498-500; Standartenbefehl 82, 22 February 1936, NA *T-175*/203/2744564.

11. Standartenbefehl 75, 7 January 1936, NA *T-175*/203/2744591; Standartenbefehl 77, 13 January 1936, NA *T-175*/203/2744578-80.

12. To gain the support of spouses, the SS invited wives to many sessions. Sturmbefehl 10, 4 March 1935, NA *T-354*/401/4112577; Sturmbefehl 11, 8 March 1935, NA *T-354*/401/4112575.

13. Führer-SS-Reiterstürme, SS-OA Rhein to SS-OA Rhein, 11 December 1934, NA *T-354*/402/4114305; Standartenbefehl 21, 21 December 1934, NA *T-175*/203/2744705; Sturmbefehl für Juni/Juli 1936, 28 May 1936, NA *T-354*/418/4138464.

14. Freiherr Hans von Wolff, commander of Equestrian Regiment 6, left the SS in 1937 to join the army, in part because he could earn more money as an army officer, but also because of his devotion to Catholi-

cism. Another equestrian leader, Pelagius Herz, commander of Equestrian Regiment 3, raised suspicions about his devotion to the Catholic Church. Although Herz had officially left the Church, a relative of his was a Catholic priest and Herz reportedly worked at the Vatican as either a painter or a photographer before Hitler became chancellor. His earlier devotion to Catholicism, nevertheless, did not harm his standing in the SS. He was, however, reprimanded for lying about his membership in a lodge during the 1920s. Führer-SS-OA West to SS-Personalamt, 4 June 1937, BDC, SS Officer File, Hans von Wolff; Undated document compiled by SS-*Hauptsturmführer* Gräfe, BDC, SS Officer File, Pelagius Herz.

15. Anlage zum Standarten-Sonderbefehl von 11 January 1935, 11 January 1935, NA *T-175*/203/2744701-02.

16. Ibid.; Standarten-Sonderbefehl-Führer-15. SS-Reiterstandarte, 11 January 1935, NA *T-175*/203/2744700.

17. Sturmbefehl 32, 18 December 1934, NA *T-354*/401/4112596; Standartenbefehl 61, 20 August 1935, NA *T-175*/203/2744647; Standartenbefehl 69, 24 October 1935, NA *T-175*/203/2744617.

18. Standartenbefehl 70, 6 November 1935, NA *T-175*/203/2744611; 1 December 1938, NA *T-354*/358/4064046.

19. RFSS to Chef-SS-Amt, 21 February 1934, NA *T-354*/400/4112536-39.

20. Ibid.

21. The SS and SA honored Rothkirch at a retirement party in September 1934, recognizing "his extraordinary service to the training of the SA and SS equestrian units." Donations from all equestrian leaders provided the famed cavalryman with a special gift. Ibid.; Inspekteur des Reitsports, 3 September 1934, NA *T-354*/401/4113173; Führer-SS Reitersturm-SS-OA Rhein to SS-Oberabschnittreiterführer, undated, NA *T-354*/401/4112591.

22. Leadership conferences also included social activities such as attending an equestrian event and visiting a stud farm. Dienstplan für den SS-Reiter-Unterführerslehrgang am 2. und 3. Febr. 35, 24 January 1935, NA *T-354*/401/4112561; Führer-SS-OA Rhein to SS-Amt, Reichsführung SS, 4 June 1934, NA *T-354*/401/4112822.

23. 21. SS-Reiterstandarte to SS-Reiterstürme 1, 2, 3, 4, NZ/R21, 29 May 1936, NA *T-354*/418/4138309; SS-R1/R21, 24 September 1937, NA *T-354*/354/418/4138367; Dienstplan für Reiter-SS-Führer und Unterführer, undated, NA *T-354*/400/4112127-32.

24. Führer -3/R24 to 24 Reiterstandarte, 15 August 1936, NA *T-354*/358/4064367; SS-Reitersturm Hof-Saale to 24 SS-Reiterstandarte, 11 May 1936, NA *T-354*/358/4064457.

25. SS-Reitersturm Hof-Saale to 24. SS-Reiterstandarte, 11 May 1936,

NA *T-354*/358/4064457; Führer-SS-Reitersturm Hof-Saale to 24. SS-Reiterstandarte, 18 August 1936, NA *T-354*/358/4064456.
26. Führer-SS-Reitersturm 3/17 to 17. SS-Reiterstandarte, Nürnberg, 19 February 1937, NA *T-354*/358/4064361; Führer-SS-Reitersturm 4/17 to 17. SS-Reiterstandarte, Regensburg, 19 August 1937, NA *T-354*/359/4064699.
27. Shalka, "The General-SS in Central Germany," 286.

Chapter 3

1. "Die Kavallerie-Schule Hannover," *DSK*, 17 July 1935, 8; "SS-Reitschule Forst," *DSK*, 13 August 1938, 3; "Eine Stolze Bilanz," *DSK*, 12 January 1938, 4; "Das Glück der Erde," *DSK*, 19 August 1937, 4.
2. The genteel world of equestrianism hardly softened Weber's coarse nature. During a hurdling race in Riem, horrified spectators gathered as an SS officer unsuccessfully attempted to kill a lame horse. The horse survived one shot which prompted shouts and protests from the group. Weber emerged to scold the inept SS horse killer and to quiet the gathering. He belted one observer, knocking him to the ground. Warnings and intimidating gestures from the stocky Bavarian quickly dispersed the onlookers. SS Card, BDC, SS Officer File, Christian Weber; *VB*, 26 July 1935, Trevor-Roper, *The Last Days*, 156.
3. "Das Glück der Erde," *DSK*, 19 August 1937, 4; "SS-Reitschule Forst," *DSK*, 13 August 1936, 3.
4. Standartenbefehl 76, 10 January 1936, NA *T-175*/203/2744587; Standartenbefehl 73, 6 December 1936, NA *T-175*/203/2744600.
5. Chef-SS-Hauptamt, 13 August 1935, NA *T-354*/401/4112723.
6. SS Card, RFSS to Gervers, 28 April 1937, BDC, SS Officer File, Wilhelm Gervers; SS Card, Personalien, Führer-SS-Abschnitt XX to Herrn Polizeigeneral Daluege, 8 May 1934, and Oberstleutnant Mörschel to Führer-SS-Abschnitt XX, 24 September 1934, BDC, SS Officer File, Hanns Mörschel.
7. Dienstlaufbahn, and Führer-SS-Abschnitt XX to SS-OA Nord, 27 August 1934, BDC, Mörschel.
8. Berichtigung, 18 February 1938, NA *T-175*/149/2676932; Reit u.Fahrlehrgang für Führer, Unterführer, und Männer, 5 August 1938, NA *T-354*/444/4176259.
9. BDC, SS Officer File, Hans von Salviati.
10. Mörschel to SS-Gruppenführer Pohl, 27 April 1937, BDC, Mörschel.
11. Ibid.; SS-Gruppenführer Pohl to SS-Obergruppenführer Heissmeyer, 26 April 1937, and SS-Gruppenführer Pohl to Schmitt, 8 April 1938, BDC, Mörschel.

12. Ibid

13. "Grundlegende Ausbildung der SS," *DSK*, 23 March 1939, 4; Führer-6. SS-Reiterstandarten to SS-OA West, BDC, SS Officer File, Rolf Becher; Chef-Kommandoamt-Allgemeine SS to SS-Führungshauptamt, NA *T-175*/149/2676927; Verwaltungschef-SS to Chef-SS-Hauptamt, undated, NA *T-175*/37/2547190-91.

14. Heissmeyer to Chef-Persönlicher Stab, RFSS, 24 March 1939, NA *T-175*/37/2547181; Inspekteur-SS-Reitschulen to Chef-SS-Hauptamt, 17 March 1939, NA *T-175*/37/2547185-89.

15. Ibid.

16. Inspekteur-SS-Reiterei to Chef-SS-Hauptamt, 20 March 1939, NA *T-175*/37/2547182-84.

17. Ibid.

18. Inspekteur-SS-Reitschulen to Chef-SS-Hauptamt, 17 March 1939, NA *T-175*/37/2547185-89.

19. SS-Hauptreitschule München-Reim to RFSS, 6 September 1938, NA *T-175*/37/2547215; "Chronik der SS-Hauptreitschule München," (Courtesy Mark C. Yerger).

20. It seems unlikely that he served in a Free Corps unit as he claimed. "Der Reiter Hermann Fegelein," *DSK*, 21 January 1943, 6; "Das Ritterkreuz für SS Standartenführer Hermann Fegelein," *DSK*, 2 April 1942, 6;"Lebenslauf, RuS Fragebogen, and Ortsgruppenführer H. V. Leiban to Abt. Ortsgruppenführer, 15 August 1931, BDC, SS Officer File, Hermann Fegelein.

21. Lebenslauf, SS Officer Card, and Personnel Referent-SS-OA Süd to RFSS, 21 November 1935, BDC, Fegelein.

22. "SS gewann Deutsches Springderby," *DSK*, 8 July 1937, 4. Germany won gold in all equestrian events at the 1936 Berlin Olympics.

23. From January to August 1939, the Main Riding School won 62 events — it had won only 48 times in 1937 and 1938 combined. It also placed in 70 other events during 1939. "Chronik der SS-Hauptreitschule München" (Courtesy Mark C. Yerger.)

24. SS Card, and "SS-Hauptführer Temme siegte im Grossen Preis von Ostpreussen," 12 July 1937, *VB*, in BDC, SS Officer File, Günter Temme; "Auch in Dortmund erfolgreich," 30 March 39, *DSK*,4; "Triumph der SS-Reiterei," 14 April 1938, *DSK*, 20.

25. Personal Bericht, BDC, Temme.

26. Aufstellung über die militärische Dienstzeit der Führer der SS-Hauptreitschule, undated, NA *T-175*/37/2547180; SS Card, and Kommandeur-SS-Hauptreitschule (Fegelein) to RFSS, 21 October 1938, BDC, SS Officer File, Martin von Barnekow. Herbert Schönfeldt, a skilled equestrian and experienced cavalryman, joined Fegelein in Munich in 1938 after serving nine years at the Hannover Cavalry School.

27. NA *T-175*/37/2547193; Ergebnisse des Turniers in Stuttgart, 12 March 1939, NA *T-175*/37/2547182; Fegelein to RFSS, 13 April 1938, NA *T-175*/37/2547175-79.

28. Ibid.

29. Inspekteur-SS-Reitschulen to RFSS, 28 June 1939, NA *T-175*/37/2547147.

30. Führer-SS-OA Main to SS-Hauptamt, Inspekteur-Reiterei, 22 September 1938, NA *T-354*/357/4063286; Führer-SS-Reitersturm 1/R 17 to SS-OA Main, 24 March 1938, NA *T-354*/358/4064102; Führer-SS-Reitersturm 2/R 17 to SS-OA Main, 14 March 1938, NA *T-354*/358/4064103; Führer-17. SS-Reiterstandarte to SS-OA Main, 12 March 1938, NA *T-354*/358/4064107.

31. Christian Weber to SS-Gruppenführer Wolff, 5 February 1938, NA *T-175*/37/2547244-46

32. Fegelein to RFSS, 9 September 1938, NA *T-175*/37/2547175-79.

33. Fegelein to RFSS, 20 September 1938, BDC, SS Officer File, Hermann Fegelein.

34. Fegelein to RFSS, 6 September 1938, NA *T-175*/37/2547215-17.

35. Fegelein to RFSS, 13 April 1939, NA *T-175*/37/2547175-79; Fegelein to RFSS, 29 Juni 1939, NA *T-175*/37/2547151-54.

Chapter 4

1. Koehl, *The Black Corps*, 40.

2. Führer-SS-OA Rhein to SS-Amt, Reichsführung-SS, 4 June 1934, NA *T-354*/401/4112838; Chef-Führungsabteilung to SS-OA, 16 August 1934, NA *T-354*/400/4112350; Chef-Führungsabteilung to SS-OA Rhein, 5 September 1934, NA *T-354*/400/4112320.

3. Inspekteur-Reitsports to Gruppenreiterführer, Oberabschnitts-reiterführer, Chefreiterführer, 1 October 1934, NA *T-354*/401/4113162; Inspekteur-Reitsports to Chefreiterführer, Gruppenreiterführer, Chefreiterführer-SS, Oberabschnittsreiterführer, 19 October 1934, NA *T-354*/401/4113139; SS-Reitersturm 3 to SS-Reitersturm SS-OA Rhein, 28 August 1934, NA *T-354*/401/4112794; 7 February 1935, NA *T-354*/401/4112730.

4. Sonderbefehl, 12 November 1934, NA *T-354*/401/4112604; 18 June 1934, NA *T-354*/402/4114390; Sturmbefehl 27, 10 November 1934, NA *T-354*/401/4112607.

5. Standartenbefehl 69, 24 October 1935, NA *T-175*/203/2744616.

6. Bericht über die Feststellungen bei der 13. SS-Reiterstandarte, 23 May 1938, Vernehmungsniederschrift, 18 May 1938, BDC, SS Officer File, Hans Floto.

7. Ibid.

8. RFSS, 20 June 1939, BDC, Floto.

9. SS Card, Dienstlaufbahn, BDC, SS Officer File, Rudolf Freiherr von Geyr.

10. Protokoll, Lebenslauf, and Beschluss, 28 November 1934, BDC, SS Officer File, Dr. Fritz Hausamen.

11. Lebenslauf, Dienstlaufbahn, a letter to Chef-SS-Hauptamt, 6 August 1935, Führer-SS-OA Südwest to RFSS, 19 August 1935, Führer-SS-OA Südwest to SS-Hauptamt, 12 November 1935, in BDC, SS Officer File, Dr. Fritz Hausamen.

12. RFSS-SS-Befehl, 1 July 1938, NA *T-175*/37/2547301; Führer-SS-OA Nordwest to RFSS, 7 July 1938, NA *T-175*/37/2547299.

13. Ibid.

14. Chef-SS-Hauptamt to RFSS, 19 July 1938, NA *T-175*/37/2547297.

15. Pohl to Chef-SS-Hauptamt, 3 February 1939, NA *T-175*/37/2547279; Braune Band-Deutschland to Chef-SS-Hauptamt, 6 September 1938, NA *T-175*/37/2547206; RFSS, Persönlicher Stab to Inspekteur-SS-Reiterei, 31 March 1939, NA *T-175*/37/2547260; Inspekteur-SS-Reiterei to RFSS, Persönlicher Stab, 14 April 1939, NA *T-175*/37/2547259.

16. RFSS, SS-Befehl, 25 April 1939, NA *T-175*/37/2547257; Verwaltungschef-SS to Inspekteur-SS-Reiterei, 3 March 1939, NA *T-175*/37/2547276.

Chapter 5

1. Döscher, *Das Auswärtige Amt im Dritten Reich*, 116.

2. Lebenslauf, BDC, SS Officer File, Eberhard von Künsberg.

3. Stellenbesetzung, 1 September 1934, BDC, SS Officer File, Eberhard von Künsberg; Standartenbefehl 54, 5 July 1935, NA *T-175*/203/2744659; Standartenbefehl 61, 20 August 1935, NA *T-354*/203/2744648.

4. Stabsführer OA Main to SS Reiterabschitt V, 25 September 1935, BDC, SS Officer File, Eberhard von Künsberg.

5. Führer-15. SS-Reiterstandarte to Chefreiterführer-SS, 20 December 1934, Chef-SS-Amt to SS-OA Süd, 10 January 1935, Chef-SS-Hauptamt to von Künsberg, 11 March 1935, a letter from Chefreiterführer-SS, 25 March 1935, and an SD report, 11 February 1935, BDC, SS Officer File, von Künsberg.

6. Ibid.

7. Stabsführer-SS-OA Süd to 31. SS-Standarte, 9 April 1935, Führer-15. SS-Reiterstandarte to SS-Reiterabschnitt V, 11 May 1935, and Führer-SS-Reitersturm 3/15 to 15-SS-Reiterstandarte, 10 May 1935, BDC, SS Officer File, von Künsberg.

8. Führer-31. SS-Standarte to Stabsführer-SS-Abschnitt XXVII, 10 April 1935, Führer-31. SS-Standarte to SS-Abschnitt, 30 April 1935, and Führer-SS Abschnitt to SS-OA Süd, 15 April 1935, BDC, von Künsberg.

9. Standartenarzt, 15. SS-Reiterstandarte to Führer-15. SS-Reiterstandarte, 9 May 1935, Stellungnahme des Rechtsberaters, 21 May 1935, and Lebenslauf, BDC, von Künsberg; Künsberg to sämtliche Einheiten der 15.SS-Reiterstandarte, 11 June 1935, NA *T-175/203/2744668*; Standartenbefehl 75, 7 July 1936, NA *T-175/203/2744593*.

10. Jonathon Petropoulos, *Art as Politics in the Third Reich* (Chapel Hill and London: The University of North Carolina Press, 1996), 319.

11. "SS-Reiterei," *DSK*, 6 March 1935, 6.

12. Führer-SS-OA Südost to Chef-SS Hauptamt, 26 September 1935, BDC, SS Officer File, Erdmann Skudlarek; An SS court report, 12 April 37, BDC, SS Officer File, Wilhelm von Woikowski-Biedau.

13. Höhne, *The Order of the Death's Head*, 176.

14. Chef-Ausbildungswesen to Chefreiterführer and Gruppen-reiterführer, 11 August 1933, NA *T-354/400/4112546*; David Littlejohn, *The SA, 1921-45: Hitler's Stormtroopers* (London: Osprey Publishing, 1990), 23.

15. Chef-Stab to Obergruppen, Gruppen, 12 September 1933, NA *T-354/194/3852360*

16. Ibid., Aufstellung von SS-Reiterverbänden, 26 January 1934, NA *T-354/400/4112542-44*; Führer-Gruppe Westmark to Oberste SA-Führer, 13 June 1934, NA *T-354/400/4112474*.

17. Ibid., 23.

18. *IMT*, 22:159; *Nazi Conspiracy and Aggression*, 4:794.

19. Ibid.; Der Führer und Reichskanzler, 30 September 1935, Bundesarchiv Berlin/NS31/108; Littlejohn, *The SA*, 23; IMT, vol. 21:421; *Deutsches Nachrichtenbüro*, Volume 3 (Berlin), 20 April 1936.

20. "Eine Lebenfrage des deutschen Pferdesports," *Völkischer Beobachter*, 10/11 February 1935; IMT, 22:159; Affidavits of Karl Otto von der Borch and Richard Walle, NA Record Group 238, Transcripts of Hearings in Defense of Organizations, Boxes 7-9.

21. Krüger later transferred to the SS, eventually becoming Inspector of the Equestrian SS. Richtlinien für Reiterführer und Reiter für die Monate Okt./Nov., 7 September 1933, NA *T-354/194/3852388-90*.

22. SS-Reitersturm 4 to SS-Reiterstürme, SS-OA Rhein, 17 July 1934, NA *T-354/402/4114629*.

23. Führer-12 Reiterstandarte to SS-OA Nord, 22 April 1937, BA Koblenz/NS33/14.

24. Ibid.

25. Ibid.

26. Standartenbefehl 64, 7 September 1935, NA *T-175*/203/2744636; Auszug aus dem SS-Befehlsblatt 10, 15 October 1934, NA *T-354*/401/4112609.

27. Standartenbefehl 38, 27 March 1935, NA *T-175*/203/2744681.

28. 10. SS-Reiterstandarte, Verwaltung to SA-Reitersturm 3/48, 31 August 1938, NA *T-354*/444/4176649; Führer-SS-Reitersturm 2/10 to 10. SS-Reiterstandarte, 4 March 1938, NA *T-354*/443/4175355.

29. Kommandeur-SS-Hauptreitschule (Fegelein) to RFSS, 9 September 1938, NA *T-175*/37/2547211-13.

30. Ibid.

31. Ibid.

32. Werner Menzendorf, *Reitsport*, 243.

33. Excerpts from a letter from the *Deutsches Olympiade-Komitee für Reiterei* to Fegelein, 3 April 1939, NA *T-175*/37/2547163-65; Fegelein to RFSS, 6 April 1939, NA *T-175*/37/2547160-61.

34. Abschrift eines Briefes des Major Momm an SS-Standartenführer Fegelein, 5 April 1939, NA *T-175*/37/2547162.

35. Fegelein to RFSS, 6 April 1939, NA *T-175*/37/2547160-61; Persönlicher Stab, RFSS to Fegelein, 22 April 1939, NA *T-175*/37/2547159; Fegelein to RFSS, 13 April 1939, NA *T-175*/37/2547175-79..

36. Ibid.

37. Ibid.

38. The SS Main Riding School was well financed. In addition to Himmler's regular contributions, the Bavarian government donated substantial sums of money as did Weber's organization, *Das Braune Band*. RFSS to Siebert, 11 January 1938, NA *T-175*/37/2547250; RFSS to Weber, 27 May 1938, NA *T-175*/37/2547235; Fegelein to RFSS, 29 June 1939, NA *T-175*/37/2547251-54; RFSS, Persönlicher Stab to SS-Standartenführer Prof. Karl Diebitsch, 3 July 1939, NA *T-175*/37/2547149.

39. Harold Momm, *Pferde, Reiter, und Trophäen*, (Munich: Copress-Verlag, 1957), 173-74. Perhaps Momm never took Fegelein seriously and he had a similar impression of Christian Weber. He considered "the former stable hand" a fool for wanting to breed talented thoroughbreds in Bavaria, an area with insufficient pastures and grazing periods, and a generally unhealthy climate for horses. All of Germany's top breeding experts ignored Weber, Momm wrote.

Chapter 6

1. Arolsen was an isolated, rustic community in the northwest corner of Hessen-Nassau. The town was home to Prince Josias zu Waldeck-Pyrmont, the commander of *Fulda-Werra* who previously led SS Main Sector *Rhein*. Waldeck, one of the first nobles to join the SS, requested

that the headquarters of the *Fulda-Werra* be in his hometown. No equestrian unit existed in Arolsen, only the equestrian regiment's staff. The regiment rented three rooms for office space in Hause Arolsen from the main sector.

2. Robert John Shalka, "The 'General-SS' in Central Germany, 1937-1939: A Social and Institutional Study of SS-Main Sector Fulda-Werra" (Ph.D. diss., University of Wisconsin, 1972), 59-61.

3. Chefreiterführer SS to SS-Oberabschnittsreiterführer, 19 April 1934, NA *T-354*/400/4112517-9.

4. Ibid.

5. Führer-SS-Reiterstürme-SS OA Rhein to SS-OA Rhein, 4 July 1934, NA *T-354*/402/4114458; Stabsführer-SS-OA Rhein to SS-Amt, Reichsführung SS, 13 June 1934, NA *T-354*/400/4112479.

6. Rechnungsführer-SS-Reitersturm 5 to SS-Reitersturm in Frankfurt, 12 September 1934, NA *T-354*/402/4114665.

7. On one occasion, the SS postponed at the last minute an emergency roll call at the height of the harvest season without contacting Company 2. The company assembled and awaited further instructions, but no other units appeared. The company commander requested the mobilization exercise be accepted as one day of service since the men had so little time to devote to the SS. Führer-SS-Reiterstürme, SS-OA Rhein to SS-OA Rhein," 5 September 1934, NA *T-354*/402/4114371.

8. SS-Reitersturm 2, Oberursel to SS-Reiterstürme-SS-OA Rhein, 13 September 1934, NA *T-354*/400/4112328-30.

9. "Führer-SS-Reitersturm 4 to SS-Reiterstürme, SS-OA Rhein," 13 September 1934, NA *T-354*/400/4112332-33.

10. Ibid.

11. Ibid.

12. Freiwillige Feuerwehr Hattersheim, 5 September 1934, NA *T-354*/402/4114361; SS Reiterschar Eschborn to Selck, 2 September 1934, NA *T-354*/402/4114365.

13. SS Reitersturm 3 to SS Reitersturm-SS-OA Rhein, 23 July 1934, NA *T-354*/401/4113730; Führer-Sturm 3 to SS-Reitersturm-SS-OA Rhein, 19 October 1934, NA *T-354*/401/4113704; Führer-Reitersturm-SS-OA Rhein, 19 September 1934, NA *T-354*/400/4112331.

14. Führer-SS-OA Rhein to SS-Amt, 14 November 1934, NA *T-354*/402/4114683.

15. Various travel records for Oskar Hix, 13 September 1934, NA *T-354*/401/4112666; 22 September 1934, NA *T-354*/401/4112663; 10 October 1934, NA *T-354*/401/4112655; 2 November 1934, NA *T-354*/401/4112651-52; "Führer-SS-OA Rhein to SS-Amt, Reichsführung-SS," 21 September 1934, NA *T-354*/401/4113165.

16. Company strength reports, NA *T-354*/401/4113849, 4113857, 4113893, 4113914, 4113917; Verwaltungsführer-SS-Reitersturm-SS-OA Rhein, 13 March 1935, NA *T-354*/402/4114251.

17. Equestrian units also complained of a shortage of blacksmiths in the region. Führer-Reitersturms-SS-OA Rhein to SS-OA Rhein, 6 December 1934, NA *T-354*/402/4114311.

18. Travel Report, 3 April 1935, NA *T-354*/401/4112618; Shalka, "The 'General-SS' in Central Germany," 100.

19. Equestrian Company 5 dissolved in January 1937. Its members transferred to an infantry battalion of Regiment 5 in Simmein/Hunsruck. 10.SS-Reiterstandarte, Verwaltung to Verlag Deutsche Wehr, Oldenburg, 3 July 1937, NA *T-354*/444/4175824.

20. 10. SS-Reiterstandarte, 31 October 1936, NA *T-354*/481/4228270.

21. Ibid.

22. Führer-SS-Reitersturm 2/R10 to 10.SS-Reiterstandarte, 4 March 1938, NA *T-354*/443/4175355.

23. Führer-1/R10 to 10. SS-Reiterstandarte, 12 May 1938, NA *T-354*/445/4178133; Führer-1/R10 to 10.Reiterstandarte, 27 November 1937, NA *T-354*/445/4178108.

24. Shalka, "The 'General-SS' in Central Germany," 116.

25. Ibid., 117; Hans Ullrich to SS-Brigadeführer Hennicke, 17 December 1937, NA *T-354*/481/4228098-104.

26. Dr. Fritz-Herbert Wolff to Dr. Ullrich, 19 January 1938, NA *T-354*/481/4228082-89.

27. A new platoon also formed in Kassel. Ibid.; Zug Kassel, 1 December 1938, NA *T-354*/443/4175186.

28. Führer-10.SS-Reiterstandarte to SS-OA Fulda-Werra, 23 April 1937, NA *T-354*/443/4175504.

29. 10.SS-Reiterstandarte, Verwaltung to Verwaltungsamt-SS-OA Fulda-Werra, 9 January 1939, NA *T-354*/445/4178556.

30. Führer-67.Standarte to SS-Abschnitt XXVII, 1 August 1938, NA *T-354*/445/4178105; Führer 1/R10 to 10. SS-Reiterstandarte, 23 February 1938, NA *T-354*/443/4175368.

31. Führer-1/R10 to 10. SS-Reiterstandarte, 15 January 1938, NA *T-354*/445/4178113.

32. Führer-35. SS-Standarte to SS-OA Rhein, 30 April 1934, NA *T-354*/400/4112520; Stabsführer-SS-OA Rhein to 35. SS-Standarte, 28 April 1934, NA *T-354*/400/4112521.

33. Ibid.; Führer-Reiterstürme-SS-OA Rhein to SS-OA Rhein, 7 June 1934, NA *T-354*/401/4112684; 10.SS-Reiterstandarte to Zug Kassel, 1 December 1938, NA *T-354*/443/4175186.

34. 10.SS-Reiterstandarte, Verwaltung to Verwaltungsamt-SS-OA Rhein, 10 October 1936, NA *T-354*/418/4138451.

35. In January 1938, the regiment's medical unit dissolved. Only four of its members remained with the equestrian regiment. Führer-10.SS-Reiterstandarte to Führer-San R 10, 24 January 1938, NA *T-354*/445/4178120; Führer-San-Staffel R/10 to 10. SS-Reiterstandarte, 4 May 1937, NA *T-354*/444/4175829.

36. Wilhelm Schweizer to Führer-10. RS, 22 January 1937, NA *T-354*/445/4178205-06.

37. Ibid.

38. Erwin Selck to 10.SS-Reiterstandarte, 17 December 1937, NA *T-354*/444/4176758; Verwaltungschef-SS to 10.SS-Reiterstandarte, 16 February 1938, NA *T-354*/445/4178505; Rolf Becher to Heinrich, 18 December 1938, NA *T-354*/445/4177362.

39. Shalka, "The 'General-SS' in Central Germany, 378; Erwin Selck to 10.SS-Reiterstandarte, 17 December 1937, NA *T-354*/444/4176759; Niederschrift, 21 February 1938, NA *T-354*/444/4176723.

40. Dr. Georg Kränzlein to 10. SS-Reiterstandarte, 6 August 1937, NA *T-354*/444/4175593.

41. SS-Abschnitt I to RFSS, 5 July 1932, BDC, SS Officer File, Caspar Koenig.

42. Himmler sent a congratulatory letter to Koenig for the Munich company's success in a tournament in Wörishofen. Among the SS riders were Hermann and Waldemar Fegelein (their father Hanns also participated). RFSS to Koenig, 31 August 1933, and Dienstlaufbahn, BDC, Koenig.

43. Führer-SS-OA Rhein to SS-Amt, Reichsführung-SS, 17 October 1934, and Gauleitung Koblenz-Trier to Reichsführer-SS, 19 October 1934, BDC, Koenig.

44. Führer-SS-OA Rhein to Reichsführung-SS, 13 February 1935, Chef-Abteilung IV to Chef-SS-Amt, 7 November 1934, and Führer-SS-OA Rhein to Chef-Personalamt, RFSS, 27 November 1934, BDC, Koenig.

45. Dienstlaufbahn, and Führer-SS-OA Südwest to Chef-SS-Personalkanzlei, 26 April 1939, BDC, Koenig.

46. The General SS was financed by the Nazi Party. When an SS member joined the Waffen SS, a state financed organization, he effectively joined another organization and, therefore, his membership in the General SS was frozen. General SS members almost always assumed lower ranks when entering the Waffen SS.

47. Ibid.; Chef-SS-Personalhauptamt to Generalinspekteur-Verstärkten SS-Totenkopfstandarten, 14 December 1939, SS Card, BDC, Koenig.

48. SS Card, Carl von Pichl to SS-OA Mitte, and SS-OA Mitte to Reichsführung SS, BDC, SS Officer File, Carl von Pichl.

49. Personal-Bericht, 13 May 1937, and Beurteilung, 10 March 1939, BDC, von Pichl.

50. Stellenbesetzung, 17 March 1936, SS Card, and SS-OA Fulda-Werra to SS-OA Süd, BDC, von Pichl; SS Card, BDC, SS Officer File, Ludwig Lang.

51. Lebenslauf, and SS Card, BDC, SS Officer File, Rolf Becher.

52. Ibid.; Führer-10. SS-Reiterstandarte to Major Werner, 21 April 1939, NA *T-354*/445/4177311-12.

53. After World War II he authored several books on horsemanship.

54. Führer-6. Reiterstandarte to SS-OA West, 24 June 1937, and Personal-Bericht, 30 March 1937, BDC, Becher.

55. Führer-SS-OA West to SS-Personalamt, 7 May 1937, and Führer-SS-OA Fulda-Werra to Chef-SS-Hauptamt, 10 January 1938, BDC, Becher; NA *T-354*/444/4176233.

56. As might be expected, several members of the regiment also held membership in various riding clubs. Untitled document, 27 June 1939, NA *T-354*/445/4177069; Gesamterfolge der SS-Reiterei, (1938), NA *T-354*/445/4177091.

57. Führer-10.SS-Reiterstandarte to SS-OA Fulda-Werra, 14 September 1938, NA *T-354*/444/4175988.

58. Inspekteur-SS-Reiterei to SS-Oberabschnitt Reiterführer Fulda-Werra, 12 September 1938, NA *T-175*/37/2547273; 10.SS-Reiterstandarte, Verwaltung to Verwaltungsamt-SS-OA Fulda-Werra, 6 October 1938 NA *T-354*/444/4176636; Dr. Fr. H. Wolff to 10.SS-Reiterstandarte, 1 November 1938, NA *T-354*/445/4178565.

59. Becher to Mayor Werner, 21 April 1939, NA *T-354*/445/4177311-12.

60. Ibid.; 10.SS-Reiterstandarte, Verwaltung to Verwaltungsamt-SS-OA Fulda-Werra, 8 August 1939, NA *T-354*/444/4175886; Erfolge des Turnierstalls der 10. SS-Reiterstandarte, NA *T-354*/445/4177038-39; Becher to F. Rinner, 21 April 1939, NA *T-354*/445/4177315.

61. Shalka, "The 'General-SS' in Central Germany," 243.

Chapter 7

1. William L. Combs, *The Voice of the SS: A History of the SS Journal 'Das Schwarze Korps'* (New York: Peter Lang, 1989), 20.

2. Standartenbefehl 71, 14 November 1935, NA T-175/203/2744610.

3. Jackson J. Spielvogel, *Hitler and Nazi Germany: A History* (Englewood Cliffs, New Jersey: Prentice Hall, 1988), 101; Gerhard Rempel, *Hitler's Children: The Hitler Youth and the SS* (Chapel Hill: The

University of North Carolina Press, 1989), 107; J. E. Farquharson, *The Plough and the Swastika: The NSDAP and Agriculture in Germany 1928-45* (London and Beverly Hills: Sage Publications, 1976), 59.

4. Johnpeter Horst Grill, "The Nazi Party's Rural Propaganda Before 1928," *Central European History*, 15 (June 1982), 171; Heinz Höhne, *The Order of the Death's Head*, 51; Rempel, *Hitler's Children*, 108.

5. Grill, "The Nazi Party's Rural Propaganda Before 1928," 152-53; Höhne, *The Order of the Death's Head*, 51.

6. "Standartenbefehl 77," 13 January 1936, NA T-175/203/2744580.

7. Combs, *The Voice of the SS*, 18-25.

8. Jeffrey Allen Henson, "The Role of Das Schwarze Korps in the SS's Campaign Against the Catholic Church," Master's Thesis, Mississippi State University, 1997, 64.

9. "SS-Reiterei," DSK, 6 March 1935, 6.

10. Ibid.; "Reiter im Grenzland," DSK, 23 July 1936, 4; "Wer will zur Kavallerie," VB, 19 December 1936, 2.

11. "SS Reiterei," DSK, 6 March 1936, 6.

12. "Seid überall wahrhafte SS Männer," DSK, 5 August 1937, 4; "Deutschlands Schönste Turnieranstalt," DSK, 5 August 1937, 4; "Um den Reiterpreis des Reichsführers-SS," DSK, 17 October 1935.

13. "SS Reiterführer in Ostpreussen," DSK, 24 October 1935, 4.

14. "Arbeitstag in Masuren," DSK, 10 December 1936, 4.

15. For instance see "SS-Reitersiege auch in Stuttgart," DSK, 27 March 1935, 12; "930 Siege und Plazierrungen," DSK, 11 February 1937, 3; "Rückblick auf 1937: Ehrentafel der SS Reiter," DSK, 6 January 1938, 3.

16. "Münchener Turnier in der Universitätsreitschule," DSK, 29 May 1935, 4; "Prachtvolle Leistungen," DSK, 4 June 1936, 3; "Ehrentafel der SS Reiter," DSK, 6 January 1938, 3; "Grosse SS Reiterwettkämpfe in Karlsruhe," DSK, 19 June 1935, 3; "Reiter-SS im Grenzland," DSK, 23 July 1936, 14; "Um den Reiterpreis des Reichsführers-SS," DSK, 17 October 1935, 4.

17. Roger Manvell and Heinrich Fraenkel, *Himmler* (New York: G. P. Putnam's Sons, 1965), 48; Combs, *The Voice of the SS*, 376; "Reichs-Reiterwettkämpfer der SS," DSK, 6 August 1936, 3.

18. "SS Reiterei," DSK, 6 March 1935, 6; "Grundlegende Ausbildung der SS," DSK, 23 March 1939, 4.

19. "Ein Reiter ohne Furcht und Tadel," DSK, February 1935, 3; The German phrase Ein Ritter ohne Furcht und Tadel translates into English as a knight in shining armor. DSK cleverly substituted the word horseman (Reiter) for the word knight (Ritter) to describe Axel Holst.

20. Werner Menzendorf, *Reitsport: Ein Bildband*, 86, 152.

21. "Ein Reiter ohne Furcht und Tadel," DSK, February, 1935, 3; "Beste Gesamtwertung beim Internationalen Reitturnier in Riga," DSK, 15 September 1935, 3; "SS Reiterführer in Ostpreussen," DSK, 24 October 1935, 4.

22. "Das Glück der Erde," DSK, 19 August 1937, 4; "SS-Reitschule Forst," DSK, 13 August 1936, 3; Erster Sieg der SS-Reitschule Forst," DSK, 7 May 1936, 3.

23. "Die SS-Hauptreitschule," DSK, 18 August 1938, 4; "Die Neue SS-Hauptreitschule in München," DSK, 22 July 1937, 3.

24. Ibid.; "Die SS-Hauptreitschule," DSK, 18 August 1938, 4; "Die Neue SS-Hauptreitschule in München," DSK, 22 July 1937, 3; For victories by members of the school see "Im ersten Jahre ihres Bestehens," DSK, 9 December 1937, 4; "SS Reiter siegen in Rom," DSK, 9 June 1938, 4.

25. "Neue Reithalle in Berlin," DSK, 8 December 1938, 4.

26. "Reithalle aus eigenen Mitteln erbaut," DSK, 13 March 1935, 3.

27. Ibid.

28. "SS Begleitkommando für Mussolini," DSK, 7 October 1937, 4; "SS Betreute die Diplomaten," DSK, 24 September 1936, 3; DSK also praised the actions of a member of Equestrian Regiment 7 as a exemplary act of camaraderie for saving a fellow horsemen from drowning. DSK, 3 July 1935.

29. "SS Reiter in Polen," DSK, 23 November 1939, 3.

30. "Kavallerie der Waffen SS," DSK, 3 September 1942, 3; "SS Reiter griefen an," DSK, 1 October 1942, 3; "Der Kampf nach Osten," DSK, 24 January 1943, 6.

31. "Das Ritterkreuz für SS-Standartenführer Hermann Fegelein," DSK, 2 April 1942, 6; "Das Eichenlaub für SS-Oberführer Fegelein," DSK, 7 January 1943, 6; "Der Reiter Hermann Fegelein," DSK, 24 January 1943, 6, 7; "Für die Waffen SS," DSK, 7 September 1944, 6.

Chapter 8

1. Gunnar C. Boehnert, "The Third Reich and the Problem of 'Social Revolution': German Officers and the SS" in *Germany in the Age of Total War*, eds. V. Berghahn and M. Kitchen (London: Croom Helm; Totowa, N.J.: Barnes and Noble, 1981), 203; Felix Kersten, *The Kersten Memoirs* trans. Constantine Fitzgibbon and James Oliver (New York: The MacMillan Co., 1957), 245.

2. Boehnert, "The Third Reich and the Problem of 'Social Revolution,'" 203.

3. This study distinguishes between leaders and officers. A leader had control over an entire equestrian unit whereas an officer was simply

one of his subordinates who often led an equestrian company. Statistics for the equestrian units were derived using data gathered from the SS *Dienstalterslisten*, the SS officer registry, for 1934 to 1937, National Archives Microfilm *T-175* roll 204, 1938 National Archives Microfilm *T-175* roll 205, and 1942-44, National Archives Microfilm *T-611* roll 2 [hereafter cited as DAL]; and from the personnel files of equestrian unit leaders, Berlin Document Center [hereafter cited as BDC, Equestrian Leaders]; Johnpeter Grill, "Nobles in the SS: Old Wine in New Bottles?" Unpublished paper presented at the annual meeting of the Southern Historical Association, New Orleans, Louisiana, 31 October-3 November, 1990, 7, 1.

4. DAL; BDC, Equestrian Leaders; Herbert F. Ziegler, *Nazi Germany's New Aristocracy: The SS Leadership, 1925-1939* (Princeton: Princeton University Press, 1989), 63.

5. Lebenslauf, BDC, SS Officer File, Hans von Treichel.

6. Undated and untitled submission, Vernehnmung, 7 May 1934, Führer of SS-OA XII to SS-OA Südost, 11 April 1934, and SS-OA Ost to Chef-SS-Hauptamt, 9 March 1937, BDC, von Treichel.

7. Roger Manvell and Heinrich Fraenkel, *Heinrich Himmler* (London: Heinemann, 1965), 31; Karl Otman von Aretin, "Der bayerische Adel. Von der Monarchie Zum Dritten Reich," in *Bayern in der NS-Zeit*, Herausgegeben von Martin Broszat, Elke Fröhlich, and Anton Grossmann (München, Wien: R. Oldenbourg Verlag, 1981), 544, 545.

8. Lebenslauf, SS Card, and Chef-Personalkanzlei to RFSS 10 February 1939, BDC, von Salviati; "Eine Stolze Bilanz," *DSK*, 12 January 1938, 4.

9. Chef-SS Gericht to Inspekteur-SS Reitschulen, 10 March 1939, Chef-Sicherheitspolizei und SD to SS-Personalamt, 17 September 1944, Chef-SS-Personalhauptamt to RFSS, 9 September 1944, and RFSS to Chef-Sicherheitspolizei und SD, 14 October 1944, BDC, von Salviati.

10. DAL; BDC, Equestrian Leaders.

11. Ibid.; *DAL*; Ziegler, *Nazi Germany's New Aristocracy*, 63.

12. Ibid.; *DAL*; BDC, Equestrian Leaders.

13. Ibid.; *DAL*; Ziegler, *Nazi Germany*, 63.

14. Ibid., 64; *DAL*; BDC, Equestrian Leaders.

15. "Ein 60 Jähriger SS Reiter," *DSK*, 3 April 1935, 4.

16. Ziegler, *Nazi Germany's New Aristocracy*, 116, 118.

17. Ibid., 104, 105; BDC, Equestrian Leaders.

18. Ibid.; Ziegler, *Nazi Germany's New Aristocracy*, 114, 115.

19. "Führer-OA West to SS-Personalamt," 4 June 1937, SS Officer File, Hans von Wolff, BDC.

20. . BDC, Equestrian Leaders.

21. SS Card, Stammrollen-Auszug, and Chef-SS-Personalkanzlei to SS-Obergruppenführer Kurt Daluege, 13 May 1938, BDC, SS Officer File, Rudiger Wilhelm von Woikowski-Biedau.

22. Lorenz to Chef-SS-Personalkanzlei, 8 February 1938, and Chef-SS-Gericht to RFSS, SS-Personalkanzlei, 17 February 1938, BDC, von Woikowski-Biedau.

23. A summary of the SS court's findings dated 23 March 1937, BDC, von Woikowski-Biedau.

24. Ibid.

25. Ibid.

26. Einleitung (undated), Vehrnehmungsniederschrift, 5 December 1936, and Von Woikowski-Biedau to Heissmeyer, undated, BDC, von Woikowski-Biedau.

27. Vernehmungsniederschrift, 3 November 1936, BDC, von Woikowski-Biedau.

28. Chef-SS-Hauptamt to SS-Gericht, 5 April 1937, and Lorenz to Chef-SS-Gericht, 4 November 1937, BDC, von Woikowski-Biedau.

29. Reichsschatzmeister-NSDAP (Munich) to Himmler, 14 January 1938, RFSS to SS-Gericht, 23 February 1938, and Lorenz to Chef-Personalkanzlei, 8 February 1938, BDC, von Woikowski-Biedau.

30. Führer-SS-Reiterabschnitt VIII to SS-OA Mitte, 17 March 1936, Personal-Bericht und Beurteilung, undated, and Wexel to Personalreferent beim RFSS, 10 January 1937, BDC, SS Officer File, Peter Wexel.

31. At one time, the SS regarded Carl von Pichl, commander of Equestrian Regiment 10, as a good replacement for Wexel, especially since von Pichl had good rapport with army officers and Nazi Party officials active in horsemanship. The transfer never occurred and the SS dissolved Equestrian Regiment 22. Führer-SS-OA Elbe to Wexel, date unknown, Vernehmungsniederschrift, 12 November 1937, Chef-SS-Personalkanzlei to SS-Gericht, München, 4 November 1938, and Führer-SS-Reiterabschnitt VII to SS-OA Elbe, 9 May 1936, BDC, Wexel.

32. Lebenslauf, Führer-SS-OA Südost to Führer-12.SS-Reiterstandarte (Herde), 15 February 1935, Führer-SS-OA Südost to Herde, 26 February 1935, Gauorganizationsleiter to Führer-SS-OA Südost, 27 February 1936, and Führer-SS-Reiterabschnitt III to Herde, 22 March 1936, BDC, SS Officer File, Oswald Herde.

33. Führer-SS-OA Südost to RFSS, 17 August 1937, Vernehmungsniederschrift, 23 September 1937, and RFSS to Herde, 12 October 1937, BDC, Herde.

34. Lebenslauf, and Dienstlaufbahn, BDC, SS Officer File, Erdmann Skudlarek.

35. Ibid.; Führer-SS-OA Südost to Chef-SS-Hauptamt, 26 September 1935, BDC, Skudlarek.

36. SS Card, Beurteilung, and 19 August 1929, Dienstleistungszeugnis, 1 November 1933, BDC, SS Officer File, Jacob Wein.

37. Führer-SS-OA Südwest to RFSS, 10 October 1936, and Badischer Finanz- und Wirtschaftminister to Reichsführer-Schutzstaffeln-NSDAP, 18 December 1937, BDC, Wein.

38. Wein to SS-Hauptamt, 20 March 1933, and RFSS to Wein, 29 September 1938, BDC, Wein.

39. Ibid., Wein to SS-Hauptamt, 20 March 1938, a letter to Chef-Verwaltungsamt, 16 August 1938, and RFSS to Wein, 11 February 1939, BDC, Wein.

40. SS Card, Dienstleistungszeugnis, 8 March 1938, and Struve to Mazuw, 23 March 1938, BDC, SS Officer File, Karl Struve.

41. Vernehmungsniederschrift, 4 March 1938, Struve to SS-Reichsführer, SS-Gericht, 7 May 1938, and RFSS to Struve, 28 August 1938, BDC, Struve.

42. Chef-SS-Gericht to Chef-SS-Totenkopfverbände und Konzentrationslager, 8 November 1938, Führer-SS-Totenkopfverbände und Konzentrationslager to Personalchef, RFSS, 11 November 1938, and Führer-SS-OA Nordost to Chef-SS-Personalhauptamt, 4 March 1941, BDC, Struve.

43. SS Card, Dienstbeurteilung, 8 April 1935, Beurteilung-SS-Untersturmführer Gilhofer, 20 December 1935, and Gilhofer to Chef-SS Hauptamt, 9 July 1935, BDC, SS Officer File, Herbert Gilhofer.

44. Ibid., Personal=Bericht, RFSS to Gilhofer, 20 December 1935, BDC, Gilhofer.

45. SS Card, Chef-Personalkanzlei to SS-OA Nord, 27 March 1939, Beurteilung, 7 September 1938, Führer-SS-OA Donau to Chef-SS Hauptamt, 11 August 1938, and Chef-Personalamt to Inspekteur-SS Reitwesens, 16 August 1938, BDC, Gilhofer.

46. Führer-SS-OA Nord to Chef-SS Hauptamt, 31 March 1939, Inspekteur-SS-Reiterei to Personalamt-SS, 14 April 1939, and Bestätigung, 1 June 1939, BDC, Wein.

47. Hahn replaced former leader Herbert von Wuthenau who was transferred because his wife was once married to an army officer active in various equestrian organizations in East Prussia. Von Wuthenau and the SS thought it wise to transfer to another equestrian post since his ability to command an equestrian regiment could have been adversely affected by the behavior of his wife's previous husband. Von Wuthenau eventually ended up in the SS Race and Settlement Office. SS Card, Führer-

SS-OA Rhein to SS-Hauptamt, SS-Personalamt, 3 October 1936, BDC, SS Officer File, Herbert von Wuthenau. SS Card, Dienstlaufbahn, and Führer-1.SS-Reiterstandarte to Führer-SS-OA Nordost, BDC, SS Officer File, Philipp Hahn.

48. Ibid., Chef-SS-Personalkanzlei to Stellvertreter-Führers, 19 February 1938, Nationalsozialistische Deutsche Arbeiterpartei to RFSS, 14 March 1938, and Oberbürgermeiser-Stadt Pirmasens to SS-OA Nordost, 16 February 1939, BDC, Hahn.

49. SS Card, and Lebenslauf, BDC, SS Officer File, Dr. Hans Jacobson.

50. Bericht, BDC, Jacobsen.

51. A report to RFSS, SS Gericht, 19 July 1939, RFSS to Jacobson, 23 June 1941, and Chef-Hauptamt-SS Gericht to Chef-Personalhauptamt, 12 March 1943, BDC, Jacobsen.

52. Lebenslauf, and Dienstlaufbahn, BDC, SS Officer File, Dr. August Schwedler.

53. Ibid., Schwedler to Gaubeaftragten-Gau Berlin-Winterhilfswerk, 24 January 1939, and NSDAP, Amt für Volkswohlfahrt, Gau Berlin to SS-Hauptamt, 26 January 1939, BDC, Schwedler.

54. SS Oberführer Dr. Katz to Chef-Rasse und Siedlungsamt, 8 September 1943, BDC, Schwedler.

55. Jonathon Petropoulos, *Art as Politics in the Third Reich* (Chapel Hill and London: The University of North Carolina Press, 1996), 129.

56. Among them was Sepp Syr, a former member of the SS Main Riding School in Munich who transferred to von Künsberg's unit from the *Leibstandarte* Adolf Hitler, a Waffen SS unit. He was in charge of training and equipping the *Sonderkommando*.

57. A fourth battalion was later deployed in North Africa. Petropoulos, *Art as Politics*, 148-50; Personalbeurteilung, 8 June 1942, BDC, SS Officer File, Sepp Syr.

58. Eugon Kogon, *The Theory and Practice of Hell*, 81; Dienstlaufbahn, and Beförderungen in der Waffen-SS, 5 March 1943, BDC, SS Officer File, Hermann Florstedt.

59. Lebenslauf, and Dienstleistungszeugnis, (date illegible), BDC, Florstedt.

60. Another controversy developed because of his reluctance to pay off a debt and the matter was referred to the deputy *Führer*. Tom Segev, *Soldiers of Evil: The Commandants of the Nazi Concentration Camps* (New York: McGraw-Hill Book Company, 1987), 150; Führer-SS-Reiterabschnitt VI to Reichsbahndirektion, 23 October 1935, SS-OA Südwest to RFSS, Chef-SS-Hauptamt, 10 March 1936, and Stabsführer OA Rhein to Reichsführung-SS, 29 June 1936, BDC, Florstedt.

61. Dienstlaufbahn, BDC, Florstedt; Segev, *Soldiers of Evil*, 150.

Chapter 9

1. *SS Kavallerie im Osten*, 1; Yerger, *Riding East*, 8.

2. Führer-SS-OA Main to 17. SS-Reiterstandarte, 6 September 1939, NA *T-354*/358/4063822.

3. Aufstellung einer berittenen SS-Sondereinheit, 11 September 1939, NA *T-354*/358/4063564-65; Führer-SS-OA Main to 17. SS-Reiterstandarte, 10 October 1939, *T-354*/358/4063572.

4. RFSS to Inspektion-SS-Reiterei, 14 September 1939, NA *T-175*/37/2547256; RFSS to Chef-SS-Hauptamt, 31 November 1939, NA *T-175*/37/2547255.

5. Yerger, *Riding East*, 40, 42.

6. Magill joined the SS in 1933, enlisting with Equestrian Regiment 7, after serving in various cavalry units in the army from 1918-1933. He quickly transferred to SS Officer School Braunschweig as a riding instructor and commander of the school's mounted unit until called upon in September 1939, by Fegelein. Before the war, Magill was a moderately successful tournament rider. Commander of Squadron 3, Rudolf Ruge, was an instructor at the SS Officer School Bad Tölz. Yerger, *Riding East*, 40-42.

7. SS-und Selbstschutzführer im General-Gouvernment Polen to Führer-Totenkopfstandarten, 23 November 1939, NA *T-354*/654/000943-46.

8. To promote camaraderie with German armed forces, the regiment later established an officers club in Warsaw, open to all officers of the army, the police and the SD. "SS Reiter in Polen," *DSK*, 23 November 1939, 3; Casino-Ordnung, NA *T-175*/219/2756974.

9. Yerger, *Riding East*, 39-44.

10. Ibid.

11. Einsätze der 1. SS-Totenkopf-Reiterstandarte, undated, NA *T-354*/735/000107-21.

12. Despite their imposing size, horses are relatively delicate animals susceptible to a variety of diseases, some contagious. They require sleep, generally at night, and an abundance of water and food — twelve to twenty pounds of fodder daily, depending on the breed. The best fodder, oats, was usually mixed with hay and straw, although horses could also graze on grass, and even roots and aquatic plants, when feed was limited, as during the SS cavalry's later operations in the Pripet Marshes. But grazing was time-consuming; it could take up to eight hours a day. A shortage of horses in February 1940 forced the SS cavalry to buy from Poles. Infested with lice and other ailments, they could be used only after veterinary treatment. Yerger, *Riding East*, 47, 55; R. L. DiNardo, *Mechanized Juggernaut or Military Anachronism? Horse and the German Army of World War II* (New York: Greenwood Press, 1991), 11.

13. Einsätze der 1.SS-Totenkopf-Reiterstandarte, NA *T-354/735/* 000107-21.

14. Reichenwallner joined Fegelein's unit after serving in Equestrian Regiment 7.

15. Einsätze der Schwadronen nach dem 15 November 1939 nach der Aufstellung der 1.SS-Totenkopf-Reiterstandarte, NA *T-354/654/* 000737-38.

16. Reichenwallner to Stab-1.SS-Totenkopf-Reiterstandarte im Generalgouvernment Polen, 14 January 1940, NA *T-354/654/000787-88*.

17. Einsätze der 1. SS-Totenkopf-Reiterstandarte, NA *T-354/735/* 000107-21.

18. Gefechtsbericht der 1.SS-Totenkopf-Reiterstandarte, 10 April 1940, NA *T-354/739/000759-67*.

19. Ibid.

20. Erfahrungsbericht zum Gefechtsbericht vom 10.4.1940, NA *T-354/654/000825*.

21. Yerger, *Riding East*, 57-58.

22. Ibid., 63.

23. Ibid.

24. Ibid., 70; Dr. K.-G. Klietmann, *Die Waffen-SS: eine Dokumentation* (Osnabrück: Verlag "Der Freiwillige," 1965), 355.

25. Yerger, *Riding East*, 73, 75, 88-92.

26. Ready, Aim, Fire!

27. In addition to the two SS cavalry regiments, other elements of the Headquarters Staff were the 1st and 2nd Brigades, SS Volunteer Regiment Hamburg, and the Begleitungsbattaillon RFSS (Escort Battalion Reichsführer-SS). Himmler thus had over 25,000 men under his personal command. Yehoshua Büchler, "Kommandostab Reichsführer-SS: Himmler's Personal Murder Brigades in 1941," *Holocaust and Genocide Studies* I (1986), 14.

28. Ibid, 16.

29. Matthew Cooper, *The Nazi War Against Soviet Partisans, 1941-1944* (New York: Stein and Day, 1979), 35; Yerger, *Riding East*, 117.

30. Richtlinien für die Durchkämmung un Durchstreifung von Sumpf durch Reitereinheiten, NA *T-175/124/2598661-64*.

31. Quoted in Büchler, "Kommandostab Reichsführer-SS," 20.

32. Hermann Fegelein recruited Gustav Lombard to serve with him in Poland from Equestrian Regiment 7.

33. The Bicycle Reconnaissance Detachment of about 500 men was placed under the 162nd Infantry Division to confront actual partisans, and thus it had a lesser role in the slaughter of Jews. It did, however, participate in rounding up Jews. Büchler, "Kommandostab Reichsführer-

SS," 15; *Unsere Ehre heisst Treue: Kriegstagebuch des Kommandostabes Reichsführer-SS* (Vienna, Frankfurt, Zurich: Europa, 1965), 215-16.

34. *Justiz und NS-Verbrechen*, 22 vols. (Amsterdam: University Press, 1968-81), 20: 47-48.

35. *Unsere Ehre heisst Treue*, 217-20; Karla Müller-Tupath, *Reichsführers gehorsamster Becher: Eine Deutsche Karriere* Fulda: Konkret Literatur Verlag, 1982), 33-34.

36. Far from turning a blind eye away from the slaughter, several army personnel arrived during the murder campaign in Pinsk to request Jewish craftsmen. They left with about six or eight Jews. The SS Cavalry also kept Jews with requisite skills. *Justiz und NS-Verbrechen*, 20:54.

37. Crowds gathered to watch the killings and locals collected the victims discarded clothes and other items. The killers kept the most valuable loot. Magill, von dem Bach-Zelewski, and Fegelein also went to Pinsk to observe the killings. Ibid., 50-52. Ruth Bettina Birn, "Two Kinds of Reality? Case Studies on Anti-Partisan Warfare During the Eastern Campaign" in *From Peace to War: Germany, Soviet Russia and the World, 1939-1941*, ed. Bernd Wegner (Providence: Berghahn Books, 1997), 280.

38. "Zwischenbericht," Zentrale Stelle, Ludwigsburg, 204, AR-Z 296/60, 357.

39. Ibid., 1207; IMT, 22:328-29.

40. Ibid.

41. Some execution figures for Pinsk reach 11,000 for the three day operation. See Büchler, "Kommandostab Reichsführer-SS," 17; During the so-called anti-partisan operation, Magill reported finding no communists because most reports on partisan activity were exaggerated. *Unsere Ehre heisst Treue*, 220.

42. The *Ordnungspolizei* had reported killing 30,000 by that date. "Nazi Messages Reveal Secret of Jews' Slaughter," *The Times* (London), 19 May 1997, 7; Müller-Tupath, *Reichsführers gehorsamster Becher*, 33.

43. Fegelein's figure for the total number of "plunderers" executed, 15,378, falls below the sum of the number of executions reported by various cavalry units. Perhaps his total represents the entire number killed by the Cavalry Brigade when operating independently of other murder squadrons. *Unsere Ehre heisst Treue*, 214-16.

44. Yehoshua Büchler estimates 50,000 executions of Jews by the Cavalry Brigade during its operations in the Pripet Marshes. Büchler, "Kommandostab Reichsführer-SS," 20.

45. Bericht über den Einsatz der SS Kav. Brigade im Winter 1941/42, 11 February 1942, NA *T-175*/111/2635510-29.

46. Yerger, *Riding East*, 167-71; Lombard to Fegelein, undated, NA *T-175*/109/26322827.

47. Fegelein to Chef-Stab-SS-Gruppenführer Jüttner, 2 April 1942, NA *T-175*/109/2632822.

48. R.L. Dinardo and Austin Bay, "Horse-Drawn Transport in the German Army," *Journal of Contemporary History*, 23 (1988), 134; Stein, *The Waffen SS*, 221.

49. By the end of 1943, roughly 52 percent of Equestrian SS personnel had been drafted into the army, 20 percent were drafted into the Waffen SS, and 3 percent ended up in labor and other services. Only 2,762 men remained officially in the Equestrian SS, most of whom were either especially needed on the homefront or were waiting to be drafted into the army, or were unfit for combat. *Statistisch-Wissenschaftliches: Stärke der SS am 31 Dezember 1943* (Berlin: Institut des Reichsführers-SS, 1944), NA *T-175*/141/2668916-46. Vorgeschichte der SS-Kavallerie-Division, undated, NA *T-354*/640/000006-000016.

50. In 1943, the "paper war" included, among other things, sending ridiculous memoranda to SS horsemen serving in the army, reminding them to abide by the SS requirement to get married. Führer- 10. SS-Reiterstandarte to Führer-Führungstab Sturm 1, 2, 3, February 1943, NA *T-354*/444/4176439; 10. SS-Reiterstandarte to Dr. Wolff, 24 July 1941, NA *T-354*/444/4176407; Führer-Führungstab 3./10. SS-Reiterstandarte to 10.RS, 25 July 1942, NA *T-354*/444/4176466.

51. The German army briefly deployed a cavalry division in Russia but withdrew it in the fall of 1941. It was converted into the 24th Panzer Division. Dinardo and Bay, "Horse-Drawn Transport in the German Army," 141 n. 36; Stein, *The Waffen SS*, 203, 233; Yerger, *Riding East*, 209.

52. Gerald Reitlinger, *The SS: Alibi of a Nation* (Englewood Cliffs, New Jersey: Prentice Hall, Inc. 1956), 239.

53. Klietmann, *Die Waffen SS: eine Dokumentation*, 233, 303; Stein, *The Waffen SS*, 297-98.

54. Kommandeur-Hauptreitschule to RFSS, and Personal-Bericht, BDC, SS Officer File, Hermann Fegelein; "Der Reiter Hermann Fegelein," *DSK*, 24 January 1943, 6.

55. Fegelein to von Jena (Führungshauptamt), 25 February 1941, NA *T-175*/201/2742363-67.

56. Fegelein to Bittrich, NA *T-354*/654/000868-71.

57. Ibid.; Fegelein to Himmler, 16 November 1941, NA *T-175*/37/2547092-95.

58. Fegelein to von Jena (Führungshauptamt), 25 February 1941, NA *T-175*/201/2742363.

59. Verzeichnis, undated, NA *T-175*/37/25447124.

60. When asked by the Gestapo, Death's Head commander Theodore

Eicke denied any affiliation between his units and the Munich school. The riding academy, Eicke insisted, was subordinate only to Himmler. Geheime Staatspolizei to Inspekteur-Sicherheitspolizei und-SD, 8 March 1940, NA *T-175*/37/2547122-23; Suchung in der SS-Hauptreitschule in Riem (Gestapo report), 7 March 1940, NA *T-175*/37/2547120-21. Suching in der SS-Hauptreitschule Riem (SD report), 5 April 1940, NA *T-175*/37/2547118-19.

     61. Fegelein to RFSS, 14 March 1940, NA *T-175*/37/2547129-33; RFSS to Heydrich, 14 March 1940, NA *T-175*/37/2547134.

     62. RFSS, Hauptamt-SS-Gericht to RFSS, 21 May 1941, NA *T-175*/123/2648547.

     63. The letter was never sent, however, because the two discussed the matter during a meeting. RFSS to Fegelein, 31 February 1940, NA *T-175*/37/2547138-39.

     64. Aktenvermerk, 21 April 1941, NA *T-175*/37/2547104-06.

     65. RFSS to Tondock, 19 May 1941, NA *T-175*/37/2547100; Tondock to RFSS, 5 August 1941, NA *T-175*/37/2547097.

     66. RFSS to Tondock, 19 May 1941, NA *T-175*/37/2547100.

     67. *Kriegstagebuch von dem Bach-Zelewski*, BA Berlin, R 020/0000456, fol.1-117.

     68. Chef-Stab-SS Führungshauptamt to Kommandeur-SS Kavallerie-Brigade, 7 May 1942, NA *T-354*/643/507-08; Der Hermann Fegelein," *DSK*, 24 January 1943, 7; Himmler to Fegelein, 1 December 1942, Aktenotiz, 13 May 1943, "Eichenlaubträger SS-Oberführer Hermann Fegelein" (*Völkischer Boebachter* article dated 30 January 1943), BDC, SS Officer File, Hermann Fegelein.

     69. Fegelein had become sufficiently influential to be able to promote the career of one of his close associates. Kurt Becher joined Fegelein's cavalry units in the East after serving in the Equestrian SS. He was a squadron leader and an ordinance officer in the SS Cavalry Brigade before he became Fegelein's adjutant. He served with Fegelein through 1943. In 1944 Himmler sent Becher on a special assignment to Hungary to secure horses and equipment for the SS. There he took control of a major armaments and equipment factory and assisted in Adolf Eichmann's scheme to "trade" Jews scheduled for deportation (his actual role has not yet been determined). In 1945 he became special commissioner for all concentration camps. Himmler to Fegelein, 19 May 1943, Vorschlag für die Verleihung des Deutschen Kreuzes in Gold, 7 October 1943, BDC, Fegelein; Muller-Tupath, *Reichsführers gehorsamster Becher*, 8,9, 82, 121.

     70. Several scandals in early 1944 destroyed Hitler's faith in the Abwehr. Its head, Admiral Wilhelm Canaris, was arrested as a spy and

later hanged. Personal Verfügung 15 June 1944, BDC, Fegelein; IMT, 15:581; IMT, 13:325; IMT, 16:493; Peter Black, *Ernst Kaltenbrunner: Ideological Soldier of the Third Reich* (Princeton: Princeton University Press, 1984), 194.

71. H.R. Trevor-Roper ed., *The Bormann Letters: The Private Correspondence Between Martin Bormann and His Wife From January 1943 to April 1945* (London: Weidenfeld and Nicolson, 1954), xii, 152; H.R. Trevor-Roper, *The Last Days of Hitler* (New York: The MacMillan Co., 1947) 157.

72. Jochen von Lang, *The Secretary, Martin Bormann: The Man Who Manipulated Hitler*, trans. Christa Armstrong and Peter White (New York: Random House, 1978), 330-31.

73. His marriage did little to quench his appetite for members of the opposite sex. Joachimsthaler, based on the testimony of two secretaries in the bunker, believes Fegelein carried on an affair with his sister-in-law, and Hitler's future bride, Eva. Anton Joachimsthaler, *The Last Days of Hitler: The Legends, the Evidence, the Truth*, trans. Helmut Bögler, (London: Arms and Armour Press, 1996).

74. "Für die Waffen-SS," *DSK*, 7 September 1944, 6; Pressenotiz, BDC, SS Officer File, Hermann Fegelein.

75. H. R. Trevor-Roper, *The Last Days of Hitler* (New York: The MacMillan Company, 1947), 158-60, 170-71, 247-48.

76. James P. O'Donnell, *The Bunker* (Boston: Houghton Mifflin Company, 1978), 190-215.

77. Interview of Hans Fegelein by Walter Hirschfeld, 22 September 1945, U.S. Forces European Theater-Military Service Center, Institut Für Zeitgeschichte, F 135/3.

Chapter 10

1. *Nazi Conspiracy and Aggression: Opinion and Judgement*, 102; IMT, 1:255-56.

2. Ibid., 22:515.

3. Ibid., 22:158-162.

4. Affidavits of Richard Walle and Karl Otto von der Borch, Record Group 238, National Archives Collection of World War II War Crimes Records, Transcripts of Hearings in Defense of Organizations, 25 June 1946, Boxes 7-9.

5. Affidavit of Wilhelm von Woikowski-Biedau, Record Group 238, National Archives Collection of War Crimes Records, Records in Defense of Organizations, Box 4.

6. IMT 20:433.

7. Ibid., 21:352.

8. *Das Schwarze Korps* publicized the activities of SS riders in the cavalry units and in 1942 the SS published *SS Kavallerie im Osten* which promoted the connection between the Equestrian SS and the SS Cavalry.

9. Helmut Krausnick and Hans-Heinrich Wilhelm, *Die Truppe des Weltanschauungskrieges: Die Einsatzgruppen der Sicherheitspolizei und des SD, 1938-1942* (Stuttgart: Deutsche Verlags-Anstalt, 1981), 601; Mr. C.F. Rüter and Dr. D.W. De Mildt, *Die Westdeutschen Strafverfahren wegen Nationalsozialistischer Tötungsverbrechen, 1945-1997* (Amsterdam: APA-Holland University Press, 19980, 119, 134.

10. Paul Hausser, *Soldaten wie andere auch: Der Weg der Waffen-SS* (Osnabruck: Munin Verlag, 1966), 131; Paul Schmidt, *Der Statist auf der Galerie, 1945-50: Erlebnisse, Kommentare, Vergleichen* (Bonn: Athenäum-Verlag, 1951), 121.

11. IMT, 42: 522-24.

12. The prosecution of another Equestrian SS member, Gustav Lombard, for murdering Jews in eastern Europe was once considered, but was postponed and apparently never resumed. *Justiz und NS-Verbrechen*, 97-99.

13. Understanding the motivations of the killers can be a difficult task. Naturally, affidavits have to be treated with suspicion. An excellent study of non-SS personnel involved in a murder squadron is Christopher Browning's *Ordinary Germans: Reserve Police Battalion 101 and the Final Solution in Poland* (New York: Harper Collins, 1992); Birn, "Two Kinds of Reality?" 280-81.

14. "Zwischenbericht," Zentrale Stelle, 204 AR-Z, 296/60, 459, 549, 814, 1235.

15. Müller-Tupath, *Reichsführers gehorsamster Becher*, 55, 59.

16. "Zwischenbericht," Zentrale Stelle, 204 AR-Z 296/60, 720.

17. *Nazi Conspiracy and Aggression: Opinion and Judgement*, 102.

Sources

I. Archives

Berlin, Berlin Document Center.
Berlin, Bundesarchiv.
Koblenz, Bundesarchiv.
College Park, Maryland. National Archives.
Ludwigsburg, Zentrale Stelle der Landesjustizverwaltungen.
Munich, Institut für Zeitgeschichte.
Washington, D. C. National Archives.

II. Published and Printed Primary Sources

Allgemeine Wochenzeitung der Juden in Deutschland. 1965.
Das Schwarze Korps. 1935 to 1945.
Der Spiegel.
Die Lageberichte der Gestapo und des Generalstaatsanwalts Karlsruhe 1933-1945, Verfolgung und Widerstand unter dem Nationalsozialismus in Baden. ed. Jörg Schadt. Stuttgart: Verlag W. Hammer.
Dienstaltersliste der Schutzstaffel der NSDAP. Personalkanzlei. Beginning in 1942, SS-Personalhauptamt. Listings as of:

1 October 1934	Munich, 1934
1 July 1935	Berlin, 1935
1 December 1936	Berlin, 1936
1 December 1937	Berlin, 1937
1 December 1938	Berlin, 1938

1 October 1942	Berlin, 1942
1 October 1943	Berlin, 1943
1 October 1944	Berlin, 1944

C.F. Rüter and Dr. D.W. De Mildt, *Die Westdeutschen Strafverfahren wegen Nationalsozialistischer Tötungsverbrechen, 1945-1997.* Amsterdam: APA-Holland University Press, 1998.

Interational Military Tribunal. *Trial of the Major War Criminals Before the International Military Tribunal. Nuremberg 14 November 1945 - 1 October 1946.* 42 vols. Nuremberg, 1947-48.

Justiz und Nationalsozialistische Verbrechen. 22 vols. Amsterdam: University Press, 1968-81.

Kersten, Felix. *The Kersten Memoirs.* trans. Constantine Fitzgibbon and James Oliver. New York: The MacMillan Co., 1957.

Office of the United States Chief of Counsel for Prosecution of Axis Criminality. *Nazi Conspiracy and Aggression.* 8 vols. Washington: United States Government Printing Office, 1946.

—. *Nazi Conspiracy and Aggression: Opinion and Judgment.* Washington: United States Government Printing Office, 1947.

SS-Kavallerie im Osten. Herausgegeben von der SS-Kavallerie Brigade für Ihre Führer und Männer. Braunschweig: G. Westermann, 1942.

Statistisch-Wissenschaftliches. Stärke der SS am 31. Dezember 1943. Berlin: Institute des Reichsführers-SS, 1943.

Statistische Jahrbuch der Schutstaffel der NSDAP 1936. Berlin: Reichsführer-SS, 1937.

Statistische Jahrbuch der Schutstaffel der NSDAP 1937. Berlin: Reichsführer-SS, 1938.

Statistisches Jahrbuch der Schutzstaffel der NSDAP 1938. Berlin, 1939.

The Times (London). 1997.

Unsere Ehre heisst Treue, Kriegstagebuch des Kommandostabes Reichsführer-SS. Vienna, Frankfurt, Zurich: Europe Verlag, 1965.

Völkischer Beobachter. 1933-1945.

III. Secondary Sources

Ammann, Max E. *Buchers Geschichte des Pferde-Sports.* Lucerne: C.J. Bucher, 1976.

Birn, Ruth Bettina. "Two Kinds of Reality? Case Studies on Anti-Partisan Warfare during the Eastern Campaign" in *From Peace to War: Germany, Soviet Russia and the World, 1939-1941,* ed. Bernd Wegner. Providence and Oxford: Berghahn Books, 1997.

Bissinger, Franz R., and Stefan Braun. *Reiter, Fahrer, Pferde in der Geschichte des deutschen Turniersports.* Verlag Welsermuhl, 1976.

Black, Peter. *Ernst Kaltenbrunner: Ideological Soldier of the Third Reich.* Princeton: Princeton University Press, 1984.

Boehnert, Gunnar C. "The Third Reich and the Problem of 'Social Revolution': German Officers and the SS" in *Germany in the Age of Total War*, eds. V. Berghahn and M. Kitchen. London: Croom Helm; Totowa, N.J.: Barnes and Noble, 1981.

Breitman, Richard. *The Architect of Genocide: Himmler and the Final Solution.* New York: Alfred A. Knopf, 1991.

——. *Official Secrets: What the Nazis Planned, What the British and Americans Knew.* New York: Hill and Wang, 1998.

Broszat, Martin and Norbert Frei, eds. *Das Dritte Reich: Ursprünge, Ereignisse, Wirkungen.* Freiburg: Verlag Ploetz, 1983.

Browning, Christopher R. *Ordinary Germans: Reserve Police Battalion 101 and the Final Solution in Poland.* New York: Harper Collins, 1992.

Büchler, Yehoshua. "Kommandostab Reichsführer-SS: Himmler's Personal Murder Brigades in 1941." *Holocaust and Genocide Studies* 1 (1996): 11-25.

Combs, William L. *The Voice of the SS.* New York: Peter Lang Publishers, Inc., 1986.

Conot, Robert E. *Justice at Nuremberg.* New York: Harper and Row, 1983.

Cooper, Mathew. *The Nazi War Against Soviet Partisans, 1941-1944.* New York: Stein and Day, 1979.

DiNardo, R. L. *Mechanized Juggernaut or Military Anachronism: Horses and the German Army of World War II.* New York: Greenwood Press, 1991.

——, and Austin Bay. "Horse-Drawn Transport in the German Army." *Journal of Contemporary History* 23 (April 1988): 129-142.

Döscher, Hans-Jürgen. *Das Auswärtige Amt im Dritten Reich; Diplomatie im Schatten der >Endlösung<.* Berlin: Wolf Jobst Siedler Verlag GMBH, 1987.

Farquharson, J. E. *The Plough and the Swastika: The NSDAP and Agriculture in Germany, 1928-1945.* London and Beverly Hills: Sage Publications, 1976.

Gelwick, Robert Arthur. "Personnel Policies and Procedures of the Waffen-SS." Ph.D. Dissertation. University of Nebraska, Lincoln, 1971.

Gilbert, Felix with David Clay Large. *The End of the European Era, 1890-Present.* New York: W.W. Norton and Co. Inc., 1991.

Grill, Johnpeter Horst. "The Nazi Party's Rural Propaganda Before 1928," *Central European History* 15 (June 1982), 149-85.

—. "Nobles in the SS: Old Wine in New Bottles?" Unpublished paper delivered at the Southern Historical Association's 56th Annual Meeting, New Orleans, Louisiana, October 31 to November 3, 1990.

Guderian, Heinz. *Panzer Leader*. Trans. Constantine Fitzgibbon. New York: E.P. Dutton and Company Inc.

Henson, Jeffrey Allen. "The Role of *Das Schwarze Korps* in the SS's Campaign Against the Catholic Church." Masters Thesis. Mississippi State University, 1997.

Hausser, Paul. *Soldaten wie andere auch: Der Weg der Waffen-SS*. Osnabrück: Munin Verlag, 1966.

Heinze, Rolf Dittmer. *Das Buch vom Reitsport*. Berlin: Safari-Verlag, 1965.

Höhne, Heinz. *The Order of the Deaths Head*. Trans. Richard Barry. New York: Ballantine Books, 1971.

Klietmann, Dr. K. G. *Die Waffen-SS: eine Dokumentation*. Osnabrück: Verlag "Der Freiwillige," 1965.

Koehl, Robert L. *The Black Corps*. Madison: The University of Wisconsin Press, 1983.

Kogon, Eugen. *The Theory and Practice of Hell*. trans. Heinz Norden. London: Secker and Warburg, 1950.

Krausnick, Helmut and Hans-Heinrich Wilhelm. *Die Truppe des Weltanschauungskrieges: Die Einsatzgruppen der Sicherheitspolizei and des SD, 1938-1942*. Stuttgart: Deutsche Verlags-Anstalt, 1981.

Krausnick, Helmut, and others. *Anatomy of the SS State*. Trans. Richard Barry, Marian Jackson, and Dorothy Long. New York: Walker and Company, 1968.

Lang, Jochen von. *The Secretary, Martin Bormann: The Man Who Manipulated Hitler*. Trans. Christa Armstrong and Peter White. New York: Random House, 1978.

Lindner, Peter. *Hermann Florstedt: SS Führer und KZ-Lagerkommandant*. Halle/Saale: Gursky, 1997.

Littlejohn, David. *The SA, 1921-45: Hitler's Stormtroopers*. London: Osprey Publishing, 1990.

Manvell, Roger and Heinrich Fraenkel. *Himmler*. New York; G. P. Putnams's Sons, 1965.

Menzendorf, Werner. *Reitsport: Ein Bildband 1900-1972*.

Textliche Bearbeitung von Hans-Joachim von Killisch-Horn. Berlin und Hamburg: Paul Parey, 1972.

Meyer, Heinz. *Geschichte der Reiterkrieger*. Stuttgart: Verlag W. Kohlhammer, 1982.

Momm, Harold. *Pferde, Reiter und Trophäen*. Munich: Copress-Verlag, 1957.

Müller-Tupath, Karla. *Reichsführers gehorsamster Becher: Eine deutsche Karriere*. Fulda: Konkret Literatur Verlag, 1982.

O'Donnell, James P. *The Bunker*. Boston: Houghton Mifflin Company, 1978.

Padfield, Peter. *Himmler: Reichsführer-SS*. New York: Heinz Holt and Company, 1991.

Petropoulos, Jonathon. *Art as Politics in the Third Reich*. Chapel Hill and London: University of North Carolina Press, 1996.

Piekalkiewicz, Janusz. *The Cavalry of World War II*. New York: Stein and Day, 1979.

Preradovich, Nikolaus von. *Generale der Waffen-SS*. Berg am See: Kurt Vowinckel-Verlag, 1985.

Reitlinger, Gerald. *The SS: Alibi of a Nation, 1922-1945*. New York: Viking Press, 1957.

Rempel, Gerhard. *Hitler's Children: The Hitler Youth and the SS*. Chapel Hill: The University of North Carolina Press, 1989.

Richter, Klaus Christian. *Die Geschichte der deutschen Kavallerie, 1919-1945*. Stuttgart: Motorbuch Verlag, 1982.

Shalka, Robert John. "The 'General-SS' in Central Germany, 1937-1939: A Social and Institutional Study of SS-Main Sector Fulda-Werra." Ph.D. Dissertation, University of Wisconsin, 1972.

Schmidt, Paul. *Der Statist auf der Galerie, 1945-50: Erlebnisse, Kommentare, Vergleiche*. Bonn: Athenäum-Verlag, 1951.

Segev, Tom. *Soldiers of Evil: The Commandants of the Nazi Concentration Camps*. Trans. Haim Watzman. New York: McGraw-Hill Book Company, 1987.

Smith, Bradley F. *Reaching Judgement at Nuremberg*. New York: Basic Books Inc., 1977.

Smith, Paul. *Der Statist auf der Galerie, 1945-50: Erlebnisse, Kommentare, Vergleiche*. Bonn: Athenäum-Verlag, 1951.

Spielvogel, Jackson J. *Hitler and Nazi Germany: A History*. Englewood Cliffs, New Jersey: Prentice Hall, 1988.

Stein, George H. *The Waffen SS: Hitler's Elite Guard at War, 1939-1945*. Ithaca and London: Cornell University Press, 1966.

Sydnor, Charles W. *Soldiers of Destruction: The SS Death's Head Division, 1933-45*. Princeton University Press, 1977.

Trevor-Roper, H. R. *The Last Days of Hitler*. New York: The MacMillan Co., 1947.

—. *The Bormann Letters: The Private Correspondence Between Martin Bormann and His Wife From January 1943 to April 1945*. Trans. R.H. Stevens. London: Weidenfeld and Nicolson, 1954.

Von Aretin, Karl Otmar. "Der bayerische Adel. Von der Monarchie zum Dritten Reich." in *Bayern in der NS-Zeit: Herrschaft und Gesellschaft im Konflikt*. eds. Martin Broszat, Elke Fröhlich, and Anton Grossmann. Munich, Vienna: R. Oldenbourg Verlag, 1981.

Wegner, Bernd. *The Waffen SS: Organization, Ideology, and Function*. Trans. Ronald Webster. Oxford: Basil Blackwell Ltd., 1990.

Wolfson, Manfred, "The SS Leadership." Ph.D. Dissertation, University of Califonia, Berkeley, 1965.

Yerger, Mark C. *Riding East: The SS Cavalry Brigade in Poland and Russia, 1939-1942*. Atglin, PA: Schiffer Publishing, Ltd., 1996.

— *Allgemeine-SS: The Commands, Units and Leaders of the General SS*. Atglen, PA: Schiffer Publishing, Ltd., 1997.

Ziegler, Herbert F. *Nazi Germany's New Aristocracy: The SS Leadership, 1925-1939*. Princeton: Princeton University Press, 1989.

Name Index

Photos

Right: Hitler's court photographer Heinrich Hoffmann photographed Hermann Fegelein with his most recent decoration, the Oak Leaves, shortly before he assumed command of the SS Cavalry Division. (Courtesy National Archives)

Below: Fegelein in 1939 poses with SS Brigadier General Günther Claassen at the SS Main Riding School in Munich. Fegelein enjoyed touring SS officials around the impressive facility. (Courtesy Mark C. Yerger)

Above: Fegelein in early 1944 after receiving the German Cross in Gold. (Courtesy National Archives)

Below: Fegelein listens intently to Hitler's words at the Führer's birthday celebration on April 20, 1944. (Courtesy National Archives)

Above: Günther Temme, an outstanding jockey, joined the SS in 1934. In 1939 he rode for the SS Main Riding School. (Courtesy Bundesarchiv Berlin)

Right: Waldemar Fegelein, Hermann Fegelein's younger brother, was one of the best SS riders. (Courtesy Bundesarchiv Berlin)

Below: Paul Brantenaar (left) commanded Equestrian Regiment 7 in Berlin, the most fashionable of Himmler's mounted units. With him is his adjutant Wolfgang Crass. (Courtesy Mark C. Yerger)

Pages 219-221: These photographs show various mounted formations during the 1937 Reichsführer SS Challenge Cup, an all-Equestrian SS tournament in Munich. (Courtesy National Archives).

Reichsführer SS Himmler addresses his cavalry during an inspection of the Kommandostab.

The chief of the Kommandostab Reichsführer SS, Kurt Knoblauch, and Fegelein smile pleasantly as a young woman presents Himmler with flowers.

Members of the SS Cavalry Brigade use sleds to travel on the eastern front during the harsh Russian winter in 1942. The out-manned and out-gunned SS Cavalry Brigade suffered devastating losses during the winter campaign.

Himmler and his cavalry commander, Hermann Fegelein.

The Camp Men: The SS Officers Who Ran the Nazi Concentration Camp System.
French L. MacLean. Inside these pages you will meet over 960 infamous men – the officers of Nazi Germany's *Totenkopf* (Death's Head). These officers of the Death's Head, many of whom later served in the Waffen-SS, were not the bureaucrats who meticulously planned Adolf Hitler's Final Solution from behind a desk in Berlin, or those who quietly scheduled the trains that carried the victims to the camps. Quite the contrary; these men stood on the front-line of the Nazi war to exterminate the Jews. With well over one hundred photographs – a large portion previously unpublished – this is the largest collection of SS camp personnel photographs ever to appear in one work.
Size: 8 1/2" x 11" • over 140 b/w photographs, maps • 384 pp.
ISBN: 0-7643-0636-7 • hard cover • $59.95

The Field Men: The SS Officers Who Led the Einsatzkommandos - the Nazi Mobile Killing Units. French MacLean. Men lined up in four motorized columns immediately behind the German Army on June 22, 1941, as it prepared to launch Operation Barbarossa, an attack designed to win the war. The Field Men covers the entire gamut, from the organization of the units, to the SS officers who served in this scourge on the Eastern Front. Some 380 SS officers are described in full detail and extensively analyzed.
Size: 8 1/2" x 11" • over 175 b/w photos and maps • 232 pp.
ISBN: 0-7643-0754-1 • hard cover • $59.95

In Perfect Formation: SS Ideology and the SS-Junkerschule-Tölz. Jay Hatheway. Includes extensive references to original source material on the underlying SS principles of blood, soil, and struggle as they were formalized in SS ideology. In support of his intricate linkages between ideology and its realized form, Hatheway has obtained over 100 previously unpublished photos of the SS officer training academy Tölz. More than a series of buildings, the structure of the *Junkerschule* was itself a metaphor for the subset of Nazi ideology that was developed by Himmler, Darré and others to create a racially pure vanguard to lead Germany on its path toward Teutonic regeneration.
Size: 6" x 9" • over 100 b/w photographs • 192 pp.
ISBN: 0-7643-0753-3 • hard cover • $29.95

Allgemeine-SS: The Commands, Units and Leaders of the General SS. Mark C. Yerger. The commands, units and leaders of the General SS are finally compiled into a single detailed reference book for both the historian and SS memorabilia collector. The biographical data for individuals alone adds vast detail to this fascinating topic. Along with more than 120 rare photos of SS senior ranking officers and seven maps, a detailed index allows referencing of individual commands or personalities.
Size: 8 1/2" x 11" • over 120 b/w photographs, maps • 256 pp.
ISBN: 0-7643-0145-4 • hard cover • $49.95

Chronicle of the 7. Panzerkompanie 1. SS-Panzer Division"Leibstandarte." Ralf Tiemann. This chronicle of the 7.Panzerkompanie follows the unit history of a ìLeibstandarteî tank company from its creation in 1942 to the end of World War II. Compiled by former company commander and German Cross in Gold holder Ralf Tiemann, the detailed text relies on both official documentation and the personal recollections of numerous unit veterans. Exacting cartographic material allows the reader to follow all engagements in this first unit history of a "Leibstandarte" tank company available in English.
Size: 6" x 9" • over 60 b/w photos, over 30 maps, charts • 320 pp.
ISBN: 0-7643-0463-1 • hard cover • $29.95

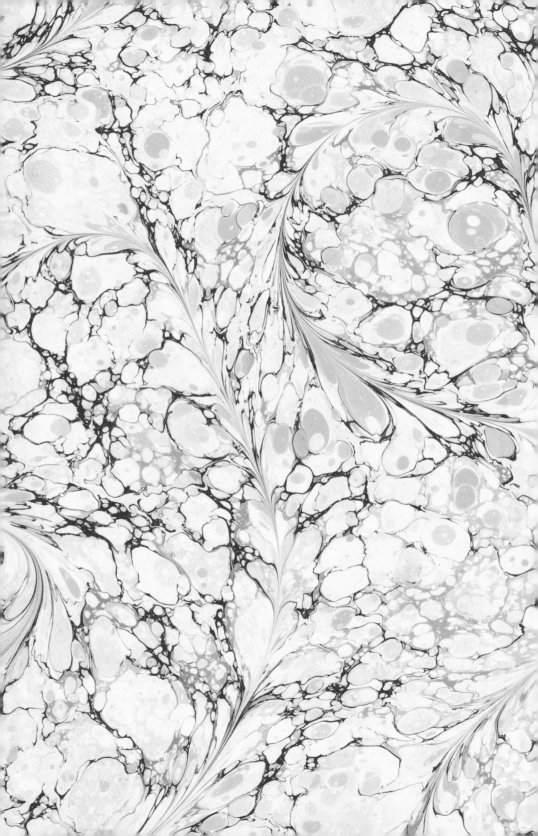